Writing Skills for Technical Students

Writing Skills for Technical Students

Sixth Edition

Delaware Technical & Community College

English Department, Jack F. Owens Campus

Upper Saddle River, New Jersey 07458

Library of Congress Cataloging-in-Publication Data
Writing skills for technical students / Delaware Technical and Community College English Department, Jack E Owens Campus. —6th ed.
p. cm.
Includes index.
ISBN-13: 978-0-13-239198-6
ISBN-10: 0-13-239198-8
1. English language—Technical English. 2. Technical writing.
I. Delaware Technical and Community College (Jack F. Owens Campus). English Dept.
PE1479.B87W75 2008
808'.0666—dc22 2007024148

Editor-in-Chief: Craig Campanella
Senior Editorial Director: Leah Jewell
Project Manager, English: Melissa Casciano
Editorial Assistant: Deborah Doyle
Director of Marketing: Brandy Dawson
Assistant Marketing Manager: Billy Grieco
Associate Managing Editor: Maureen Richardson
Full-Service Liaison: Shelly Kupperman
Senior Operations Supervisor: Sherry Lewis
Operations Specialist: Christina Amato
Composition/Full-Service Project Management: TexTech, Inc.
Production Manager and Editor: Kathy O'Connor/TexTech, Inc.
Printer/Binder: Edwards Brothers Malloy
Cover Printer: Edwards Brothers Malloy
Cover Designer: Bruce Kenselaar
Cover Illustration/Photo: Getty Images Inc.

The text of this book was written collectively by Jennifer Morley, Rob Rector, Coordinator Diana Young, Janelle Boyer, Fred Baker, Jerome Dujordan, George Ellegood, Carol Kopay, Sara Drew Lewis, Harriet Smith-Windsor, Ward Tanzer, and Ron Webster.

This book was set in 11.5/13 Garamond by TexTech International, and was printed and bound by Edwards Brothers Malloy. Cover was printed by Edwards Brothers Malloy.

Pearson Education LTD.
Pearson Education Singapore, Pte. Ltd
Pearson Education, Canada, Ltd
Pearson Education—Japan
Pearson Education Australia PTY, Limited
Pearson Education North Asia Ltd
Pearson Educación de Mexico, S.A. de C.V.
Pearson Education Malaysia, Pte. Ltd
Pearson Education, Upper Saddle River, NJ

14 13
ISBN-13: 978-0-13-239198-6
ISBN-10: 0-13-239198-8

Contents

To the Teacher xi

To the Student xiii

Student Progress Record xiv

Section One

MODULE 1 **Verbs** 1

Diagnostic Exercise 2
Action Verbs 2
Linking Verbs 4
Helping Verbs 7
Irregular Verbs 9
Verb Tense 16
Diagnostic Feedback 19
Feedback for Module 1 20

MODULE 2 **Adjectives and Adverbs** 23

Diagnostic Exercise 24
Adjectives 24
Adverbs 28
"Good" and "Well" 31
Comparison of Adjectives and Adverbs 33
Diagnostic Feedback 37
Feedback for Module 2 37

MODULE 3 **Phrases 41**

Diagnostic Exercise 42
Prepositional Phrases 42
Verbal Phrases 45
Diagnostic Feedback 50
Feedback for Module 3 51

MODULE 4 **Nouns/Possessive Nouns 53**

Diagnostic Exercise 54
Nouns 54
Functions of Nouns 55
Plural Nouns and Possessives 57
Possessive Nouns 57
Diagnostic Feedback 67
Feedback for Module 4 67

MODULE 5 **Subject–Verb Agreement 71**

Diagnostic Exercise 72
Recognizing Subjects and Verbs 72
Subject–Verb Agreement 74
Interfering Words 77
Indefinite Pronoun Subjects 79
Compound Subjects and Verbs 82
Special Problems in Agreement 84
Diagnostic Feedback 86
Feedback for Module 5 86

MODULE 6 **Pronouns 91**

Diagnostic Exercise 92
Pronouns as Subjects 93
Pronouns as Subject Complements 94
Pronouns as Direct Objects 96
Pronouns as Objects of Prepositions 97
Possessive Pronouns 99
Pronoun Rules 101

Pronoun–Antecedent Agreement 104
Diagnostic Feedback 108
Feedback for Module 6 109

MODULE 7 **Sentence Patterns 114**

Diagnostic Exercise 115
Independent Clauses 115
Dependent Clauses 118
Appropriate Clause Connectors 122
Diagnostic Feedback 129
Feedback for Module 7 130

MODULE 8 **Punctuation 133**

Diagnostic Exercise 134
Basic Sentence Punctuation Patterns 134
Other Basic Comma Rules 139
Diagnostic Feedback 149
Feedback for Module 8 150

MODULE 9 **Fragments and Run-Ons 155**

Diagnostic Exercise 157
Fragments 157
Run-Ons 159
Diagnostic Feedback 164
Feedback for Module 9 165

MODULE 10 **Paragraph Writing 169**

Diagnostic Exercise 170
Introduction 170
The Paragraph 171
Constructing the Topic Sentence 172
Choosing a Subject 172
Choosing a Controlling Idea 174
Writing the Concluding Sentence 178
Developing Unity 179

Developing Coherence 181
Organizing and Writing a Paragraph 183
The Reasons Paragraph 184
The Reasons and Examples Paragraph 186
The Pro and Con Paragraph 188
The Process Paragraph 191
Diagnostic Feedback 194
Feedback for Module 10 195

Section Two

MODULE 11 **Shifts 198**

Diagnostic Exercise 199
Shifts in Voice 200
Shifts in Tense 204
Shifts in Person 207
Shifts in Number 210
Diagnostic Feedback 216
Feedback for Module 11 217

MODULE 12 **Clarity 223**

Diagnostic Exercise 224
Pronoun Reference 224
Misplaced and Unclear Modifiers 228
Word Usage 230
Parallel Construction 235
Diagnostic Feedback 242
Feedback for Module 12 242

MODULE 13 **Accelerating Techniques 248**

Diagnostic Exercise 249
Eliminating Unnecessary Words 249
Avoiding Clichés, Slang, and "IMglish" 252
Combining Like Subjects and Verbs 255
Subordinating Ideas 257

Reducing Dependent Clauses 261
Diagnostic Feedback 268
Feedback for Module 13 268

MODULE 14 **Report Writing 273**

Review of Paragraph Writing 274
Outlining 276
Report Introductions 280
Format Tips 282
The Persuasive Report 283
Technical Procedure Report 287
Interview Report 292
Recommendation Report 298
Summary Report 303
Feedback for Module 14 310

MODULE 15 **Business Letter Writing 312**

Psychology of Business Writing 313
Planning 315
Format 316
Request Letter 323
Letter That Says "No" 324
Resumé and Letter of Application 326
The Memo 332
Transmittal Letter and Transmittal Memo 336

Glossary 341

Index 359

To the Teacher

This text is designed for the adult learner who needs a review of grammar and writing skills in order to be able to write clearly and concisely on the job. Its format provides for diagnosis, instruction, and practice in 15 self-paced modules that can be adapted to both individualized and classroom methods. There are 12 grammar modules, a module on paragraph writing, a module on report writing, and a module on business letter writing. Each module consists of a set of objectives followed by diagnostic exercises, instruction, and practice in small segments with immediate feedback. The examples used throughout are meaningful and relevant, particularly for technical students. The fundamental principles applied are as follows:

1. Test—find out what the students already know.
2. Teach—explain to them the concepts they need to know.
3. Retest—check to see that they have mastered the objectives. (If not, repeat the procedure.)

The underlying philosophy is that writing skills are built inductively; that is, students learn and practice correct grammar and usage first, then go on to build from the sentence to the paragraph to the report to the business letter.

The materials included in the Instructor's Manual are vital to an effective use of *Writing Skills for Technical Students.* The manual contains diagnostic tests for the grammar units so that you can pretest and exempt students from modules they can already apply. Also included in the manual are four module tests and two editing tests for each grammar module, final grammar tests, applied writing exercises, and extra worksheets for practice when the student does not master the instructional material.

For use with the paragraph, report, and business writing modules, the Instructor's Manual includes checklists to be used by both students and instructors to proofread and evaluate writing assignments and to note the kinds of errors made.

We believe the organization and modular format of this text will provide instructors with a flexible and effective approach to teaching students how to write well.

To the Student

This book presents a self-paced, modularized program to build your skills in grammar and writing. It is divided into two sections. Section One deals with the basic points of grammar and the writing of paragraphs. Section Two covers additional areas in the refinement of grammar plus the writing of reports and business communications.

Here's how to use the book. For each grammar module that your instructor requires you to complete, first read the objectives, then complete the Diagnostic Activities, and check your answers with the answers provided in the Feedback section at the end of the module. Study the instructional materials. Follow the directions for each Activity. At the end of each Activity, you are directed to check your responses in the Feedback section at the end of the module. You will also be directed how to proceed after completing the Activity.

The Paragraph Module progresses from the topic sentence to the outline to the writing of four important types of paragraphs. Follow the procedures indicated, checking your work with your instructor when required. After completing Section One, you will proceed in the same manner through Section Two.

Many students have been helped by the materials and methods in this book. We hope you will find it both useful and enjoyable.

STUDENT PROGRESS RECORD
Section One

NAME ____________________________

GRAMMAR MODULES

	Tests: A	B	C	D	Applied Writing	Review
1. Verbs						
2. Adjectives & Adverbs						
3. Phrases						
4. Nouns/Possessive Nouns						
5. Subject-Verb Agreement						
6. Pronouns						
7. Sentence Patterns						
8. Punctuation						
9. Fragments & Run-Ons						

Grammar Final A __________ B __________

10. Paragraph Module

	A	B	Comments
Reasons			
Reasons & Examples			
Pro & Con			
Process			
Paragraph Final			

Section Two

GRAMMAR MODULES

	Tests: A	B	C	D	Applied Writing	Review
11. Shifts						
12. Clarity						
13. Acceleration						

Grammar Final A __________ B __________

14. Report Module

	A	B	Comments
Outlining			
Technical Procedure			
Persuasion			
Interview Questions			
Interview			
Recommendation			
Summary			
Report Final			

15. Business Letters

	A	B	Comments
Request Letter			
"No" Letter			
Resumé			
Application Letter			
Memorandum			
Letter of Transmittal			
Letter Final			

Writing Skills for Technical Students

MODULE 1

Verbs

Objective: This module will give you a good foundation on which to build your sentences.

Upon completion of this module, you will be able:

- To recognize action and linking verbs.
- To identify helping verbs.
- To identify and to use correctly the principal parts of verbs, both regular and irregular.

The verb is the basic part of every sentence. In order to write correct sentences, you have to be able to recognize verbs. There are two types of verbs: action verbs, which indicate what the subject is doing, and linking verbs, which link the subject with another word in a sentence. Most verbs show action, and generally this type of verb is more forceful in a sentence.

The subject of the sentence is what the sentence is about. It is usually a noun or pronoun. A noun is the name of a person, place, thing, or idea. A pronoun takes the place of a noun.

DIAGNOSTIC EXERCISE

Identify the verb and label it as an action verb or linking verb:

1. The sales executive arranged to have the contract sent overnight.
2. The nursing assistant is certified in CPR.
3. The repair technician evaluated the water damage.
4. The flight attendant is in the cockpit with the pilot.
5. The instructor stressed the importance of careful editing.

Choose the correct form of the verb:

1. Because I was up late, I plan to (lie/lay) down when I get home from work today.
2. The waiter did not know where to (lie/lay) the bill because the table was so cluttered.
3. In my interview, I did not (sit/set) down until I was asked to do so.
4. I plan to (sit/set) the silverware out next to the plates for the dinner party.
5. Don't forget to (rise/raise) the blinds before leaving for work.

PART I: ACTION VERBS

Just as the name implies, *action verbs show action.* You can perform or *do* any action verb, either physically or mentally. Read the following examples and note that the verbs (printed in **bold** type) all show *an action that can be done.*

He **typed** the letter to Dr. Jones. (Physical action)
Jon **read** all of the material. (Physical action)
He **studied** every rule. (Mental action)

She **walks** to work. (Physical action)
Mary **spoke** at the meeting. (Physical action)
I **thought** about the experiment. (Mental action)

ACTIVITY 1-A: Identifying Action Verbs

Underline the action verbs in the following sentences.

1. The architect made copies of the drawings.
2. The secretary processed the bid specifications this morning.
3. Mary cleaned and oiled the lathe.
4. Their computer operator entered 200 new addresses.
5. Our nurses' program assists the local hospitals with many duties.
6. The hotel offers attractive accommodations for conventions.
7. A new chemical process extracts gold economically from mining residue.
8. Police officers work long hours during civil disturbances.
9. The Help Line volunteer workers saved many lives this year.
10. The prolonged strike hurts too many farmers.

Check your responses in Feedback 1-A at the end of this module. If your responses were correct, proceed to Activity 1-C. If you missed any, do Activity 1-B.

ACTIVITY 1-B: Identifying Action Verbs

Underline the action verbs in the following sentences.

1. The auctioneer sold many attractive items at low bids.
2. She drew the most practical plan for the apartment.
3. The DuPont Company prefers men for some administrative assistant positions.
4. The electrician installed a new switch on the machine.
5. One of our nurses stopped the bleeding very quickly.
6. In minutes, a computer saves hundreds of work hours.
7. After lunch, the crew assembled the surveyor's level.
8. The Ramada Inn hotel chain sold its Denver branch.
9. Bill transferred to the hospital emergency ward.
10. Doris aligned her truck's front wheels this morning.

Check your responses in Feedback 1-B at the end of this module. If your responses were correct, proceed to Part II. If you missed any, review Part I before continuing.

PART II: LINKING VERBS

Verbs that do not show action are called *linking verbs.* Only a few verbs are in this category: verbs of being (**to be, to become,** etc.) and verbs of the senses (**to feel, to smell, to taste,** etc.).

Linking verbs express some relationship between the subject and a word that follows the linking verb (see Module 2, Part I, Rule 7). The word following the linking verb may be an *adjective* (a word that describes a noun or pronoun). Its function is to describe the subject of the sentence.

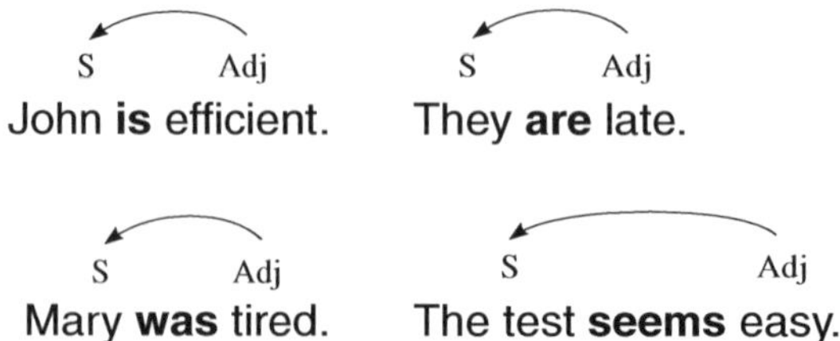

The word following the linking verb may also be a noun that renames or identifies the subject. The linking verb acts as an equal sign when the subject and the noun following the verb are one and the same.

S Noun	S Noun
Joe **is** my brother.	Mary **is** class president.
Joe = brother	Mary = president

The most common linking verb is the verb **to be** in all its forms: **be, am, is, are, was, were, been, being.**

In addition, the following are linking verbs used to express a state of being: **become, grow, seem, act, appear, stay, remain.**

Finally, these five verbs are linking verbs when used in connection with the senses: **look, feel, smell, taste, sound.**

Be careful. Some verbs, especially verbs of the senses, are linking verbs when used in one way, but they are action verbs when used in a different way. You can test the function of the sense verbs by substituting a form of the verb **to be** in their place.

Linking Verb Test

To test whether or not a verb is a linking verb, substitute **is** or **was** for the verb and see if the sentence still makes sense.

> The assignment **seems** difficult. (Can you substitute *is* for the verb *seems*? Yes. The assignment *is* difficult. *Seems* is a linking verb.)

The cake **tasted** good. (Can you substitute *was* for the verb *tasted*? Yes. The cake *was* good. *Tasted* is a linking verb.)

The following verbs are used as linking verbs. Here the subject is not doing the action of the verb.

This book **looks** good. (The book is not looking. The book *is* good.)
The pie **tastes** delicious. (The pie is not tasting. The pie *is* delicious.)
This record **sounds** scratched. (The record is not sounding. The record *is* scratched.)
The farmer **grows** tired. (The farmer is not growing; he *is* becoming tired.)

The verbs below are used as action verbs. They show what the subject is doing.

He **looks** for the memo. (Not "He *is* the memo.")
He **tastes** wine as a hobby. (Not "He *is* wine.")
The foghorn **sounds** a blast. (Not "The foghorn *is* a blast.")
The farmer **grows** cabbages. (Not "The farmer *is* cabbages.")

LINKING VERBS

Verbs of Being

All parts of **to be**: **be, am, is, are, was, were, been, being**
become grow seem act appear stay remain

Verbs of the Senses

look feel smell taste sound

ACTIVITY 1-C: Identifying Linking Verbs

Underline the linking verbs in the following sentences.

1. Hog production is second only to poultry production on the Delmarva Peninsula.
2. His word processing is the neatest in the office.
3. We are proud of our nursing program.
4. The account appeared complete.
5. The sign on the building seemed too tall for its setting.
6. Many activities for young people are challenging.
7. All the electrical circuits seem to have adequate power.

8. The news reporter remained calm during the interview.
9. Most meals at the plant cafeteria taste delicious.
10. The air-conditioned rooms felt good today.

Check your responses in Feedback 1-C at the end of this module. If your responses were correct, proceed to Activity 1-E. If you missed any, do Activity 1-D.

ACTIVITY 1-D: Identifying Linking Verbs

Circle the linking verbs in the following sentences. Draw one line under the subject and two lines under the noun or adjective to which it is linked.

1. In this newspaper column, one sentence is as lengthy as a paragraph.
2. Wild cherry trees seem susceptible to web-weaving insects.
3. The judge appears thoughtful.
4. Stale coffee generally tastes horrible.
5. The aroma from that restaurant smells inviting.
6. Our accountant was trustworthy.
7. This electric wire feels hot.
8. Our new generator is much more efficient.
9. I am happy with the new design.
10. He became an excellent wastewater operator in a very short time.

Check your responses in Feedback 1-D at the end of this module. If your responses were correct, proceed to Activity 1-E. If you missed any, review Part II before continuing.

ACTIVITY 1-E: Identifying Linking and Action Verbs

Underline the verbs in the following sentences. In the spaces provided, identify them as A (action) or L (linking).

_______ 1. Your comments are valid.

_______ 2. The final paragraph suggests a meeting.

_______ 3. This example supports my viewpoint.

_______ 4. The letters were ready on time.

_______ 5. Each worker seems competent.

_______ 6. Marcia looks capable of good work.

_______ 7. Problems occur in that area often.

_______ 8. An unclear letter causes misunderstanding.

_______ 9. The filing system appears orderly.

_______10. All of the reports fell on the floor.

Check your responses in Feedback 1-E at the end of this module. If your responses were correct, proceed to Part III. If you missed any, do Activity 1-F.

ACTIVITY 1-F: **Identifying Linking and Action Verbs**

Underline the verbs in the following sentences. In the spaces provided, identify them as A (action) or L (linking).

_______ 1. All these accounts are current.

_______ 2. We sampled those cultures earlier.

_______ 3. The center also provides responsible daycare.

_______ 4. His plea affected my decision.

_______ 5. Pigs are marketable after being weaned.

_______ 6. Justice seems abstract at times.

_______ 7. He listened carefully to the truck's engine.

_______ 8. During the electrical storm, everyone felt tense.

_______ 9. That student carried the engineer's measuring chain.

_______10. The administrative assistant prepared an extra copy of our report.

Check your responses in Feedback 1-F at the end of this module. If your responses were correct, proceed to Part III. If you missed any, review Part II.

PART III: HELPING VERBS

Sometimes the verb is expressed using more than one word. The complete verb consists of a main verb and one or more helping verbs, which precede it. When locating the complete verb in a sentence, be sure to indicate any helping verbs as well as the verb they help. In the following examples, the helping verbs are in bold type.

has erased	**might have** been
will be coming	**can** say
should have gone	**is** finished

Listed below are the most commonly used helping verbs. These helpers may be used singly or in groups with the main verb.

HELPING VERBS

am	do	must
are	had	shall
be	has	should
been	have	was
can	is	were
could	may	will
did	might	would

Helping verbs are often separated from the main verb by an adverb such as **not, never, always,** etc. These words are not part of the verb. Likewise, the contraction **n't** on the end of a negative verb (were**n't,** does**n't,** etc.) is not part of the complete verb.

	COMPLETE VERB
I **did** not **see** you at the safety meeting.	did see
He **can** always **type** it again for his boss.	can type
Are you still **going** to the company party?	are going
Weren't you **surveying** the lot?	were surveying

NOTE When a sentence is in the form of a question, the helping verb is separated from the main verb by the subject.

ACTIVITY 1-G: Complete Verbs

Underline the complete verb. Remember that the complete verb consists of all helping verbs and the main verb but does not include adverbs.

1. She is covering the story for the local newspapers.
2. Pat may have already done the internship.
3. Were you planning to attend the seminar?
4. Mary Smith has written the report for the meeting.
5. Mr. Dukes has already proofread the report.
6. We are making several changes in the architect's drawing.

7. Will you complete the experiment before noon?
8. Mrs. Jones's work should have been done earlier than his.
9. He is doing all of the construction himself.
10. I must attend the meeting tomorrow in St. Louis.

Check your responses in Feedback 1-G at the end of this module. If your responses were correct, proceed to Part IV. If you missed any, review Part III before continuing.

PART IV: IRREGULAR VERBS

Learning the principal parts of verbs will help you use the correct verb form. The *principal parts* are the present, the past, the past participle, and the present participle.

The **past participle** is the form that must be used with a helping verb (see the list of Helping Verbs in Part III). Examples of the past participle with a helping verb are **has walked, had seen, is given, was ended, were broken, has been sent,** etc.

The **present participle** is the form ending in **-ing**, and it uses a helping verb: **is helping, are writing, is scheduling,** etc.

Regular verbs make their past and past participle forms by adding **-d** or **-ed** to the present tense form of the verb.

PRESENT	PAST	PAST PARTICIPLE	PRESENT PARTICIPLE
walk	walked	(have) walked	(are) walking
hope	hoped	(have) hoped	(are) hoping
save	saved	(have) saved	(are) saving
polish	polished	(have) polished	(are) polishing

Irregular verbs *do not* form their past and past participle forms by adding **-d** or **-ed** to the present tense verb. Irregular verbs form their past and past participle in various ways: (1) by changing the vowel in the verb (changing *rise* to *rose*); (2) by adding **-n** or **-en** (changing *drive* to *driven*); (3) by making no change at all (*bet, bet, bet*); or (4) by changing the word completely (changing *bring* to *brought*).

Principal Parts of Common Irregular Verbs

Four principal parts of common irregular verbs are given in the following alphabetical list. Consult a dictionary when you are in doubt about the principal parts of other irregular verbs. Learn the forms below and then do Activity 1-H.

PRESENT	PAST	PAST PARTICIPLE	PRESENT PARTICIPLE
begin	began	(have) begun	(are) beginning
break	broke	(have) broken	(are) breaking
bring	brought	(have) brought	(are) bringing
burst	burst	(have) burst	(are) bursting
choose	chose	(have) chosen	(are) choosing
come	came	(have) come	(are) coming
do	did	(have) done	(are) doing
drink	drank	(have) drunk	(are) drinking
drive	drove	(have) driven	(are) driving
eat	ate	(have) eaten	(are) eating
fly	flew	(have) flown	(are) flying
give	gave	(have) given	(are) giving
go	went	(have) gone	(are) going
know	knew	(have) known	(are) knowing
lend	lent	(have) lent	(are) lending
lose	lost	(have) lost	(are) losing
ride	rode	(have) ridden	(are) riding
run	ran	(have) run	(are) running
see	saw	(have) seen	(are) seeing
sing	sang	(have) sung	(are) singing
speak	spoke	(have) spoken	(are) speaking
swim	swam	(have) swum	(are) swimming
take	took	(have) taken	(are) taking
throw	threw	(have) thrown	(are) throwing
write	wrote	(have) written	(are) writing

ACTIVITY 1-H: Irregular Verbs

Complete each sentence by supplying the correct past or past participle of the verb indicated.

1. *begin* I had already ____________ to write the memo.
2. *come* He ____________ to the meeting at 10 A.M.
3. *choose* Has everyone ____________ a conference hour?
4. *do* Norman ____________ the work on the computer.
5. *break* He has ____________ his new keyboard.

6. *burst* The test tube had ___________ from intense heat.

7. *do* They ___________ what was required by the job.

8. *burst* The automobile tire ___________ yesterday.

9. *bring* Have you ___________ your lunch?

10. *come* He had ___________ from the other office.

11. *drink* Have you ___________ a cup of coffee yet?

12. *go* He has ___________ to the meeting in Boston.

13. *give* Don ___________ him the check last month.

14. *fly* He could have ___________ to New York in three hours.

15. *drive* We have ___________ the company car.

16. *go* When the snowstorm came, everyone ___________ home early.

17. *speak* Have you ___________ to your supervisor yet?

18. *sing* The trio has ___________ at our meetings many times.

19. *know* We found that only one ___________ the correct procedure.

20. *ride* A member of the firm has ___________ over to see the new property.

21. *see* Dr. Allen ___________ him at the seminar.

22. *take* She should have ___________ the lab reports with her.

23. *swim* I could not have ___________ that distance without help.

24. *throw* The car swerved and ___________ everyone to one side.

25. *write* His boss has ___________ several reports on this product.

26. *bring* He should have ___________ the safety reports to the conference.

27. *eat* Last night we ___________ at the new restaurant.

28. *lend* He __________ me his microscope for the experiment.

29. *lose* We almost __________ our drawings.

30. *eat* I should have __________ earlier.

Check your responses in Feedback 1-H at the end of this module. If you missed any, review the list of principal parts before continuing.

Six Confusing Irregular Verbs

The following pairs of irregular verbs require special attention because they are especially troublesome. First of all, learn the six verbs, their meanings, and their principal parts.

PRESENT	PAST	PAST PARTICIPLE WITH HELPER	PRESENT PARTICIPLE WITH HELPER	MEANING
lie	lay	have lain	are lying	*to recline, rest*
lay	laid	have laid	are laying	*to put, place something* (takes a direct object)
sit	sat	have sat	are sitting	*to take a sitting position, to rest in a chair*
set	set	have set	are setting	*to place something* (takes a direct object)
rise	rose	have risen	are rising	*to go upward on one's own power*
raise	raised	have raised	are raising	*to lift something; to bring up; to increase in amount* (takes a direct object)

From the definitions, you will notice that the second verb in each pair (**lay, set, raise**) is a verb of motion that shows action done to "something." In a sentence, this "something" will be a **direct object**—a noun that follows the verb and receives the action of the verb. The direct object answers the question "whom?" or "what?" after the verb.

Direct Object Test

To find out if the verb has a direct object, ask the question "what?" or "whom?" after the verb.

Helen laid the book on the table. (**Laid** is the verb. Laid *what*? Laid *book—book* is the direct object.)

The landlord raised my rent. (**Raised** is the verb. Raised *what*? Raised *rent—rent* is the direct object.)

Jim lay down to rest. (**Lay** is the verb. Lay *what*? There is no answer—no direct object in this sentence.)

All forms of the verbs **lay**, **set**, and **raise** can take a direct object. Don't be confused by **lay** (the past form of **lie**), which cannot take a direct object, as we saw in the example "Jim lay down to rest."

When in doubt about the correct form of these troublesome verbs, try the direct object test. It is an easy way to settle the issue.

Synonym Test

A second test you can try is substituting a synonym (word with the same meaning) for the word in the sentence. Decide which meaning of the troublesome verb fits in the sentence (*rest* or *put? go upward* or *lift?*). Place the synonym in the sentence. Then check the chart to see which form of the verb to use.

SYNONYM: I *reclined* on the couch all afternoon.
CORRECT VERB: I **lay** on the couch all afternoon.
SYNONYM: The custodian *lifted* the window.
CORRECT VERB: The custodian **raised** the window.

When in doubt, the synonym test can help you decide which verb fits the meaning. Of course, you must also use the correct principal part of the verb.

ACTIVITY 1-I: Six Confusing Irregular Verbs

Two verbs are given in parentheses. Read each sentence carefully and underline the correct verb form. Apply the direct object test and the synonym test.

1. Where did you (lie/lay) the drawings?
2. The student nurse (rose/raised) a question concerning medication.
3. He asked the technician to (sit/set) the microscope on the counter.
4. The architect had (lain/laid) the drawing in its proper place.
5. When she finished the book, she (rose/raised) from her chair.
6. The custodian (rose/raised) the defective window.
7. Mary was thinking how nice it would be to (lie/lay) on the beach instead of (sitting/setting) in the office.
8. (Sit/Set) the computer on the table next to the desk.
9. Please (sit/set) the calculator on the counter when you are finished.
10. We asked the electronics technician to (rise/raise) the amperage.
11. John was asked to (rise/raise) money for an immunization clinic in Los Angeles.
12. In measuring the plot, he had to read the figures on the chart that (lay/laid) on the ground.
13. Andy (rose/raised) the shade after the film was over.

14. Bill (sat/set) at the desk for two hours without getting up.
15. Temperatures will (rise/raise) as summer progresses.

Check your responses in Feedback 1-I at the end of this module. If your responses were correct, proceed to Activity 1-J. If you missed any, review Six Confusing Irregular Verbs before continuing.

ACTIVITY 1-J: Six Confusing Irregular Verbs

Insert the correct form of the verbs indicated. Apply the direct object test and the synonym test. Be sure to use the proper form of the verb, according to the time expressed in the sentence.

Lie or *Lay*

1. I ____________ down on the sofa when I am tired.
2. Right now I am ____________ on the sofa.
3. Yesterday I ____________ on the sofa until noon.
4. All afternoon I have ____________ on the sofa.
5. Yesterday I was ____________ on the sofa when you called.
6. Where should I ____________ the bricks for the foundation?
7. Right now I am ____________ the bricks for the foundation.
8. Yesterday I ____________ the bricks for the foundation.
9. All afternoon I have ____________ the bricks for the foundation.
10. Yesterday I was ____________ the bricks for the foundation.

Sit or *Set*

11. May I ____________ on the chair?
12. Right now I am ____________ on the chair.
13. Yesterday I ____________ on the chair by the window.
14. All afternoon I have ____________ on the chair.

15. Yesterday I was __________ on the chair.

16. Today I can't __________ the menus on the tables.

17. Right now I am __________ the menus on the tables.

18. Yesterday I __________ the menus on the tables.

19. All afternoon I __________ menus on the tables.

20. Yesterday I was __________ menus on the tables.

Rise or *Raise*

21. Watch the weather balloons __________ in the air.

22. Right now the weather balloons are __________ in the air.

23. Yesterday the weather balloons __________ in the air.

24. All afternoon the weather balloons have __________ in the air.

25. Yesterday the weather balloons were __________ in the air.

26. Please __________ the window.

27. Right now I am __________ the window.

28. Yesterday I __________ the window.

29. All afternoon I have __________ and lowered the window.

30. Yesterday I was __________ the window every hour.

Check your responses in Feedback 1-J at the end of this module. If you missed any, review Six Confusing Irregular Verbs, the Direct Object Test, and the Synonym Test. Then proceed to Activity 1-K.

ACTIVITY 1-K: Six Confusing Irregular Verbs

Fill in the chart below with the correct forms of the verbs indicated. Commit the chart to memory, and you will always know which form to use. In the sentences that follow, replace the synonym in italics with the correct form of the verb from the chart.

PRESENT	PAST	PAST PARTICIPLE	PRESENT PARTICIPLE
sit (*rest*)			
set (*put*)			
lie (*rest, recline*)			
lay (*put*)			
rise (*go up*)			
raise (*lift up*)			

________ 1. The nurse asked the patient to *rest* in the wheelchair, but she was already *reclining* in bed.

________ 2. Please *put* your printout on the table.

________ 3. The hot air *went up* to the ceiling.

________ 4. The administrative assistant *remained seated* at his desk all day.

________ 5. Have you *put* the ledger on the desk?

________ 6. The printout has *rested* on the desk all day.

________ 7. I *put* it there myself.

________ 8. The weather balloon has *gone up* above the trees.

________ 9. The athlete *lifted* the weights up over his head.

________10. The nurse had *put* the syringe on the nightstand.

Check your responses in Feedback 1-K at the end of this module. If you missed any, review Part IV. Then proceed to Part V for a discussion of various verb tenses.

PART V: VERB TENSE

The four principal parts of verbs are used to form the various verb tenses. **Tense** refers to the time expressed by the verb: present, past, or future.

1. The *present tense* expresses present action. It is formed by using the first principal part of the verb (also known as the base form of the verb).

NOTE For third-person singular subjects (**he, she, it**), add **-s** or **-es**.

Pharmacists **fill** prescriptions every day.
The pharmacist **fills** prescriptions every day.

- It may also express present condition.
  She **is** happy.
- It may also express a statement that is ongoing.
  Freedom of speech **is** a right that is granted to all Americans.
- It may also express habitual action.
  He **drinks** tea every morning.
- It may also express future time.
  The banquet **begins** at 7 o'clock tonight.
- It also expresses literary or general scientific truths.
  Shakespeare **uses** animal imagery frequently in his plays.

2. The *past tense* expresses past action. It is formed by using the second principal part of the verb. Add **-d** or **-ed** for regular verbs. For irregular verbs, see the section on irregular verbs earlier in this module.

   The pharmacist **filled** the prescription yesterday.

   - It may also express past condition.
     She **was** sad yesterday.

NOTE No helping verb is used with this tense.

3. The *future tense* expresses future time. It is formed by using **will** with the first principal part (**present tense**).

   The pharmacist **will fill** the prescription.

4. The *present perfect tense* expresses action that was begun in the past and has recently been completed. It is formed by using **have** or **has** plus the **past participle.**

   The pharmacist **has filled** the prescriptions.

   - It may also express habitual or continual action that began in the past and has continued into the present.
     He **has** not **drunk** alcohol for two years.

5. The *past perfect tense* expresses action that was completed before another past action. It is formed by using **had** plus the **past participle.**

   The pharmacist **had filled** the prescription before he left for lunch.

6. The *future perfect tense* expresses action that will be completed by or before a certain time in the future. It is formed by using **will have** plus the **past participle.**

   The pharmacist **will have filled** the prescriptions by 5 P.M.

7. The *present progressive tense* expresses action in progress. It is formed by using the verb **am, is,** or **are** plus the **present participle (-ing** form).

   The pharmacist **is filling** the prescription as fast as he can.

8. The *past progressive tense* expresses action in progress sometime in the past. It is formed by using the verb **was** or **were** plus the **present participle.**

   The pharmacist **was filling** the prescription when the customer came in.

9. The *future progressive tense* expresses action that will continue for some time. It is formed by using **will be** plus the **present participle.**

   The pharmacist **will be filling** prescriptions for hours.

10. The *present perfect progressive tense* expresses action that began in the past and continues to the present or possibly into the future. It is formed by using **have** or **has** plus **been** plus the **present participle.**

    The pharmacist **has been filling** prescriptions for 10 years.

11. The *past perfect progressive tense* expresses a continuous action in the past that has been completed. It is formed by using **had** plus **been** plus the **present participle.**

    The pharmacist **had been filling** prescriptions for 35 years when he retired.

12. The *future perfect progressive tense* expresses a continuous action or condition until a certain time in the future. It is formed by using **will** plus **have** plus **been** plus the **present participle.**

    The pharmacist **will have been filling** prescriptions for 35 years when he retires.

ACTIVITY 1-L: Editing Practice

Writers tend to rely too heavily on linking verbs for communication purposes. In the following paragraph, replace all linking verbs with action verbs and edit for correct verb form. You can change the wording, but do not eliminate sentences or change the meaning of the paragraph.

It is apparent that most workers will have to continue their education while on the job. Attending classes while working full time is difficult to manage, but those who have began to pursue advanced coursework offer many helpful suggestions. First, they let it be know that workers need to realize if they have tooken enough courses to advance in their jobs. It is important for workers to know when they have ran out of skills to advance. Second, they suggest that workers don't just set around waiting for someone else to do the work. Sometimes, it becomes apparent that the level of skills needed for the job has raised. Finally, they seem to have came to the conclusion that time management skills will be the core for success. Workers who have choosen to pursue advanced coursework can benefit from this advice.

Check your responses in Feedback 1-L at the end of this module.

ACTIVITY 1-M: **Editing Practice**

Underline all of the verbs in this paragraph, and identify each as either a linking verb or an action verb.

Recent studies have shown that it is not just important what employees say in their communications, but also how they say it. Having emotional intelligence in business communications is important, especially when communicating with supervisors. For instance, when employees are asked to comment on a project approved or completed by a supervisor, they must be careful to be both honest and tactful. It can be awkward critiquing the work of a superior, but most bosses want thoughtful feedback, not just a patronizing affirmation. However, supervisors also do not want to be undercut in front of their employees, so when making a criticism, employees should remember to be discreet and should also be prepared to offer solutions to problems that they have found. Effective communication is one of the most important factors in maintaining a productive, efficient workplace, and most businesses value employees who are concise, straightforward, thorough, and courteous in their communications.

Check your responses in Feedback 1-M at the end of this module.

DIAGNOSTIC FEEDBACK

Identify the verb and label it as an action verb or linking verb:

1. The sales executive <u>arranged</u> (action) to have the contract sent overnight.
2. The nursing assistant <u>is</u> (linking) certified in CPR.
3. The repair technician <u>evaluated</u> (action) the water damage.
4. The flight attendant <u>is</u> (linking) in the cockpit with the pilot.
5. The instructor <u>stressed</u> (action) the importance of careful editing.

Choose the correct form of the verb:

1. Because I was up late, I plan to (lie/lay) down when I get home from work today.
2. The waiter did not know where to (lie/lay) the bill because the table was so cluttered.
3. In my interview, I did not (sit/set) down until I was asked to do so.
4. I plan to (sit/set) the silverware out next to the plates for the dinner party.
5. Don't forget to (rise/raise) the blinds before leaving for work.

FEEDBACK FOR MODULE 1

Feedback 1-A

1. made
2. processed
3. cleaned, oiled
4. entered
5. assists
6. offers
7. extracts
8. work
9. saved
10. hurts

Feedback 1-B

1. sold
2. drew
3. prefers
4. installed
5. stopped
6. saves
7. assembled
8. sold
9. transferred
10. aligned

Feedback 1-C

1. is
2. is
3. are
4. appeared
5. seemed
6. are
7. seem
8. remained
9. taste
10. felt

Feedback 1-D

1.	sentence	is	lengthy
2.	trees	seem	susceptible
3.	judge	appears	thoughtful
4.	coffee	tastes	horrible
5.	aroma	smells	inviting
6.	accountant	was	trustworthy
7.	wire	feels	hot
8.	generator	is	efficient
9.	I	am	happy
10.	He	became	operator

Feedback 1-E

1. L—are
2. A—suggests
3. A—supports
4. L—were
5. L—seems
6. L—looks
7. A—occur
8. A—causes
9. L—appears
10. A—fell

Feedback 1-F

1. L—are
2. A—sampled
3. A—provides
4. A—affected
5. L—are
6. L—seems
7. A—listened
8. L—felt
9. A—carried
10. A—prepared

Feedback 1-G

1. is covering
2. may have done
3. were planning
4. has written
5. has proofread
6. are making
7. will complete
8. should have been done
9. is doing
10. must attend

Feedback 1-H

1. begun
2. came
3. chosen
4. did
5. broken
6. burst
7. did
8. burst
9. brought
10. come
11. drunk
12. gone
13. gave
14. flown
15. driven
16. went
17. spoken
18. sung
19. knew
20. ridden
21. saw
22. taken
23. swum
24. threw
25. written
26. brought
27. ate
28. lent
29. lost
30. eaten

Feedback 1-I

1. lay
2. raised
3. set
4. laid
5. rose
6. raised
7. lie/sitting
8. set
9. set
10. raise
11. raise
12. lay
13. raised
14. sat
15. rise

Feedback 1-J

1. lie
2. lying
3. lay
4. lain
5. lying
6. lay
7. laying
8. laid
9. laid
10. laying
11. sit
12. sitting
13. sat
14. sat
15. sitting
16. set
17. setting
18. set
19. set
20. setting
21. rise
22. rising
23. rose
24. risen
25. rising
26. raise
27. raising
28. raised
29. raised
30. raising

Feedback 1-K

Check the answers in your chart against the chart on page 12.

1. sit, lying
2. set *or* lay
3. rose
4. sat
5. set *or* laid
6. lain
7. set *or* laid
8. risen
9. raised
10. set *or* laid

Feedback 1-L

Corrected verb forms are underlined; linking verbs are italicized, and their sentences have been edited in bold to show one way to eliminate the linking verb. You may have other wording that is correct.

It *is* apparent that most workers (**Apparently, most workers**) will have to continue their education while on the job. Attending classes while working full time *is* difficult to manage (**Attending classes while working full time demands good time management**), but those who have begun to pursue advanced coursework offer many helpful suggestions. First, they let it be known that workers need to realize if they have taken enough courses to advance in their jobs. It *is* important for workers to know when they have run out of skills to advance (**The importance of recognizing when they have run out of skills to advance tops their list of hints**). Second, they suggest that workers don't just *sit* around waiting for someone else to do the work. Sometimes, it *becomes* apparent that the level of skills needed for the job has risen (**Sometimes, the level of skills needed for the job rises**). Finally, they *seem* to have *come* (**Finally, they have come**) to the conclusion that time management skills *will be* (**will comprise**) the core for success. Workers who have chosen to pursue advanced coursework can benefit from this advice.

Feedback 1-M

Recent studies have shown (action) that it is (linking) not just important what employees say (action) in their communications, but also how they say (action) it. Having emotional intelligence in business communications is (linking) important, especially when communicating with supervisors. For instance, when employees are asked (action) to comment on a project approved or completed by a supervisor, they must (action) be careful to be both honest and tactful. It can be (linking) awkward critiquing the work of a superior, but most bosses want (action) thoughtful feedback, not just a patronizing affirmation. However, supervisors also do not want (action) to be undercut in front of their employees, so, when making a criticism, employees should remember (action) to be discreet and should also be prepared (action) to offer solutions to problems that they have found (action). Effective communication is (linking) one of the most important factors in maintaining a productive, efficient workplace, and most businesses value (action) employees who are (linking) concise, straightforward, thorough, and courteous in their communications.

MODULE 2

Adjectives and Adverbs

Objective: In this module, you will learn the functions of two types of describing words, the adjective and the adverb.

Upon completion of this module, you will be able:

- To identify the functions of the adjective and the adverb in the sentence.
- To use the comparison process for adjectives and adverbs.

DIAGNOSTIC EXERCISE

Underline and identify the adjective or adverb in each sentence and draw an arrow to the word it modifies.

1. The assistants struggled to complete the complicated task.
2. We were warmly welcomed at the reception.
3. The driver missed the turn on the windy road.
4. The misleading statement caused a controversy.
5. The accountant deliberately manipulated the figures.

Underline the correct word and draw an arrow to the word it modifies.

1. She speaks very (good, well), so she was chosen as the moderator.
2. We had a (good, well) meeting and accomplished many tasks.
3. If she feels (good/well) enough, she will attend the conference.
4. He plans to be the (most promoted/more promoted) manager in the office.
5. The delivery company is reported to be the (faster/fastest) and (most/more) dependable in the area.

PART I: ADJECTIVES

Here are eight rules that will help you to use adjectives correctly.

Rule 1. *Adjectives describe or modify nouns and pronouns.* They answer certain questions.

What kind? The **efficient** secretary was hired yesterday.
Which one? **That** system is very simple.
How many? **Six** men attended the meeting.
How much? **Some** coffee was left for our break.
We bought **enough** paper for five reports.

Rule 2. *Adjectives usually come before the noun or pronoun they modify.*

The new printer produces **clear** print.

Occasionally, you may use adjectives *after* the word they modify for emphasis or variety. Set these adjectives off with commas.

The bank, **old** and **unpainted,** was finally rebuilt.
Billing records, **corporate** or **personal,** are stored in our computer.

Rule 3. *The adjectives* **a, an,** *and* **the** *are called articles.* Use **a** before words beginning with a consonant sound and **an** before words beginning with a vowel sound.

Go strictly by **sound,** not by whether the word begins with a consonant or vowel.

an egg	**a** factory	**the** keyboard
an hour (*h* is silent)	**an** upper berth	**the** report
a union (consonant y sound)	**an** envelope	**the** meeting
an onion	**an** honor	**the** blueprint

Rule 4. *The pronouns* **this, that, these,** *and* **those** *may be used as adjectives to point out or identify a particular noun.* They agree in number and are placed directly before the noun they modify. Use **this** and **that** before a singular noun; use **these** and **those** before a plural noun.

SINGULAR	PLURAL
this kind	these kinds
that type	those types
this company	these companies
that office	those offices

Rule 5. *Indefinite pronouns do not refer to a specific person, place, or thing. Some indefinite pronouns, such as* **each, one, any, many, some,** *and* **all,** *can be used either as adjectives or as pronouns.* As adjectives, they are followed by a noun. As pronouns, they are not followed by a noun.

Noun

ADJECTIVE: **Each** task will be completed in time.

PRONOUN: **Each** will be completed in time. (The noun *task* has been replaced by the pronoun *each.*)

Noun

ADJECTIVE: **Many** technicians are needed.

PRONOUN: **Many** are needed. (The noun *technicians* has been replaced by the pronoun *many.*)

Rule 6. *Two or more consecutive adjectives may be used to modify the same noun. These adjectives are called* **coordinate adjectives.** Notice the punctuation. Commas are placed between the adjectives *but not between the final adjective and the noun.* If the word "and" makes sense in place of the comma, you need the comma. Also, if you can logically reverse the adjectives, you need the comma (see Module 6, Part II, Rule 3, for further discussion).

She is **an industrious, efficient, hard-working** accountant.

He is engaged in **dangerous, exciting** work.

Rule 7. *Adjectives are often used after linking verbs.* You will remember that linking verbs do not show action; they link the subject to a word that follows the verb. The most common linking verbs are listed below (for more about linking verbs, see Module 1, Part II).

LINKING VERBS

act	feel	remain	sound
appear	grow	seem	stay
be (is, am, etc.)	look	smell	taste
become			

In the following pattern, the adjective tells something about the subject.

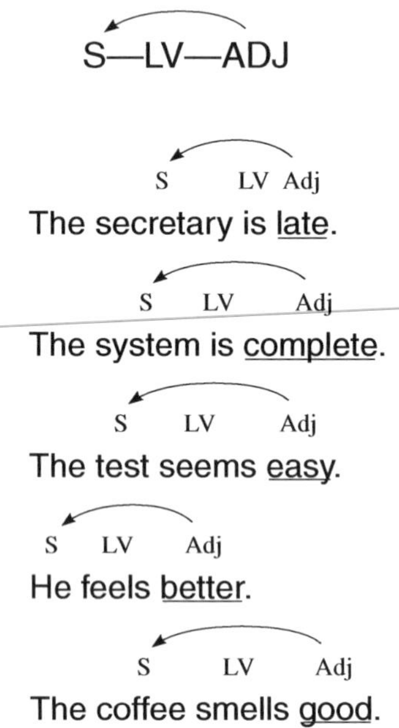
S—LV—ADJ
S LV Adj
The secretary is late.
S LV Adj
The system is complete.
S LV Adj
The test seems easy.
S LV Adj
He feels better.
S LV Adj
The coffee smells good.

Sometimes, as in the pattern below, another word comes between the linking verb and the adjective. That word is usually an adverb, which describes the adjective (see Part II, Rule 2).

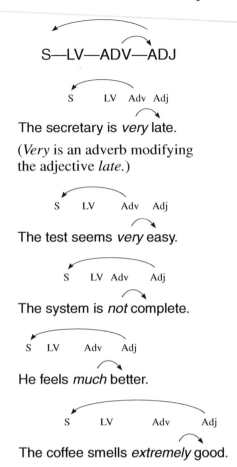

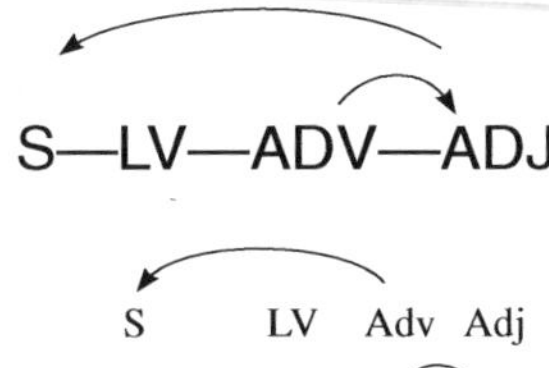

The secretary is *very* late.

(*Very* is an adverb modifying the adjective *late*.)

S LV Adv Adj

The test seems *very* easy.

S LV Adv Adj

The system is *not* complete.

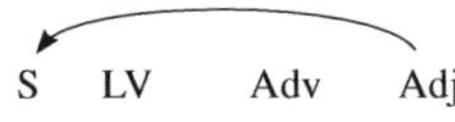

He feels *much* better.

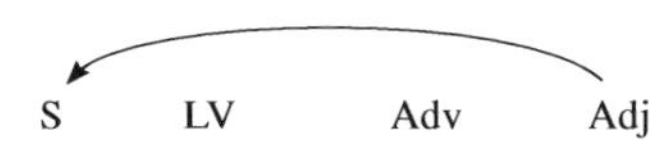

The coffee smells *extremely* good.

Rule 8. *Nouns can sometimes function as adjectives when they are used to modify other nouns.*

I handed in the *book* report.

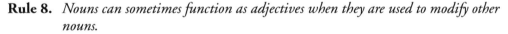

The *computer* programmer worked on the new application.

ACTIVITY 2-A: **Adjectives**

Underline each word that is used as an adjective. Then draw an arrow to the noun it describes or modifies.

1. Many technicians are needed to complete the hard work.
2. The tired nurse was required to chart relevant information.
3. New drawings were completed for each of the three projects.

4. Old, broken equipment was to be replaced.
5. The new technician reported all vitally important data to the supervisor.
6. The retired owner of the three motels was honored at a delicious dinner last night.
7. Each supervisor was required to write monthly reports.
8. The updated computer system is difficult to understand.
9. Report valid test results immediately to the supervisor.
10. A large envelope was mailed without a complete address.

Check your responses in Feedback 2-A at the end of this module. If your responses were correct, proceed to Part II. If you missed any, review Part I; then do Activity 2-B.

ACTIVITY 2-B: Adjectives

Underline all words used as adjectives.

1. She was in a carefree, gay mood while working on the new plan.
2. These ten processors are in good condition.
3. More people were hired than we expected.
4. Please consider all applicants before the final decision is made.
5. Very old records can be found in the department files.
6. The young, highly educated man was the first one to be promoted.
7. Inform the employees that the newly repaved lot is ready for immediate use.
8. The new green machine in the business office will be used to ease the transmitting of existing records.
9. Control systems are used many times to prevent an excessive buildup of unusable inventory.
10. An introductory tour of the recently enlarged facilities will be scheduled for all new employees.

Check your responses in Feedback 2-B at the end of this module. If your responses were correct, proceed to Part II. If you missed any, review them before continuing.

PART II: ADVERBS

These four rules will help you to avoid errors in using adverbs.

Rule 1. *The adverb modifies or describes a verb, an adjective, or another adverb.*

- *Modifying a verb:*

  He speaks **cheerfully.** (The adverb **cheerfully** describes the verb **speaks.** It tells *how* he performs the action.)

- *Modifying an adjective:*

  He speaks in an **exceedingly** cheerful fashion. (The adverb **exceedingly** modifies the adjective **cheerful.** It does not tell *how* he speaks, but *how* cheerful.)

- *Modifying another adverb:*

  He speaks **very cheerfully.** (The adverb **very** modifies the adverb **cheerfully. Cheerfully** tells *how* he speaks. **Very** tells *how* **cheerfully** he speaks.)

Rule 2. *Adverbs often answer the questions* **when, where, how, how often,** *or* **to what extent.**

When?	The board met **recently.**
Where?	John sat **there** in the office.
How?	Ellen works **fast.**
How much?	This faucet leaks **slightly.**
How often?	John drove to town **frequently.**

Rule 3. *Most adverbs are formed by adding* **-ly** *to the adjective form.*

ADJECTIVES: swift, slow, warm, cold

ADVERBS: swiftly, slowly, warmly, coldly

- A number of adjectives ending in **-y** change the **-y** to **-i** before the **-ly** ending of the adverb: **happy** ⟶ **happily; easy** ⟶ **easily; merry** ⟶ **merrily,** etc.
- However, the ending **-ly** is not always the sign of the adverb: **very, much, little, almost, often, there,** etc.
- Some adjectives end in **-ly**:

  The **friendly** (Adj) salesman sold a **lovely** (Adj) quilt to an **ugly,** (Adj) **lonely** (Adj) tourist.

- Note also that sometimes the adverb and the corresponding adjective have the same form:

He had a **fast** (Adj) grip on the pen. (The adjective **fast** modifies the noun *grip*, answering the question "what kind?")

He held **fast** (Adv) to the pen. (The adverb **fast** modifies the verb *held* and answers the question "held how?")

To distinguish between adjectives and adverbs, use this chart:

	MODIFY	ANSWER THE QUESTIONS	
ADJECTIVES	nouns	what kind?	how much?
	pronouns	which one?	how many?
ADVERBS	verbs	how?	to what extent?
	adjectives	where?	how often?
	other adverbs	when?	

Rule 4. *The following words always function as adverbs:*

ADVERBS			
not	very	quite	too
never	often	seldom	always

ACTIVITY 2-C: Adverbs

Underline each adverb and draw an arrow to the word it modifies or describes.

1. Write all the results accurately and neatly.
2. The police officer slowly approached the quiet man.
3. The committee met recently and quickly discussed the proposal.
4. Slowly pour the solution into the beaker.
5. The newly appointed foreman shouted loudly to his men.
6. Mr. Greer was formerly employed at Sears.
7. He was not very well prepared for the meeting.
8. He is late for work quite often.
9. Jane was very excited about her job.
10. Tilt the vial slightly so that the liquid will flow evenly.

Check your responses in Feedback 2-C at the end of this module. If your responses were correct, proceed to Part III. If you missed any, review Part II; then do Activity 2-D.

ACTIVITY 2-D: Adverbs

Underline all adverbs.

1. She was in a serious mood while working diligently on the new plan.
2. These computers are in extremely good condition.

3. More people have been hired lately than we ever expected.
4. Please consider carefully each applicant before we finally make a decision.
5. Billing records can be found easily in the updated files.
6. The highly educated man was the first one to be promoted.
7. Inform the employees soon that the newly repaved parking lot is ready for immediate use.
8. The very heavy machine in the business office will be used easily in the transmitting of existing records.
9. Control systems are often used to prevent an excessively unusable inventory.
10. Fortunately, a tour of the vastly enlarged facilities will be scheduled later for all new employees.

Check your responses in Feedback 2-D at the end of this module. If your responses were correct, proceed to Part III. If you missed any, review before continuing.

PART III: "GOOD" AND "WELL"

Two very common words that are often misused are **good** and **well.** As a general rule, use **good** as an adjective; use **well** as an adverb except when it means "in good health."

Rule 1. **Good** *is usually an adjective.* It precedes a noun or follows a linking verb.

He has a **good** skill.
Adj Noun
He is **good** in accounting.
LV Adj
The rain felt **good**.
LV Adj

Rule 2. **Well** *is usually an adverb that describes* how.

He speaks **well.** Grapes grow **well** here.

She supervises **well.** They are doing **well.**

Rule 3. *When* **well** *means* in good health, *it is an adjective and goes with a linking verb.*

Compare the uses of **good** and **well** in the following sentences.

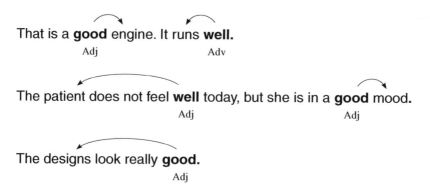

That is a **good** engine. It runs **well.**
Adj Adv

The patient does not feel **well** today, but she is in a **good** mood.
Adj Adj

The designs look really **good.**
Adj

ACTIVITY 2-E: Good—Well

Underline the correct word and draw an arrow to the word it describes.

1. Because of the move, Sam had to quit a (good/well) job.
2. Each administrative assistant must write and type (well/good).
3. I can type (good/well) if the computer works (good/well).
4. If you speak (well/good), you will get the job.
5. The mechanic noticed that the car did not run (good/well).
6. She was late for the meeting because she did not feel (well/good).
7. The new foreman works (good/well) with his men.
8. The staff members ate at Brown's, where the food was (good/well) and prepared (good/well).
9. The nurse told the patient that his pulse was (well/good) and he looked (good/well).
10. The new machine runs (good/well).

Check your responses in Feedback 2-E at the end of this module. If your responses were correct, proceed to Part IV. If you missed any, review Part III; then proceed to Activity 2-F.

ACTIVITY 2-F: Good—Well

Underline the correct word.

1. She was in a (good/well) mood while typing the memo.
2. These new computers are in (good/well) condition.
3. Consider (good/well) each applicant.
4. Personnel records are found easily in files that are kept (good/well).

5. The applicant was educated (good/well).
6. The new parking lot is in (good/well) shape.
7. The machine in the business office works (good/well).
8. We were given a (good/well) tour of the new facility.
9. The new schedule for employees works (good/well).
10. Nurses must learn to give injections (good/well).

Check your responses in Feedback 2-F at the end of this module. If your responses were correct, proceed to Part IV. If you missed any, review before continuing.

PART IV: COMPARISON OF ADJECTIVES AND ADVERBS

Adjectives and adverbs have *degrees of comparison:* the positive, the comparative, and the superlative. The positive (base form) describes *one* entity; the comparative is used when comparing *two;* the superlative is used when comparing *three or more.*

Frank drafted **new** designs. (positive)
His designs are **newer** than Henry's. (comparative)
Frank and Henry's designs are **the newest** in the department. (superlative)

Comparison of Adjectives

The following table shows the positive, comparative, and superlative forms of a few common adjectives.

POSITIVE	COMPARATIVE	SUPERLATIVE
fast	faster	fastest
slow	slower	slowest
fine	finer	finest
happy	happier	happiest
careful	more (less) careful	most (least) careful
beautiful	more (less) beautiful	most (least) beautiful

To form the comparative degree, add **-er** or use the words **more** or **less.** For the superlative, add **-est** or use **most** or **least.** In general, long adjectives (over two syllables) do not use **-er** or **-est.**

NOTE The article the signals the superlative in many cases.

Here are some adjectives that are irregular in form:

POSITIVE	COMPARATIVE	SUPERLATIVE
good, well	better	best
little	less	least
much, many	more	most
bad	worse	worst

Comparison of Adverbs

The following table shows the comparative and superlative forms of several common adverbs. Note that **fast** may function as an adjective as well as an adverb.

POSITIVE	COMPARATIVE	SUPERLATIVE
fast	faster	fastest
slowly	more (less) slowly	most (least) slowly
promptly	more (less) promptly	most (least) promptly
carefully	more (less) carefully	most (least) carefully
easily	more (less) easily	most (least) easily

ACTIVITY 2-G: Comparison

Underline the correct degree of comparison.

1. Pat is the (faster/fastest) typist in the office.
2. He spoke (more calmly/most calmly) to his employees than did Ted.
3. That experiment was (more difficult/most difficult) than the last one.
4. Of all the replies, his was the (more prompt/most prompt).
5. Mary was (more dependable/most dependable) than Rose.
6. Who is the (fastest/faster) one to solve the equation?
7. The assistant was the (most prompt/more prompt) to answer calls.
8. These results must be tallied (most carefully/more carefully) than all the other ones.
9. Employees who have had the vaccine are (least/less) susceptible to the disease than those who have not had the vaccine.
10. My new job requires more work and, therefore, allows me (less/least) time to relax.

Check your responses in Feedback 2-G at the end of this module. If your responses were correct, proceed to Activity 2-I. If you missed any, review Part IV; then do Activity 2-H.

ACTIVITY 2-H: Comparison

Underline the correct degree of comparison.

1. Jim is the (more efficient/most efficient) of all the electricians.
2. The boss shouted (more loudly/most loudly) than before.
3. The lab results were the (more impressive/most impressive) of all the data.
4. Of the two truck drivers, Sam is (weaker/weakest).
5. Kate was (more effective/most effective) as a receptionist than Belinda.
6. Who is the (faster/fastest) typist in all the offices?
7. The applicant who got the job was (more prompt/most prompt) than his colleague.
8. Evaluate the results (more carefully/most carefully) than you did last time.
9. Molly received the (fewest/fewer) responses of all the graduates to her letter of application.
10. There is (less/least) time for coffee breaks.

Check your responses in Feedback 2-H at the end of this module. If your responses were correct, proceed to Activity 2-I. If you missed any, review before continuing.

ACTIVITY 2-I: Identification of Adjectives and Adverbs

Identify the italicized words as adjectives (Adj) or adverbs (Adv).

1. The *elderly* patient looks *well* today.
2. *Any* suggestion will be read and considered *immediately*.
3. Our results will be evaluated *quickly* by the *three* technicians.
4. The data machine will function *correctly* when the material is fed *properly* into it.
5. He *recently* compiled the data and wrote a *lengthy* report.
6. Mr. Bonner will respond *adequately* to your *last* question.
7. That man is *less likely* to be promoted to foreman than his *young* co-worker.
8. The building, *dilapidated* and *crumbling*, is to be razed before the *new* parking lot can be constructed.
9. The *new* drawing looked *good* to the architect.
10. Please return the *old* printouts to Mr. Grant's office before *late* afternoon.

Check your responses in Feedback 2-I at the end of this module. If you missed any, do Activity 2-J.

ACTIVITY 2-J: Identification of Adjectives and Adverbs

Identify the italicized words as adjectives (Adj) or adverbs (Adv).

1. The *concrete* bridge was *sturdily* built.
2. *All* plans for the ceremony are being worked out *carefully*.
3. The statistics will be calculated *rapidly* by the *new* computer.
4. The boss was *very upset* about the breakdown.
5. A *skillful* technician is *seldom* unemployed for a *long* time.
6. Mr. Newton will call *later* in response to your *recent* message.
7. *Fringe* benefits should be *carefully* examined when a *new* job is being considered.
8. Marcy's job, *exciting* and *challenging*, has made her *very happy*.
9. The bridge appears *quite sturdy*.
10. The *noon* flight to Dulles Airport was *late*.

Check your responses in Feedback 2-J at the end of this module. If you missed any, review before continuing.

ACTIVITY 2-K: Editing Practice

Edit the following paragraph for correct forms of adjectives, adverbs, and comparatives. Then circle any five adjectives (other than A, AN, or THE), and underline any five different adverbs.

Changes in health insurance have forced workers to rethink much more careful their health plans. In the past, it was easy to be very lackadaisical about health care options, but carelessness now could result in financial ruin more easier. Because of the highly competitive field and rising costs for health care, plans are constantly requiring workers to assume part of the costs and to follow detailed procedures. Workers should maintain healthier lifestyles so they can stay good. The important thing is to read health literature so that it will be more easily to compare if one plan is best than another. Otherwise, workers could be paying exceedingly more premiums than they should.

Check your responses in Feedback 2-K at the end of this module.

ACTIVITY 2-L: Editing Practice

Edit the following paragraph for correct forms of adjectives, adverbs, and comparatives. Then circle any five adjectives (other than A, AN, or THE), and underline any five different adverbs.

Kimberly thought that returning to college after fifteen years might be the more difficult thing she had ever done. First of all, she did not know how to type good, and it seemed that all of her assignments were to be completed using a word processing program. Second, after being away from school for so long, she found the amount of reading assigned overwhelming, and she wasn't sure how she would complete it all since she also had responsibilities to her family and to her current employer. However, her instructor quickly put her mind at ease when he pointed out that her experience managing a demanding family, being accountable at work, and taking responsibility for a variety of tasks definitely gave her an advantage over some students who have not had those kinds of experiences. She was little worried after speaking with her teacher, and she soon began to eager anticipate her upcoming challenges in her new role as a student.

Check your responses in Feedback 2-L at the end of this module.

DIAGNOSTIC FEEDBACK

Underline and identify the adjective or adverb in each sentence and draw an arrow to the word it modifies.

1. The assistants struggled to complete the complicated task.
2. We were warmly welcomed at the reception.
3. The driver missed the turn on the windy road.
4. The misleading statement caused a controversy.
5. The accountant deliberately manipulated the figures.

Underline the correct word and draw an arrow to the word it modifies.

1. She speaks very (good, well), so she was chosen as the moderator.
2. We had a (good, well) meeting and accomplished many tasks.
3. If she feels (good/well) enough, she will attend the conference.
4. He plans to be the (most promoted/more promoted) manager in the office.
5. The delivery company is reported to be the (faster/fastest) and (most/more) dependable in the area.

FEEDBACK FOR MODULE 2

Feedback 2-A

1. Many technicians
   the hard work
2. The tired nurse
   relevant information
3. New drawings
   the three projects
4. Old, broken equipment
5. The new technician

all important data
the supervisor

6. The retired owner
the three motels
a delicious dinner
last night
7. Each supervisor
monthly reports
8. The updated computer system
difficult system
9. valid test results
the supervisor
10. A large envelope
a complete address

Feedback 2-B

1. a, carefree, gay, the, new
2. These, ten, good
3. More
4. all, the, final
5. old, the, department
6. The, young, educated, the, first
7. the, the, repaved, ready, immediate
8. The, new, green, the, business, the, existing
9. Control, many, an, excessive, unusable
10. An, introductory, the, enlarged, all, new

Feedback 2-C

1. Write accurately, neatly
2. slowly approached
3. met recently; quickly discussed
4. Slowly pour
5. newly appointed; shouted loudly
6. formerly was employed
7. not, well prepared; very well
8. quite often; often late
9. very excited
10. Tilt slightly; flow evenly

Feedback 2-D

1. diligently
2. extremely
3. lately, ever
4. carefully, finally
5. easily
6. highly
7. soon, newly
8. very, easily
9. often, excessively
10. Fortunately, vastly, later

Feedback 2-E

1. good job
2. write, type well
3. type well; works well
4. speak well
5. run well
6. she well (in good health)
7. works well
8. good food; prepared well
9. good pulse; looked well
10. runs well

Feedback 2-F

1. good
2. good
3. well
4. well
5. well
6. good
7. well
8. good
9. well
10. well

Feedback 2-G

1. fastest
2. more calmly
3. more difficult
4. most prompt
5. more dependable
6. fastest
7. most prompt
8. more carefully
9. less
10. less

Feedback 2-H

1. most efficient
2. more loudly
3. most impressive
4. weaker
5. more effective
6. fastest
7. more prompt
8. more carefully
9. fewest
10. less

Feedback 2-I

1. elderly (adj)
   well (adj)
2. Any (adj)
   immediately (adv)
3. quickly (adv)
   three (adj)
4. correctly (adv)
   properly (adv)
5. recently (adv)
   lengthy (adj)
6. adequately (adv)
   last (adj)
7. less (adv)
   likely (adv)
   young (adj)
8. dilapidated (adj)
   crumbling (adj)
9. new (adj)
   good (adj)
10. old (adj)
    late (adj)

Feedback 2-J

1. concrete (adj)
   sturdily (adv)
2. All (adj)
   carefully (adv)
3. rapidly (adv)
   new (adj)
4. very (adv)
   upset (adj)

5. skillful (adj)
   seldom (adv)
   long (adj)
6. later (adv)
   recent (adj)
7. Fringe (adj)
   carefully (adv)
   new (adj)
8. exciting (adj)
   challenging (adj)
   very (adv)
   happy (adj)
9. quite (adv)
   sturdy (adj)
10. noon (adj)
    late (adj)

Feedback 2-K

NOTE Changes in form are italicized. Adverbs are underlined; adjectives are in bold.

Changes in **health** insurance have forced workers to rethink much more *carefully* their **health** plans. In the past, it was **easy** to be very **lackadaisical** about **health care** options, but carelessness *now* could result in **financial** ruin more *easily*. Because of the highly **competitive** field and **rising** costs for **health** care, plans are constantly requiring workers to assume part of the costs and to follow **detailed** procedures. Workers should maintain **healthier** lifestyles so they can stay ***well.*** The **important** thing is to read **health** literature so that it will be ***easier*** to compare if **one** plan is ***better*** than another. Otherwise, workers could be paying exceedingly **more** premiums than they should.

Feedback 2-L

NOTE Changes in form are italicized. Adverbs are underlined; adjectives are in bold.

Kimberly thought that returning to college after **fifteen** years might be the *most* **difficult** thing she had ever done. First of all, she did not know how to type *well*, and it seemed that all of her assignments were to be completed using a **word processing** program. Second, after being away from school for so long, she found the amount of reading assigned **overwhelming,** and she wasn't sure how she would complete it all since she also had responsibilities to her family and to her **current** employer. However, her instructor quickly put her mind at ease when he pointed out that her experience managing a **demanding** family, being accountable at work, and taking responsibility for a variety of tasks definitely gave her an advantage over some students who have not had those kinds of experiences. She was less worried after speaking with her teacher, and she soon began to *eagerly* anticipate her upcoming challenges in her **new** role as a student.

MODULE 3

Phrases

Objective: In this module, you will learn to identify and use two kinds of phrases.

Upon completion of this module, you will be able:

- To define a phrase.
- To identify the prepositional phrase and its function in the sentence.
- To identify the verbal phrase and its function in the sentence.

A phrase is a group of words serving as a single unit within a sentence and having the following characteristics:

1. A phrase contains neither a subject nor a verb.
2. A phrase cannot stand by itself as a grammatically complete sentence but must always be part of a sentence.

There are two kinds of phrases, *prepositional* and *verbal*.

DIAGNOSTIC EXERCISE

Underline the prepositional phrases.

1. We met in the small office at the rear of the building because our conference room is under construction.
2. In the last decade, we have seen many technological advances.
3. The box on the floor needs to be moved to the closet in the back.
4. Two of the employees were suspended without pay.
5. The luggage on the plane was sent to the wrong destination.

Underline the prepositional phrases and circle the verbal phrases.

1. She felt that it was important to see the project herself before making any hasty decisions.
2. Working two jobs was starting to feel overwhelming for the shift nurse.
3. The car, swerving quickly, barely missed the debris in the road.
4. When they completed the project, they made plans to meet for a celebration dinner.
5. Having two interviews in one day was not only hectic, but also stressful.

PART I: PREPOSITIONAL PHRASES

A **prepositional phrase** is a group of words that contains (1) a preposition, (2) the object of the preposition, which is a noun or pronoun, and (3) all modifiers of that object. Like all phrases, it is a part of a sentence, not a sentence in itself.

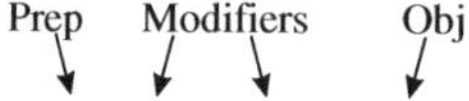

The manager **in the navy suit** read your letter.

In the prepositional phrase "in the navy suit," **in** is the preposition, **suit** is the object, and **the** and **navy** modify the object **suit**.

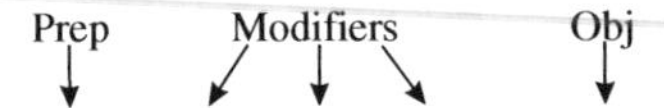

Coffee was available during the first 4-H meeting.

In the prepositional phrase "during the first 4-H meeting," **during** is the preposition, **meeting** is the object, and **the**, **first**, and **4-H** modify the object **meeting**.

NOTE A word must have an object to be used as a preposition in a sentence.

Object Test

To find out if a word has an object, ask "what?" or "whom?" after the word. If there is an answer, the word has an object.

in the suit (in *what?* in *suit—suit* is the object)

during the meeting (during *what?* during *meeting—meeting* is the object)

for my employers (for *whom?* for *employers—employers* is the object)

He looked above. (above *what?* There is no answer. There is no object. *Above* is not being used as a preposition here. It is an adverb.)

Study the following list of some of the more common prepositions. Learn to recognize them quickly so you can identify and use them in sentences.

PREPOSITIONS

about*	beneath	in*	throughout*
above	beside	inside	to
across	besides	into	toward*
after*	between	like	under
against	beyond	near*	underneath
along	but (meaning "except")	of	until*
amid		off	unto
among	by*	on*	up
around*	down	outside	upon
at*	during*	over	with
before*	except	past*	within*
behind	for*	since*	without
below	from*	through*	

NOTE The asterisk (*) indicates prepositions that often begin a *time phrase*; that is, a phrase that answers the question "when?" For example: **about** 10 o'clock, **in** the evening, **on** Tuesday.

Some prepositions consist of a combination of two or more words. The following examples are just a few of the many possibilities.

accompanied by	in addition to
along with	in back of
as well as	in front of
because of	next to
by means of	together with

ACTIVITY 3-A: Prepositional Phrases

Underline the prepositional phrases in the sentences below.

1. I heard about the position from my friend.
2. He moved the car into the shop for repairs.
3. A portrait of the company's founder hangs on the wall of her office to the left of her desk.
4. In the morning, we report for work at the factory.
5. He got the idea for his invention from the supervisor.

Check your responses in Feedback 3-A at the end of this module. If your responses were correct, proceed to Activity 3-C. If you missed any, review the list of prepositions and then do Activity 3-B.

ACTIVITY 3-B: Prepositional Phrases

Underline the prepositional phrases in the sentences below.

1. The loose bolt fell under the machine.
2. The company's picnic is held every July in the park near the old grandstand.
3. The drawings are in the top drawer of the gray filing cabinet.
4. The police officer stopped the car that was doing 65 in a 30-mile speed zone.
5. In spring, the horticulture department is busy with planting.

Check your responses in Feedback 3-B at the end of this module. If your responses were correct, proceed to Activity 3-C. If you missed any, review the list of prepositions before continuing.

ACTIVITY 3-C: Prepositional Phrases

Underline the 10 prepositional phrases in the sentences below.

1. As we watched from the door of his office, we saw the executive.
2. The new computer in the office has been praised by the staff.

3. The retailers have postponed their meeting for three weeks.
4. The decision on the drawings was made by the committee.
5. The office for the new president will be completed on time by the crew.

Check your responses in Feedback 3-C at the end of this module. If your responses were correct, proceed to Part II. If you missed any, review Part I before continuing.

PART II: VERBAL PHRASES

A **verbal** is a verb form used as another part of speech. Like all phrases, a verbal phrase has neither a subject nor a verb. It cannot stand alone but must always be part of a sentence.

A **verbal phrase** is composed of a verbal, its object (if any), and its modifiers (if any). There are three types of verbals: **infinitives, participles,** and **gerunds.**

Three Types of Verbals

1. *Infinitives:* **"to" plus a verb.** Infinitives may be used as nouns, adjectives, or adverbs. When used as nouns, infinitives may function as subjects, direct objects, or subjective complements.

   to go, to type, to write, to be, etc.

2. *Participles:* **present participles** (**-ing** form) and **past participles.** The participle form by itself, without a helper verb, functions as an adjective.

   Present participle: going, singing, walking, etc.
   Past participle: played, walked, given, heard, lent, etc.

3. *Gerunds:* **-ing form of the verb used as a noun.**

   swimming, fishing, hunting, etc.

The following rules will help you recognize the three types of verbals. You will not have to know them by name. Remember that a verbal phrase does not contain the verb of the sentence. In the examples below, the verbals are underlined, and the verbs of the sentences are in bold type.

Rule 1. Present participles and gerunds are identical in form: both end in **-ing.** The difference is in their use.

Running **is** good exercise. (Here *running* is a gerund, used as a subject of the sentence. It is a verbal, so there is no helping verb.)

He **was running** in the lab. (**Was running** is the verb.)

The running water **filled** the beaker. (Here *running* is a participle, used as an adjective modifying *water.*)

Rule 2. A participle (or participle phrase) functions as an adjective in a sentence. It modifies a noun or pronoun. In the examples below, the arrows point to the noun modified by the underlined participle.

The running water **has filled** the beaker.

The detective sitting in the car **has reported** for duty.

Standing high on a metal frame, the foreman **shouted** directions.

Having been filled with gas, the car **was** ready for the trip.

❑ ***Punctuation Tip:***

Punctuation with participles varies, but, generally, if there is a sentence following an introductory participle, the phrase is set off with a comma. Interrupting participles depend on whether they are essential or nonessential. (See Module 8 for more information on punctuating essential and nonessential clauses.)

Rule 3. The past participle is made from the past tense of the verb; however, it is not being used as the verb in the sentence. It usually ends in **-d** or **-ed,** such as **talked.** Some past forms of verbs are irregular, such as **sang** or **went.**

The Buick, sold yesterday, **was** in good condition.
Broken from mistreatment, the computer **was sent** away for repairs.
The report, written with accuracy, **revealed** many company strengths.

NOTE There are no helping verbs in front of the verbals.

Rule 4. A verbal or verbal phrase that is a gerund must serve as a noun in a sentence. This noun may function as the *subject, direct object, subject complement,* or the *object* of a preposition.

Subject
Counseling juveniles **has become** my vocation.

Direct Object
We **like** doing our work early.

Obj of Prep
Through counseling, many students **determine** their job capabilities.

Sub Complement
Her favorite part of the course **was** the writing.

Rule 5. A verbal phrase that is an infinitive may serve as a noun, adjective, or adverb. As a noun, the infinitive or infinitive phrase may function as the *subject, direct object,* or *subjective complement* of the sentence.

NOTE Do not confuse the infinitive, *to + verb* (as in **to walk**), with the prepositional phrase, *to + noun* (as in **to school**) or *to + pronoun* (as in **to him**).

Subject
To counsel a juvenile **requires** patience.

Direct Object
We **like** to repair cars that need attention.

Sub Complement
His immediate goal **is** to complete the course.

Adjective
The decision to dissolve the partnership **was** a difficult one.

Adverb
He **was hired** to train the U.S. Olympic Swim Team.

❑ ***Punctuation Tip:***

Since gerunds function as nouns in the sentence, they are usually not set off with commas.

ACTIVITY 3-D: **Verbal Phrases**

Circle the complete verb in each sentence so you won't confuse it with the verbal phrases. Then underline any verbal phrases that you spot. Do not worry about which type of verbal phrase you find. Simply look for the verbal signals: *to + verb*, *-ing* form without a helper, and past form without a helper.

1. They were too timid to ask for more money.
2. Capturing their attention, the speaker referred to their problem areas.
3. Taking care, one can avoid errors.
4. The car, dented in the accident, was the plant manager's.
5. Believing in all their promises was hard for the new employee.
6. Walking quickly, he entered the conference room.
7. To read a report quickly can be a helpful skill.
8. Programming a computer requires much skill.
9. Seeing the unsatisfactory results, he tried a new plan of attack.
10. He enjoyed operating the machine alone.

Check your responses in Feedback 3-D at the end of this module. If your responses were correct, proceed to Activity 3-F. If you missed any, review the definitions of verbals in Part II and then do Activity 3-E.

ACTIVITY 3-E: Verbal Phrases

Circle the complete verb in each sentence so that you won't confuse them with verbal phrases. Then underline any verbal phrases that you spot. Do not worry about which type of verbal phrases you find. Look for the verbal signals.

1. Calling the supervisor, the plant manager requested two more workers for the graveyard shift.
2. The police officers, seeing the speeding car, climbed into their car and drove after it.
3. Hearing the report, the social worker called the agency.
4. Determining the results was the job of the technician.
5. Experimenting with new chemicals can be a dangerous job.
6. To operate the machine can be difficult.
7. Mr. Smith enjoyed working throughout the summer.
8. Speaking with her partner, the president began the new project.
9. Rising early is not much fun for the worker.
10. He liked to calculate the results immediately.

Check your responses in Feedback 3-E at the end of this module. If your responses were correct, proceed to Activity 3-F. If you missed any, review Part II before continuing.

ACTIVITY 3-F: Verbal and Prepositional Phrases

Circle the complete verb in each sentence. Then underline and label all phrases V for verbal or P for prepositional. Some sentences contain more than one phrase. The first sentence has been done as an example.

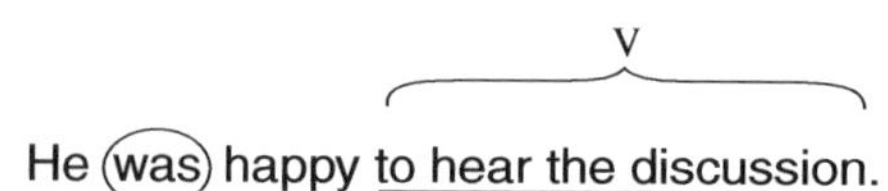

1. The man with the briefcase is the applicant.
2. Organizing a conference, state or local, requires detailed plans.
3. Seeing the manager was a pleasant surprise.
4. Gaining her boss's approval was important to Jane.
5. Becoming an architect requires much dedication.
6. The supervisor speaking with the workers encouraged them to finish their job before noon.
7. She became an expert in social work through her job as a counselor in a summer camp.
8. Rising to a towering height, the construction looked beautiful.

9. For many years, the gap between the employer and the employee has been widening gradually.
10. The student was not present to hear the discussion about citations.

Check your responses in Feedback 3-F at the end of this module. If your responses were correct, proceed to Activity 3-G. If you missed any, review Part II before continuing.

ACTIVITY 3-G: Review

Circle the complete verbs. Then underline all phrases and, using the blanks to the left of each sentence, label them P for prepositional or V for verbal.

1. ______ Ms. Banks, will you fax an acceptance to the seminar chairman?
2. ______ Taking blood can be difficult.
3. ______ We seldom attend both of the meetings.
4. ______ At the building site, Mr. Blake noticed a broken glass.
5. ______ The employees are allowed to use the administrative lounge.
6. ______ The foremen were encouraged to speak their grievances.
7. ______ Drafting a new plan is difficult.
8. ______ The lawyer was asked to meet the judge later.
9. ______ To cater luncheons is hard work.
10. ______ The staff parking lot is near the main building.

Check your responses in Feedback 3-G at the end of this module.

ACTIVITY 3-H: Editing Practice

Underline five verbal phrases and place parentheses around five prepositional phrases in the following paragraph.

Working with a study group can prove to be very beneficial to students. Many studies have been performed on this topic, and all indicate that students can raise their grades substantially if they take time to work together. In writing, there are various applications of the study group. Groups can help with brainstorming ideas for reports. Furthermore, they can be helpful when proofreading a draft. Members can help each other by creating practice activities for skill work. Participating in a writing group, students can learn from each other and share thoughtful ideas and critiques with their colleagues.

Check your responses in Feedback 3-H at the end of this module.

ACTIVITY 3-I: Editing Practice

Underline five verbal phrases and place parentheses around five prepositional phrases in the following paragraph.

Paying for a college education can be costly and overwhelming. Students often must be creative in order to cut expenses while they are in college. For instance, buying used books instead of new texts can often save money. Carpooling with other students is another way to cut travel costs. If students budget carefully, affording a college education can be within their reach.

Check your responses in Feedback 3-I at the end of this module.

DIAGNOSTIC FEEDBACK

Underline the prepositional phrases.

1. We met in the small office at the rear of the building because our conference room is under construction.
2. In the last decade, we have seen many technological advances.
3. The box on the floor needs to be moved to the closet in the back.
4. Two of the employees were suspended without pay.
5. The luggage on the plane was sent to the wrong destination.

Underline the prepositional phrases and circle the **verbal phrases.**

1. She felt that it was important ***to see*** the project herself before **making any hasty decisions.**
2. **Working two jobs** was starting **to feel** overwhelming for the shift nurse.
3. The car, **swerving quickly,** barely missed the debris in the road.
4. When they completed the project, they made plans **to meet** for a celebration dinner.
5. **Having two interviews** in one day was not only hectic, but also stressful.

FEEDBACK FOR MODULE 3

Feedback 3-A

1. about the position
   from my friend
2. into the shop
   for repairs
3. of the company's founder
   on the wall
   of her office
   to the left
   of her desk
4. In the morning
   for work
   at the factory
5. for his invention
   from the supervisor

Feedback 3-B

1. under the machine
2. in the park
   near the old grandstand
3. in the top drawer
   of the gray filing cabinet
4. in a 30-mile speed zone
5. In spring
   with planting

Feedback 3-C

1. from the door
   of his office
2. in the office
   by the staff
3. for three weeks
4. on the drawings
   by the committee
5. for the new president
   on time
   by the crew

Feedback 3-D

1. were *to ask for more money*
2. *Capturing their attention* referred
3. *Taking care* can avoid
4. *dented in the accident* was
5. *Believing in all their promises* was
6. *Walking quickly* entered
7. *To read a report quickly* can be
8. *Programming a computer* requires
9. *Seeing the unsatisfactory results* tried
10. enjoyed *operating the machine alone*

Feedback 3-E

1. *Calling the supervisor* requested
2. *seeing the speeding car* climbed, drove
3. *Hearing the report* called
4. *Determining the results* was
5. *Experimenting with new chemicals* can be
6. *To operate the machine* can be
7. enjoyed *working throughout the summer*
8. *Speaking with her partner* began
9. *Rising early* is
10. liked *to calculate the results immediately*

Feedback 3-F

1. *with the briefcase* (P) is
2. *Organizing a conference* (V) requires
3. *Seeing the manager* (V) was
4. *Gaining her boss's approval* (V) was *to Jane* (P)
5. *Becoming an architect* (V) requires
6. *speaking with the workers* (V) encouraged *to finish their job* (V) *before noon* (P)
7. became *in social work* (P) *through her job* (P) *as a counselor* (P) *in a summer camp* (P)
8. *Rising to a towering height* (V) looked
9. *For many years* (P) *between the employer and the employee* (P) has been widening
10. Was present *to hear the discussion* (V) *about citations* (P)

Feedback 3-G

1. P *to the seminar chairman* will fax
2. V *Taking blood* can be
3. P *of the meetings* attend
4. P *At the building site* noticed
5. V *to use the administrative lounge* are allowed
6. V *to speak their grievances* were encouraged
7. V *Drafting a new plan* is
8. V *to meet the judge later* was asked
9. V *To cater luncheons* is
10. P *near the main building* is

Feedback 3-H

Working (with a study group) can prove to be very beneficial (to students). Many studies have been performed (on this topic), and all indicate that students can raise their grades substantially if they take time to work together. (In writing), there are various applications (of the study group). Groups can help (with brainstorming ideas) (for reports). Furthermore, they can be helpful when proofreading a draft. Members can help each other (by creating practice activities) (for skill work). Participating (in a writing group), students can learn (from each other) and share thoughtful ideas and critiques (with their colleagues).

Feedback 3-L

Paying (for a college education) can be costly and overwhelming. Students often must be creative (in order to cut expenses) while they are (in college). (For instance), buying used books instead (of new texts) can often save money. Carpooling (with other students) is another way to cut travel costs. If students budget carefully, affording a college education can be (within their reach).

MODULE 4

Nouns/Possessive Nouns

Objective: This module will introduce you to nouns, which are central for communication purposes.

Upon completion of this module, you will be able:

- To identify various kinds of nouns.
- To distinguish between plural nouns and possessive nouns.
- To apply two rules governing the apostrophe to show possession.
- To use the five-step process to form possessives.

Like verbs, nouns are part of the core of any sentence. By definition, a ***noun*** is a person, place, thing, or idea. Nouns can be singular or plural, and they can be proper (capitalized) or common (not capitalized). There are also **collective nouns,** which indicate groups.

DIAGNOSTIC EXERCISE

Underline all of the nouns in the following sentences, including the noun antecedent (and circle its pronoun).

1. The instructor plans her lessons well in advance.
2. The students gathered their materials and went to the library.
3. The student council has its meetings on the third Wednesday of each month.
4. When the customers arrived, the store was locked, and they were not able to get in.
5. The daycare manager lost her job because of a poor work ethic.

Underline the correct pronoun.

1. The syllabus on the desk is (your's/yours).
2. The committee held (its/it's) last meeting in the spring.
3. The technician (whose/who's) error caused the misdiagnosis has agreed to resign.
4. (It's/Its) difficult to predict the outcome.
5. The paper shredder is (ours/our's), so don't leave it here.

PART I: NOUNS

Here are some examples of different forms of nouns:

PERSON	PLACE	THING	IDEA	PROPER	COMMON	COLLECTIVE
employee	cafeteria	pen	memory	Kathy	girl	committee
citizen	lab	cup	approval	Sunday	calendar	class

ACTIVITY 4-A: Identifying Nouns

Underline the nouns in the following sentences.

1. The architect submitted his drawings for the bid.
2. The nurses will take their boards on Monday.
3. The jury cannot seem to come to a decision.

4. The Board of Education meets every third week of the month.
5. The virus in the network can be eliminated with this program.
6. The company reviewed its policy on personal leave.
7. Each accountant must be responsible for his own clients.
8. The daycare has additional hours available for people on the late shift.
9. Counselors meet weekly with their probation clients.
10. Therapy in a group seems to be working for these patients.

Check your responses in Feedback 4-A at the end of this module. If your responses were correct, proceed to Part II. If you missed any, review Part I and do Activity 4-B before continuing.

ACTIVITY 4-B: **Identifying Nouns**

Underline the nouns in the following sentences.

1. Companies are stressing the ethics of proper use of the computer during the workday.
2. The therapists went to the convention to become familiar with new techniques.
3. Auto mechanics are learning to deal with highly sophisticated computers in cars.
4. The Washington Monument in our nation's capital is one of the most recognized buildings in the world.
5. Several workers attended the seminar on job discrimination.
6. Employees are very concerned with their job retirement plans because of recent changes in the Social Security Program.
7. The phlebotomist is currently analyzing samples of blood.
8. The patients on the third floor have ambulatory privileges.
9. Licensure depends on a variety of conditions according to individual states.
10. The company sent a summary of its financial condition to its stockholders.

Check your responses in Feedback 4-B at the end of this module. Then proceed to Part II.

PART II: FUNCTIONS OF NOUNS

Nouns have various functions in sentences. They appear throughout sentences where they can be subjects and objects. In addition, nouns are antecedents of pronouns. An **antecedent** is the word a pronoun replaces. The antecedent must be clearly established before a pronoun can be substituted for it. Antecedent nouns and pronouns, therefore, must agree in gender (male, female, neuter) and number (singular, plural). For a more detailed discussion of this concept, see Module 6, Pronoun–Antecedent Agreement, and Module 11, Shifts in Number.

The **greenhouses** are being renovated, so **they** should be ready next month.

Mr. Stevens met with **his employees**, and **he** told **them** to be ready to work overtime.

ACTIVITY 4-C: Locating Antecedents and Pronouns

Underline the noun antecedent and circle its pronoun in the following sentences.

1. Many healthcare workers are concerned with their stress levels.
2. The receptionist is responsible for making her calls first thing each morning.
3. The state troopers complete their training after their coursework.
4. The committee made its decision late last night.
5. Ms. Barto sent her resume to companies on the West Coast.
6. The electronics students spend their free time in lab.
7. CNAs can earn their certification.
8. Internships are available after students complete their first year of studies.
9. That radiologist travels to her community's outreach centers.
10. The company changed its family leave policy.

Check your responses in Feedback 4-C at the end of this module. If your responses were correct, proceed to Part III. If you missed any, review Part II and do Activity 4-D before continuing.

ACTIVITY 4-D: Locating Antecedents and Pronouns

Underline the noun antecedent and circle its pronoun in the following sentences.

1. The nurse found his stethoscope on his rear view mirror.
2. Each computer workstation has its own printer.
3. All employees must submit their overtime by noon today.
4. The lab assistant showed her students how to dissect the pig.
5. The welders know that their safety is top priority.
6. Some accountants prefer to work from their homes.
7. The probation officer met with her clients today.
8. The daycare posts its hours on a website.
9. The advisory board submitted its recommendations.
10. The convention announced its sessions in a spring brochure.

Check your responses in Feedback 4-D at the end of this module. If your responses were correct, proceed to Part III. If you missed any, review before continuing.

PART III: PLURAL NOUNS AND POSSESSIVES

One of the key attributes of nouns is that they can be singular or plural. Plural nouns often get confused with possessive formations because they SOUND alike, so it is critical to know how to differentiate between use of a plural noun and a singular or plural possessive. For example, look at the following sentence to see how the plural noun formation sounds the same as both of the possessive formations. The meanings, however, are quite different.

All the **programmers'** (plural possessive) supervisors presented the **programmers** (plural noun) with a certificate that would reimburse each **programmer's** (singular possessive) tuition costs for networking training.

When writing correspondence, it is easy to get confused with plurals and possessives. Therefore, the following sections of the module will help you to use possessive nouns and to form them correctly using a simple five-step process. Then you will get some editing practice on differentiating among the formations.

PART IV: POSSESSIVE NOUNS

The **apostrophe** is a punctuation mark used to show possession in nouns and indefinite pronouns. Here is the basic rule: *If the word you wish to make possessive ends in* **s**, *add an apostrophe after the* **s**; *if the noun does not end in* **s**, *add an apostrophe and an* **s**.

Rule 1. *Don't worry about whether the noun is singular or plural. Just concern yourself with whether or not it ends in* **s**.

NOUN	SINGULAR POSSESSIVE	PLURAL POSSESSIVE
man	man's	men's
woman	woman's	women's
supervisor	supervisor's	supervisors'
boss	boss'	bosses'
Jones	Jones'	Joneses'

INDEFINITE PRONOUN	
everyone	everyone's
anybody	anybody's

There is a simple five-step process to help you locate and form a possessive. Here is a sentence to use as an example:

The news in the Student Center is about students grades.

Step 1: Locate nouns or indefinite pronouns ending in **s.**

The **news** in the Student Center is about **students grades.**

Step 2: Check to see if there is a noun to the right.

The **news** in the Student Center is about **students grades.**
There is no noun to the right of **news.**
There is no noun to the right of **grades.**
There is a noun to the right of **students.**

Step 3: Substitute the phrase *belonging to* or *of* to determine if possession is being shown.

grades of students

NOTE There is nothing belonging to **news** or **grades;** therefore, possession is not being shown. Be sure to check all nouns ending in **s** to see if they are possessive or if they are merely plural. **News** is a singular noun ending in **s** (an exception to the rule of the way most nouns form their plurals); **grades** is a plural noun showing no possession.

Step 4: Determine if the possessive noun or indefinite pronoun is singular or plural.

Students is plural because the sentence is talking about the grades of more than one student.

Step 5: Turn the *belonging* to phrase around again, this time using the apostrophe to show that the noun is possessive. If the possessive noun ends in **s,** add only an apostrophe. If the noun does not end in **s,** add an apostrophe and an **s.**

students' grades

Corrected sentence:

The news in the Student Center is about students' grades.

Now, apply the five-step approach to a slightly different sentence:

The news in the Student Center is about a students grades.

Step 1: Locate the nouns or indefinite pronouns ending in **s.**

news, students, grades

Step 2: Check to see if there is a noun to the right.

a students grades

NOTE Be sure to check for words that qualify whether the noun is singular or plural, such as **a, an, each,** and **every.**

Step 3: Substitute the phrase *belonging to* or *of* to determine if possession is being shown.

the grades of a student

NOTE Include any qualifying words that indicate whether the noun is singular or plural.

Step 4: Determine if the possessive noun or indefinite pronoun is singular or plural.

A student is singular.

Step 5: Turn the *belonging* to phrase around again, this time using the apostrophe to show that the noun is possessive. If the possessive noun ends in **s,** add only an apostrophe. If the noun does not end in **s,** add an apostrophe and an **s.**

a student's grades

Corrected sentence:

The news in the Student Center is about a student's grades.

Now, do one more example before you try to use the five-step method for using the apostrophe to show possession. This time, the example will have a possessive indefinite pronoun instead of a noun.

The cafeteria tables should be free of anyones books.

Step 1: Locate the nouns or indefinite pronouns ending in **s.**

tables, anyones, books

Step 2: Check to see if there is a noun to the right of it.

anyones books

Step 3: Substitute the phrase *belonging* to or *of* to determine if possession is being shown.

books belonging to anyone

Step 4: Determine if the possessive noun or indefinite pronoun is singular or plural.

Anyone is singular.

Step 5: Turn the *belonging to* phrase around again, this time using the apostrophe to show that the noun or pronoun is possessive.

anyone's books

Corrected sentence:

The cafeteria tables should be free of anyone's books.

Now it is time for you to try your hand at applying the five-step approach to solving possessive problems.

ACTIVITY 4-E: **Apostrophe**

Sample sentence:

The retailers meetings are held on Wednesdays and Fridays.

Step 1: Locate the nouns or indefinite pronouns ending in **s.**
Step 2: Check to see if there is a noun to the right.
Step 3: Substitute the *belonging to* or *of* phrase to determine if possession is being shown.
Step 4: Determine if the possessive noun or indefinite pronoun is singular or plural.
Step 5: Turn the belonging to phrase around, using the apostrophe to show possession.

Corrected sentence:

____

Sample sentence:

A computers keys need repair because of careless operators.

Step 1: ______________________________

Step 2: ______________________________

Step 3: ______________________________

Step 4: ______________________________

Step 5: ______________________________

Corrected sentence:

____

Sample sentence:

Everybodys printouts are on the shelves.

Step 1: ______________________________

Step 2: ______________________________

Step 3: ______________________________

Step 4: ______________________________

Step 5: ______________________________

Corrected sentence:

____

Check your responses in Feedback 4-E. If you missed any, review the five-step process before proceeding to Activity 4-F.

ACTIVITY 4-F: Apostrophe

Provide the correct possessive form.

1. everyone ______________________________
2. foreman ______________________________
3. Ross ______________________________
4. Lindquists ______________________________
5. accountants ______________________________
6. child ______________________________

7. retailers ____________________
8. women ____________________
9. Davises ____________________
10. waitress ____________________
11. company ____________________
12. companies ____________________

Check your responses in Feedback 4-F at the end of this module. If you missed any, review Rule 1 before continuing.

Rule 2. *Make sure that possession is being shown by seeing if there is something that belongs to the noun. To do this, reverse the possessive phrase (such as the* **dog's bone***) and use a prepositional phrase* (**bone of the dog**).

the book's pages *becomes* the pages of the book
the man's hat *becomes* the hat of the man
the policeman's badge *becomes* the badge of the policeman (Singular)
the policewomen's badges *becomes* the badges of the policewomen (Plural)
the boats in the harbor (Can't turn phrase around—not possessive; no apostrophe needed)

NOTE In some situations, there is no "belonging." Certain nouns may be possessive in form only.

a day's wages
a nickel's worth

ACTIVITY 4-G: Apostrophe

Show possession with an apostrophe instead of the prepositional phrase.

Example: the trial of the defendant *becomes* the defendant's trial.

1. the efficiency of the reporter ____________________
2. the work of the women ____________________
3. the duties of tomorrow ____________________
4. the manual of the student ____________________
5. the automobile of the company ____________________

6. the hat of the manager ______________________
7. the safety shoes of the workers ______________________
8. the hard hat of the electrician ______________________
9. the saw of the carpenter ______________________
10. the yellow shoes of Mrs. David ______________________

Check your responses in Feedback 4-G at the end of this module. If your responses were correct, proceed to Rule 3. If you missed any, review the five-step process and then do Activity 4-H.

ACTIVITY 4-H: Apostrophe

Show possession with an apostrophe instead of the prepositional phrase.

1. the CAD station of the architect ______________________
2. the syringes of the nurses ______________________
3. the ledger of the company ______________________
4. a vacation of two weeks ______________________
5. the work of one day ______________________
6. the administrative assistants of the boss ______________________
7. the administrative assistant of the boss ______________________
8. the administrative assistants of the bosses ______________________
9. the administrative assistants of Mr. Jones ______________________
10. the paychecks of the women ______________________

Check your responses in Feedback 4-H at the end of this module. If your responses were correct, proceed to Rule 3. If you missed any, review before continuing.

Rule 3. Use an apostrophe after the last noun in a series to show joint possession.

Bill, Henry, and **Fred's** project

My aunt and **uncle's** anniversary

Mom and **Dad's** car

Rule 4. Use an apostrophe with each name when two or more persons possess something individually.

> **Hemingway's** and **Steinbeck's** novels
> my **sister's** and my **brother's** salaries

ACTIVITY 4-I: Apostrophe

Provide the correct possessive form.

1. the cars of Pat and Mike (different cars)

___

2. the room of Eileen and Gail (same room)

___

3. the tools of Dan and Fred (same tools)

___

4. the tools of Dan and Fred (different tools)

___

5. the lunch of Ann and Sherry (same lunch)

___

Check your responses in Feedback 4-I at the end of this module. If your responses were correct, proceed to Rule 5. If you missed any, review Rules 3 and 4 and do Activity 4-J.

ACTIVITY 4-J: Apostrophe

Provide the correct possessive form.

1. the offices of Griffin and Kelly (same offices)

___

2. the offices of Griffin and Kelly (different offices)

___

3. the ears of Joe and Carl (different ears)

___

4. the boat of Dave and Wayne (same boat)

___

5. the apartments of Marston and Santana (different apartments)

___

Check your responses in Feedback 4-J at the end of this module. If you missed any, review before proceeding to Rule 5.

Rule 5. *A company name is singular. Even though it may be composed of several names, it is one unit. In order to make a company name possessive, you need to add only one apostrophe to the last name.*

the lumber of Smart and Jordan	Smart and Jordan's lumber
the baby powder of Johnson and Johnson	Johnson and Johnson's baby powder
the toothpaste of Procter and Gamble	Procter and Gamble's toothpaste
the cigarettes of Benson and Hedges	Benson and Hedges' cigarettes
the rating of Standard and Poor	Standard and Poor's rating

ACTIVITY 4-K: Apostrophe

Provide the correct possessive form.

1. the law offices of Morgan and Anderson

____

2. the products of Johnson and Johnson

____

3. the cafeteria of Townsend and Baker

____

4. the firm of Jones and Jones

____

5. the equipment of Mead and Johnson

____

Check your responses in Feedback 4-K at the end of this module. If your responses were correct, proceed to Rule 6. If you missed any, review Rule 5 and do Activity 4-L.

ACTIVITY 4-L: Apostrophe

Provide the correct possessive form.

1. the machinery of Smith, Jones & Brown

____

2. the acreage of Ayres and Hull Farms

____

3. the hospital facilities of Scott and White

____

4. the catalog of L.L. Bean

____

5. the merchandise of Sears and Roebuck

____

Check your responses in Feedback 4-L at the end of this module. If you missed any, review before proceeding to Rule 6.

Rule 6. *Never use an apostrophe with the possessive pronouns.*

POSSESSIVE PRONOUNS

yours ours theirs its his whose hers

When you speak, there is no distinction in sound between **its** and **it's,** between **theirs** and **there's,** or between **whose** and **who's.** When you write, however, it's important to make a distinction. None of the possessive pronouns ever takes an apostrophe.

> **It's** is a contraction for **it is.**
> **Who's** is a contraction for **who is.**
> **There's** is a contraction for **there is.**

Fix clearly in your mind that **its** (*no apostrophe*) is the possessive form of **it.** When you write **it's** (*with apostrophe*), you mean **it is.**

> **It's** time for the secretarial staff to take **its** coffee break.

ACTIVITY 4-M: Apostrophe

Underline the correct pronoun.

1. The new lab reports are (your's/yours).
2. (Whose/Who's) printouts were left in the computer room?
3. (It's/Its) results will show on the graph.
4. (There's/Theirs/Their's) are the best.
5. The syringe is (her's/hers).
6. (Ours/Our's) is in the filing cabinet.
7. (Whose/Who's) going to proofread the letter?
8. (It's/Its) time for a salary increase.
9. (Theirs/There's/Their's) no more fuel in the gas tank.
10. (Yours/Your's) are in the office.

Check your responses in Feedback 4-M at the end of this module. If your responses were correct, proceed to the Apostrophe Review. If you missed any, review Rule 6 and do Activity 4-N.

ACTIVITY 4-N: Apostrophe

Underline the correct pronoun.

1. The book lost (it's/its) cover.
2. (Your's/Yours) are in the desk.

3. He brought us (our's/ours).
4. (Whose/Who's) computer is unplugged?
5. (Whose/Who's) typing now?
6. (Theirs/There's/Their's) no way to check the records.
7. (Theirs/There's/Their's) are in the file folder.
8. The briefcase is (her's/hers).
9. (It's/Its) pages are torn.
10. (It's/Its) in the wrong place.

Check your responses in Feedback 4-N at the end of this module. If you missed any, review before proceeding to the Apostrophe Review.

Apostrophe Review

Before your last practice using possessives, let's review the basic rule:

If a possessive noun ends in s, add **'**.
If a possessive noun does not end in s, add **'s.**

ACTIVITY 4-O: Editing Practice

Provide the correct possessive form.

The architects drawing revealed a large square building with an open courtyard in its center. Staff members offices opened onto the courtyard. Everyones desk had a view of a lovely colored fountain. Each employees chair was positioned to make the most of the restful fountain. Harris and Farmers design firm was credited with the imaginative layout. People from miles around came to observe the buildings design features.

Check your responses in Feedback 4-O at the end of this module.

ACTIVITY 4-P: Editing Practice

Provide the correct possessive form.

The colleges plans for renovations of the computer labs will begin in the spring. The plans include installing state of the art technological devices, such as a smart board for displaying computer images and table-top monitors for each student. In fact, each students desk will be equipped with headphones and a glare shield. Decker and Tuckers technology firm has designed the rooms layout, and the administrations approval was unanimous. The administrators were thrilled with the design of the room, its open layout, and the spacious instructors area that includes a desk, podium, printer, and whiteboard.

Check your responses in Feedback 4-P at the end of this module.

DIAGNOSTIC FEEDBACK

Underline all of the nouns in the following sentences, including the **noun antecedent** and circle its pronoun.

1. The instructor plans her lessons well in advance.
2. The students gathered their materials and went to the library.
3. The student council has its meetings on the third Wednesday of each month.
4. When the customers arrived the store was locked, and they were not able to get in.
5. The daycare manager lost her job because of a poor work ethic.

Underline the correct pronoun.

1. The syllabus on the desk is (your's/yours).
2. The committee held (its/it's) last meeting in the spring.
3. The technician (whose/who's) error caused the misdiagnosis has agreed to resign.
4. (It's/Its) difficult to predict the outcome.
5. The paper shredder is (ours/our's), so don't leave it here.

FEEDBACK FOR MODULE 4

Feedback 4-A

1. The architect submitted his drawings for the bid.
2. The nurses will take their boards on Monday.
3. The jury cannot seem to come to a decision.
4. The Board of Education meets every third week of the month.
5. The virus in the network can be eliminated with this program.
6. The company reviewed its policy on personal leave.
7. Each accountant must be responsible for his own clients.
8. The daycare has additional hours available for people on the late shift.
9. Counselors meet weekly with their probation clients.
10. Therapy in a group seems to be working for these patients.

Feedback 4-B

1. Companies are stressing the ethics of proper use of the computer during the workday.
2. The therapists went to the convention to become familiar with new techniques.
3. Auto mechanics are learning to deal with highly sophisticated computers in cars.
4. The Washington Monument in our nation's capital is one of the most recognized buildings in the world.

5. Several workers attended the seminar on job discrimination.
6. Employees are very concerned with their job retirement plans because of recent changes in the Social Security Program.
7. The phlebotomist is currently analyzing samples of blood.
8. The patients on the third floor have ambulatory privileges.
9. Licensure depends on a variety of conditions according to individual states.
10. The company sent a summary of its financial condition to its stockholders.

Feedback 4-C

1. Many health care workers are concerned with (their) stress levels.
2. The receptionist is responsible for making (her) calls first thing each morning.
3. The state troopers complete (their) training after their coursework.
4. The committee made (its) decision late last night.
5. Ms. Barto sent (her) resume to companies on the West Coast.
6. The electronics students spend (their) free time in lab.
7. CNAs can earn (their) certification.
8. Internships are available after students complete (their) first year of studies.
9. That radiologist travels to (her) community's outreach centers.
10. The company changed (its) family leave policy.

Feedback 4-D

1. The nurse found (his) stethoscope on (his) rear view mirror.
2. Each computer workstation has (its) own printer.
3. All employees must submit (their) overtime by noon today.
4. The lab assistant showed (her) students how to dissect the pig.
5. The welders know that (their) safety is top priority.
6. Some accountants prefer to work from (their) homes.
7. The probation officer met with (her) clients today.
8. The daycare posts (its) hours on a website.
9. The advisory board submitted (its) recommendations
10. The convention announced (its) sessions in a spring brochure.

Feedback 4-E

Sample sentence 1: The retailers meetings are held on Wednesdays and Fridays.
Step 1: retailers, meetings, Wednesdays, Fridays
Step 2: retailers meetings
Step 3: meetings of retailers
Step 4: **Retailers** is plural.
Step 5: retailers' meetings.
Corrected sentence: The retailers' meetings are held on Wednesdays and Fridays.

Sample sentence 2: A computers keys need repair because of careless operators.
Step 1: computers, keys, operators
Step 2: computers keys
Step 3: keys belonging to a computer

Step 4: **A computer** is singular. (Note the qualifying word a.)
Step 5: computer's keys.
Corrected sentence: A computer's keys need repair because of careless operators.

Sample sentence 3: Everybodys printouts are on the shelves.
Step 1: everybodys, printouts, shelves
Step 2: everybodys printouts
Step 3: printouts belonging to everybody
Step 4: **Everybo**dy is a singular indefinite pronoun.
Step 5: everybody's printouts
Corrected sentence: Everybody's printouts are on the shelves.

Feedback 4-F

1. everyone's
2. foreman's
3. Ross's
4. Lindquists'
5. accountants'
6. child's
7. retailers'
8. women's
9. Davises'
10. waitress's
11. company's
12. companies'

Feedback 4-G

1. the reporter's efficiency
2. the women's work
3. tomorrow's duties
4. the student's manual
5. the company's automobile
6. the manager's hat
7. the workers' safety shoes
8. the electrician's hard hat
9. the carpenter's saw
10. Mrs. David's yellow shoes

Feedback 4-H

1. the architect's CAD station
2. the nurses' syringes
3. the company's ledger
4. two weeks' vacation
5. one day's work
6. the boss' administrative assistants
7. the boss' administrative assistant
8. the bosses' administrative assistant
9. Mr. Jones' administrative assistant
10. the women's paychecks

Feedback 4-I

1. Pat's and Mike's cars
2. Eileen and Gail's room
3. Dan and Fred's tools
4. Dan's and Fred's tools
5. Ann and Sherry's lunch

Feedback 4-J

1. Griffin and Kelly's offices
2. Griffin's and Kelly's offices
3. Joe's and Carl's ears
4. Dave and Wayne's boat
5. Marston's and Santana's apartments

Feedback 4-K

1. Morgan and Anderson's law offices
2. Johnson and Johnson's products
3. Townsend and Baker's cafeteria
4. Jones and Jones' firm
5. Mead and Johnson's equipment

Feedback 4-L

1. Smith, Jones & Brown's machinery
2. Ayres and Hull Farms' acreage
3. Scott and White's hospital facilities
4. L.L. Bean's catalog
5. Sears and Roebuck's merchandise

Feedback 4-M

1. yours
2. Whose
3. Its
4. Theirs
5. hers
6. Ours
7. Who's
8. It's
9. There's
10. Yours

Feedback 4-N

1. its
2. Yours
3. ours
4. Whose
5. Who's
6. There's
7. Theirs
8. hers
9. Its
10. It's

Feedback 4-O

The architect's drawing revealed a large square building with an open courtyard in its center. Staff members' offices opened onto the courtyard. Everyone's desk had a view of a lovely colored fountain. Each employee's chair was positioned to make the most of the restful fountain. Harris and Farmer's design firm was credited with the imaginative layout. People from miles around came to observe the building's design features.

Feedback 4-P

The college's plans for renovations of the computer labs will begin in the spring. The plans include installing state of the art technological devices, such as a smart board for displaying computer images and table-top monitors for each student. In fact, each student's desk will be equipped with headphones and a glare shield. Decker and Tucker's technology firm has designed the room's layout, and the administration's approval was unanimous. The administrators were thrilled with the design of the room, its open layout, and the spacious instructor's area that includes a desk, podium, printer, and whiteboard.

MODULE 5

Subject–Verb Agreement

Objective: This module provides practical methods for checking subject–verb agreement, one of the most important aspects of good writing.

Upon completion of this module, you will be able:

- To identify correct subject–verb agreement by applying practical methods of sentence analysis.

DIAGNOSTIC EXERCISE

Draw one line under the subject and two lines under the verb.

1. The accountant for the company plans to file the paperwork today.
2. The employees at the conference were honored for their research.
3. Three times a year, the senior executives on the project meet for a week-long brainstorming retreat.
4. The analyst on the project was disturbed by his findings.
5. The first responder on the scene is expected to act quickly to respond to the crisis.

Draw one line under the subject and two lines under the verb.

1. Neither the teacher nor the students (are/is) expected to come in because of the inclement weather.
2. The administrative assistants and the executive (plans/plan) to meet today at noon.
3. Each of the students (stay/stays) after class to help with the project.
4. Economics (is/are) the main reason why she chose a community college.
5. There (is/are) three proposed solutions to the drainage problem.

PART I: RECOGNIZING SUBJECTS AND VERBS

As the first step in mastering subject–verb agreement, you must be able to recognize the subject and the verb of a sentence. In Module 1, you learned about two types of verbs, action verbs and linking verbs, and you were shown how to recognize them in a sentence.

- To find the action verb, ask yourself what word shows action, either physical or mental.

  The paint spattered on the drawing board. (What word shows action? **Spattered** is the verb.)

  The technician learned quickly. (What word shows action? **Learned** is the verb. Here the action is mental.)

- To recognize a linking verb, remember that most linking verbs are forms of the verb **to be**. The forms **is**, **am**, **are**, **was**, and **were** link the subject to another word in the sentence, usually a noun or an adjective (see Module 1, Part II, Linking Verbs).

  I **was** a student. (**Was** links *I* with *student*, a noun.)

  He **is** competent. (**Is** links *He* with *competent*, an adjective.)

- Other verbs of being and verbs of the senses may also be linking verbs. When in doubt, you can try the Linking Verb Test. Substitute **is** or **was** for the verb and see if the sentence still makes sense.

Linking Verb Test

The assignment **seems** difficult. (The assignment **is** difficult. Linking verb.)
The cake **tasted** good. (The cake **is** good. Linking verb.)
He **tasted** the cake. (He **is** the cake. Not logical; not a linking verb.)

Subject Test

Once you have located the verb, it is easy to find the subject. Try putting *Who* or *What* in front of the verb. The answer is your subject. The **subject** of a sentence is what the sentence is talking about. It is usually a noun or pronoun. A noun names a person, place, thing, or idea. A pronoun takes the place of a noun. Note that most subjects precede verbs. Now go back and do this with all the previous examples:

What **spattered**? (The *paint* spattered. *Paint* is the subject.)
Who **learned**? (The *technician* learned. *Technician* is the subject.)
Who **was**? (*I* was. *I* is the subject.)
Who **is**? (*He* is. *He* is the subject.)
What **seems**? (The *assignment* seems. *Assignment* is the subject.)
What **tasted**? (The *cake* tasted. *Cake* is the subject. Notice that no action is expressed here. The cake is not doing the tasting.)

NOTE Gerunds, which are the *-ing* form of a verb, can serve as a subject. If so, they are singular.

Planning introductions and conclusions of reports **takes** special attention.

ACTIVITY 5-A: Recognizing Subjects and Verbs

Draw one line under the subject and two lines under the verb.

1. Your reports are due in the main office by Friday.
2. I attended the morning conference with my two assistants.
3. The technician with the advanced training went to the lab after lunch.
4. He gave a referral to his friend without telling the doctor.
5. The instrument in question is on the top shelf.
6. Her drawings for the new house needed a few changes.

7. Surveying the Ladd property requires four assistants.
8. Mr. Raymond frequently requested all of the day shift to attend the meeting.
9. We asked your supervisor to give us a break before midnight.
10. The assistant in the other office typed four letters for Mrs. Gableton.

Check your responses in Feedback 5-A at the end of this module. If your responses were correct, proceed to Part II. If you missed any, review Part I and do Activity 5-B.

ACTIVITY 5-B: Recognizing Subjects and Verbs

Draw one line under the subject and two lines under the verb.

1. Harry's drawing of the landscape won the blue ribbon.
2. Ordering new software requires a special purchase order.
3. The surveyor from the inspector's office studied the landscape carefully.
4. The nurse from the doctor's office took several vials of my blood.
5. They are Jane's foster parents.
6. The truck driver without hesitation leased a new tractor-trailer.
7. Last night he bought 50 shares of common stock.
8. We sharpened the blades on the lawnmowers.
9. Yesterday I replaced the worn-out light switch.
10. A nurse from the second floor took his temperature this morning.

Check your responses in Feedback 5-B at the end of this module. Then proceed to Part II.

PART II: SUBJECT–VERB AGREEMENT

The subject and verb of a sentence must agree in number. **Number** refers to singular or plural. **Singular** refers to one. **Plural** refers to more than one.

- A *singular subject* requires a *singular verb.*

The surveyor writes a report.

singular subject / singular verb

- A *plural subject* requires a *plural verb.*

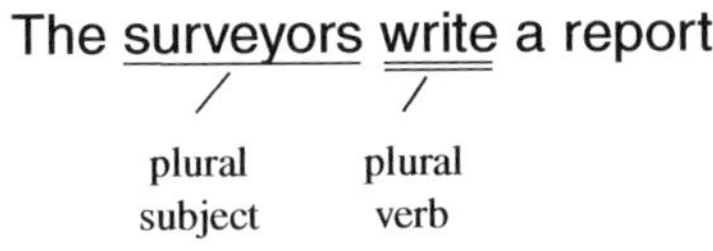

Subject Forms

As a helpful guide, remember that most verbs in the third-person singular, present tense, end in a single **s**: he *walks*, she *thinks*, it *shows*, he *has*, etc. The ending **s** on a verb signals that the verb is singular and requires a singular subject. The ending **s** on a subject, however, usually signals that the subject is plural and requires a plural verb, one that does not end in **s**.

NOTE Agreement is usually a *present tense* problem, except for such past tense irregular verbs as **was.**

The student reports to the class.

S on the VERB indicates SINGULAR.

The students report to the class.

S on the SUBJECT indicates PLURAL.

- Exceptions to this general guide include the following subjects, which end in **s** but take a singular verb.

  Mumps is a highly contagious disease.
  The waitress has been hired for the lunch shift.
  My boss is a fair person.
  Mathematics is harder than English for me.
  Physics has to be taught well.
  Economics is a complicated subject.

- A company or corporation, even if it consists of many names, is considered a single body and, therefore, requires a singular verb.

  Williams, Wright, & Wilson is a law firm in Dover.
  Chucker, Inc., is a large transportation company.

- There are also certain nouns, known as **collective nouns**, which usually refer to a group but use a singular verb. You will learn more about collective nouns in Module 11, Shifts.

  The committee is meeting today.
  The news is shocking.
  The city council meets today.

ACTIVITY 5-C: Subject–Verb Agreement

Some of the following sentences are incorrect because their subjects and verbs do not agree. Draw one line under the subject and two lines under the verb in each sentence; if the sentence is incorrect, cross out the verb and write the correct verb above it.

1. Mathematics are hard for many people.
2. The boss ride to the construction site daily.
3. The workers are ready to begin laying the bricks.
4. The Riker Company were to call back early this morning.
5. The hotel rooms was to be opened by Memorial Day weekend.
6. The employees were to attend the special program at noon.
7. The two nurses was to be on duty from 3 to 11 P.M.
8. Three people wants to be interviewed for the opening in the Accounting Department.
9. All our employees stays at motels on field trips.
10. Mr. Bruce were to conduct the special meeting for the technicians.

Check your responses in Feedback 5-C at the end of this module. If your responses were correct, proceed to Part III. If you missed any, review Part II and then do Activity 5-D.

ACTIVITY 5-D: Subject–Verb Agreement

Some of the following sentences are incorrect because their subjects and verbs do not agree. Draw one line under the subject and two lines under the verb in each sentence; if the sentence is incorrect, cross out the verb and write the correct verb above it.

1. The duties was time consuming.
2. The late news meets the deadline every day.
3. Allison, Merk & Mann plan to picnic at Crater Lake this year.
4. The whole system drain into the swamp.
5. The eastern farmers was dependent upon subsistence.
6. The computer operators needs to learn how to program the new DELL.

7. On every school day, two crossing guards helps with the traffic.
8. Economics is interesting to most people.
9. The drawings show the details of the new addition to the building.
10. Good counseling are necessary to reduce delinquency.

Check your responses in Feedback 5-D at the end of this module and proceed to Part III.

PART III: INTERFERING WORDS

When the verb directly follows its subject in a sentence, you will have little trouble making the subject and verb agree. Your trouble may come when the subject and verb are separated by other words. Sometimes prepositional phrases come between the subject and its verb. Recall that the object of the preposition is a noun or pronoun. Do not confuse this noun or pronoun with the subject of the sentence.

Study the examples below. The subjects and verbs are in bold print, and prepositional phrases are italicized.

The **performance** *of the assistant* **was** excellent.

The **decision** *of the personnel managers* **is** final.

The **supervisor,** *as well as the managers,* **was** upset about the result.

The **employer,** *together with the employees,* **does** her best.

The **president,** *along with the reporters,* **is** on the way to Washington.

NOTE The prepositional phrase is set off by a pair of commas if it is a nonessential interrupter (See Module 8, Rule 5). Subjects are never within these commas.

ACTIVITY 5-E: Interfering Words

Draw one line under the subject and two lines under the verb. To help you locate the subject, put parentheses around the interfering prepositional phrases.

1. The construction of the new buildings was begun yesterday.
2. The computer, in addition to two printers, needs to be repaired.
3. A combination of these procedures is certain to succeed.
4. Mr. Long, together with his associates, attends every business meeting.
5. The firm of McCabe & Walston is able to print the survey results.
6. Politics, along with economics, is a complicated subject.

7. The young men on our shift are going for job interviews next week.
8. John, along with his two assistants, has a promotion to consider.
9. Jane, together with her sister, has a degree in Computer Information Systems Technology.
10. Your contribution, in addition to other people's, fosters the success of the project.

Check your responses in Feedback 5-E at the end of this module. If your responses were correct, proceed to Activity 5-G. If you missed any, review Part III and do Activity 5-F.

ACTIVITY 5-F: **Interfering Words**

Draw one line under the subject and two lines under the verb. To help you locate the subject, put parentheses around the interfering prepositional phrases.

1. An assistant for an educational organization needs a broad vocabulary.
2. The interior designs of the house show details of historic value.
3. The engineer of the firm recommends choosing a site before planning a house.
4. The wiring in these houses doesn't meet the specifications.
5. A truck with two sets of dual rear wheels is built for heavy loads.
6. Her weekly articles in our local paper are quite interesting.
7. The serum for the new virus is available at the hospital.
8. Most prisons in the state need to be redesigned.
9. The larger hotels in Atlantic City offer several recreational activities.
10. A medical lab assistant at County Memorial Hospital is usually quite busy.

Check your responses in Feedback 5-F at the end of this module and proceed to Activity 5-G.

ACTIVITY 5-G: **Subject–Verb Agreement**

Draw one line under the subject and two lines under the correct verb. In sentences with a prepositional phrase between the subject and the verb, put parentheses around the prepositional phrase.

1. Employees of the plant (is/are) on strike.
2. Clearness in oral and written communications (is/are) necessary to success.
3. His objections to the proposal (seem/seems) unreasonable.
4. Certain pieces of the equipment (need/needs) to be replaced often.
5. Her skill in dictation (appears/appear) to be her only positive asset.

6. The two therapy rooms (are/is) closed until next Wednesday.
7. Bob's drawing, together with his schematics, (were/was) submitted for approval.
8. The charts (was/were) to be returned yesterday.
9. The nurses (record/records) the blood type for the doctor.
10. A reporter, because of training and experience, (reports/report) the facts accurately.

Check your responses in Feedback 5-G at the end of this module. If your responses were correct, proceed to Part IV. If you missed any, review Part III before continuing.

PART IV: INDEFINITE PRONOUN SUBJECTS

When indefinite pronouns (such as **anybody, everyone, many**) are used as the subject of a sentence, students often make mistakes in subject–verb agreement. **Indefinite pronouns** are nonspecific references (there is no indication as to who they are), but the way they are used indicates whether they are singular or plural. This is what you need to know in order to make the verb agree in number with the subject.

Most indefinite pronouns are always singular, a few are always plural, and a third group can be singular or plural, depending on the meaning of the sentence.

ALWAYS SINGULAR. Indefinite pronouns that are always singular include:

each	one	everybody	someone
anyone	everyone	nobody	either
anybody	no one	somebody	neither

The word **everybody** may cause trouble because it seems to refer to several individuals. To avoid confusion, think of everybody as "every single body," and you won't be tempted to use a plural verb. The same principle applies to all the words in this category.

Everybody (*every single body individually*) who can attend is encouraged to participate.

Everyone (*every single one*) has his own ideas about social services.

Each (*each one*) of the students buys her own book.

Neither (*not either one*) of the technologies is very easy.

ALWAYS PLURAL. The following indefinite pronouns always take a plural verb:

both	few	many	several

Several of the members were late.
Few of my friends are on my shift.
Both of your letters are acceptable.

SINGULAR OR PLURAL. Depending on the meaning of the sentence, the following indefinite pronouns are sometimes singular and sometimes plural (this is not a complete list):

all	most	half
any	none	part
	some	

These words are usually followed by a prepositional phrase, and the object of the preposition shows whether to use the singular or the plural. For instance, **all** of something singular uses a singular verb; **all** of something plural uses a plural verb.

All of the machine looks clean. (Singular)
All of the machines look clean. (Plural)
Most of the report was lost. (Singular)
Most of the reports were lost. (Plural)

With the words **none** or **any,** the choice depends on whether you are emphasizing the singular or the plural meaning.

None of the books has arrived. (Emphasizes the singular: *not one book*)
None of the books have arrived. (Emphasizes the plural: no books)

ACTIVITY 5-H: **Indefinite Pronoun Subjects**

Draw one line under the subject and two lines under the correct verb. Put parentheses around the prepositional phrase that comes between the subject and verb.

1. Each of the managers (grades/grade) the assignments promptly.
2. One of the experiments (was/were) not finished.
3. All of our repair work (is/are) done in the back shop.
4. Every one of my drawings (is/are) too small.
5. Some of these errors (is/are) careless.
6. A few of the books (were/was) found.

7. Everybody in these cities (pay/pays) a municipal tax.
8. None [not a single one] of the supervisors (approves/approve) of our project.
9. Everyone (is/are) able to complete the assignment.
10. Neither of us (work/works) on Saturday.

Check your responses in Feedback 5-H at the end of this module. If your responses were correct, proceed to Activity 5-J. If you missed any, review Part IV and then do Activity 5-I.

ACTIVITY 5-I: Indefinite Pronoun Subjects

Draw one line under the subject and two lines under the correct verb. Put parentheses around the prepositional phrase that comes between the subject and verb.

1. Each of the administrative assistants (type/types) 60 words per minute.
2. Neither of the house plans (has/have) a large living room.
3. Most of the information (has/have) been entered into the computer.
4. Everybody at the hotel (like/likes) the new swimming pool.
5. All of the work (was/were) completed by noon.
6. A few of the pine trees (has/have) an unknown disease.
7. Some of the switches (need/needs) to be replaced.
8. Neither of the newspapers (print/prints) news about South America.
9. One of the accounts (show/shows) figures on depreciation of equipment.
10. Each of the truck drivers (own/owns) an 18-wheel rig.

Check your responses in Feedback 5-I at the end of this module. If your responses were correct, proceed to Activity 5-J.

ACTIVITY 5-J: Indefinite Pronoun Subjects

Draw a line under the subject and two lines under the correct verb. Put parentheses around the prepositional phrase that comes between the subject and verb.

1. Both of those supervisors (advise/advises) the others in the shop.
2. The auditors at the state agency (was/were) ready to work.
3. A crate of strawberries (is/are) selling for $12 today.
4. The trucks on our highways (has/have) slowly put the locomotive out of business.
5. Each of the computer operators (was/were) working on a different shift.

6. The technicians in the lab (recognizes/recognize) many molds by color.
7. One of the students (is/are) employed at the Halfway House.
8. Neither of the detectives (choose/chooses) to work alone on the case.
9. A doctor, in addition to a nurse, (make/makes) regular visits in the hospital.
10. The roof, along with the chimney, (need/needs) repairing.

Check your responses in Feedback 5-J at the end of this module. Then proceed to Part V.

PART V: COMPOUND SUBJECTS AND VERBS

A **compound subject** has two or more parts that are joined by a connecting word such as **and, or,** or **nor**. A compound subject may be singular or plural depending on what the connecting word is.

- If the parts of the subject are joined by **and,** the subject is plural and takes a plural verb.

  A keyboard and monitor are to be used in every class.
  Tom, Mary, and Clark want to participate in the seminar.

- If two singular subjects are joined by **or** or **nor**, the verb must be singular.

  Either the manager or the supervisor is ready for the union meeting.

  Note that the sentence does not say, "Both the *manager* and *supervisor are* ready." It says, "Either the *manager* is ready or the *supervisor is* ready." It is helpful to take each subject by itself first.

  Neither John nor Jim is to be the new foreman. (John is not; Jim is not.)

- If the two parts of the subject are joined by **or** or **nor** but one part is singular and one is plural, then the *verb agrees with the subject closer to it.*

  Either the judge or the lawyers are wrong. (lawyers are, PLURAL)
  Either the lawyers or the judge is wrong. (judge is, SINGULAR)

- If a subject takes two or more verbs, each verb must agree with the subject. Verbs having the same subject are known as a **compound verb.**

  The administrative assistant types and takes dictation well.
  The engineers come to work by bus and leave by train.
  A nurse or a doctor is on duty or answers the phone.
  Suppliers neither stock nor backorder such items.
  The good driver uses judgment and pays attention.

ACTIVITY 5-K: Subject–Verb Agreement

Draw one line under the subjects and two lines under the correct verbs. Circle the connecting word for a clue to which verb to use.

1. Neither the box nor the wooden crates (was/were) damaged in the accident.
2. Either Sam or his father (is/are) going to drive us to the plane.
3. Neither the supplies nor the book (has/have) been delivered.
4. Private proprietorship and free trade (is/are) aspects of capitalism.
5. Neither Fred nor George (have/has) enough energy to complete the job or (want/wants) to do it.
6. Engineering and architecture (involve/involves) different skills.
7. Randy, his roommate, and his brother (has/have) a new summer business.
8. Either the employees or the employer (is/are) wrong.
9. Neither the college nor the senior high school (has/have) enough lab supplies or (hire/hires) qualified teachers.
10. Either Monday or Tuesday (appear/appears) to be the only time for the interview.

Check your responses in Feedback 5-K at the end of this module. If your responses were correct, proceed to Part VI. If you missed any, review Part V and then do Activity 5-L.

ACTIVITY 5-L: Subject–Verb Agreement

Draw one line under the subjects and two lines under the correct verbs. Circle the connecting word.

1. Neither rancher nor farmer (specializes/specialize) in more than one crop or (try/tries) to irrigate the land.
2. On the damaged boardwalk after the storm, the hammering and sawing (was/were) ceaseless.
3. Either dark green or dark blue (absorb/absorbs) more solar heat than black.
4. For example, neither the pick-up nor the vans (was/were) built to carry such heavy machinery.
5. Energy and empathy (help/helps) the social worker in many ways.
6. Land, sea, or air (is/are) directly affected by many pollutants.
7. Neither an assistant nor a stenographer (accept/accepts) the responsibility of a report's content and (take/takes) the blame for errors.
8. Science and technology (help/helps) the nurse in many ways.
9. The soil type and the topography (is/are) important when building a highway.

10. In many retirement situations, only a pension and social security (offers/offer) support.

Check your responses in Feedback 5-L at the end of this module. Then proceed to Part VI.

PART VI: SPECIAL PROBLEMS IN AGREEMENT

When a sentence begins with **here**, **there**, **where**, **which**, or **what**, the subject will follow the verb (V–S order). In this reversed order, there must still be agreement of the verb and subject. To check, pick out and state the subject and verb in S–V order and make sure they do agree.

V S S–V
There are two designs you can make. (Designs are)
There is a job opening at the plant. (Opening is)
Here are the supplies you ordered. (Supplies are)
Where are the plans and report? (Plans and report are)
What is he, the draftsman or the technician? (He is)

NOTE To be sure what the subject is, mentally rearrange the sentence in the subject–verb (S–V) order.

Sometimes with this pattern, sentences begin with a prepositional phrase, followed by the verb, then the subject. Again, in this V–S order, verb and subject must agree.

V S
At the end of the hall is an office. (Office is)

V S
To the right of the desk were three chairs. (Chairs were)

ACTIVITY 5-M: Special Problems in Agreement

Draw one line under the subject and two lines under the verb. Put parentheses around all the prepositional phrases in each sentence. Mentally rearrange the sentence in S–V order.

1. On the table there (is/are) computers and calculators.
2. Here (is/are) the drawings for the motel.
3. In the lab there (was/were) two Bunsen burners.
4. Near the filing cabinet there (is/are) some blank forms.
5. At the end of the hall there (is/are) a room to be used for special meetings.
6. There on the desk (was/were) my three reports.

7. Here in written form (is/are) my reason for accepting the proposal.
8. Beside the new lab, there (is/are) a row of chairs.
9. Which (is/are) the new men for the job?
10. Where (is/are) your reports and experiment results?

Check your responses in Feedback 5-M at the end of this module. If you missed any, review Part VI and do Activity 5-N.

ACTIVITY 5-N: Special Problems in Agreement

Draw one line under the subject and two lines under the correct verb. Put parentheses around all the prepositional phrases in each sentence. Mentally rearrange the sentence in S–V order.

1. Frequently, there (was/were) more printouts for the systems analyst.
2. In the spring schedule there (is/are) too many ball games scheduled.
3. There (is/are) many truck body styles.
4. Over here on the table (is/are) the display of portable computers.
5. Near the end of the hall there (is/are) a service desk and an information center.
6. What (was/were) John's temperature and blood pressure?
7. Before you leave, where (is/are) the specifications for this transmission?
8. Which (is/are) your favorite styles of business letters?
9. Where (does/do) the architect and the surveyor research the history of this lot?
10. There behind the door (is/are) the master switch for all the lights.

Check your responses in Feedback 5-N at the end of this module. Then proceed to Activity 5-O, Editing Practice.

ACTIVITY 5-O: Editing Practice

Edit only verbs as needed in the following paragraph using subject–verb agreement rules discussed in this module.

Once the committee of executives and marketing staff meet and decide which five candidates' credentials best match the needs of the company, scheduling of interviews are necessary. All of the committee members is required to be present for the planning meetings to formulate the questions and for the interviews. The two new members of the staff and the first vice president is excited to be part of the process. Neither the other staff members nor the president are as excited, but they are aware of the importance of this process.

Check your responses in Feedback 5-O at the end of this module.

ACTIVITY 5-P: Editing Practice

Edit the following paragraph for subject–verb agreement errors.

There is many advantages to attending a community college. First, a student who chooses a community college usually find that the community college offer a variety of programs, degrees, certificates, and transfer options. Second, almost everyone in the United States have access to a local community college. Furthermore, neither the parents nor the student accrue a large debt paying for the community college courses since they are often quite affordable. Even though economics are often the reason many students choose to attend a community college, convenience and a variety of degree options are also benefits of studying locally.

Check your responses in Feedback 5-P at the end of this module.

DIAGNOSTIC FEEDBACK

Draw one line under the subject and two lines under the **verb**.

1. The accountant for the company plans to file the paperwork today.
2. The employees at the conference were honored for their research.
3. Three times a year, the senior executives on the project meet for a week-long brainstorming retreat.
4. The analyst on the project was disturbed by his findings.
5. The first responder on the scene is expected to act quickly to respond to the crisis.

Draw one line under the subject and two lines under the correct verb.

1. Neither the teacher nor the students (are/is) expected to come in because of the inclement weather.
2. The administrative assistants and the executive (plans/plan) to meet today at noon.
3. Each of the students (stay/stays) after class to help with the project.
4. Economics (is/are) the main reason why she chose a community college.
5. There (is/are) three proposed solutions to the drainage problem.

FEEDBACK FOR MODULE 5

Feedback 5-A

1. reports are
2. I attended
3. technician went
4. He gave
5. instrument is
6. drawings needed
7. Surveying requires
8. Mr. Raymond requested
9. We asked
10. assistant typed

Feedback 5-B

1. drawing won
2. Ordering requires
3. surveyor studied
4. nurse took
5. They are
6. driver leased
7. he bought
8. We sharpened
9. I replaced
10. nurse took

Feedback 5-C

1. Mathematics is
2. boss rides
3. workers are
4. The Riker Company was
5. rooms were
6. employees were
7. nurses were
8. people want
9. employees stay
10. Mr. Bruce was

Feedback 5-D

1. duties were
2. news meets
3. Allison, Merk & Mann plans
4. system drains
5. farmers were
6. operators need
7. guards help
8. Economics is
9. drawings show
10. counseling is

Feedback 5-E

1. construction (of the new buildings) was begun
2. computer (in addition to two printers) needs
3. combination (of these procedures) is
4. Mr. Long (together with his associates) attends
5. firm (of McCabe & Walston) is
6. Politics (along with economics) is
7. men (on our shift) are going
8. John (along with his two assistants) has
9. Jane (together with her sister) has
10. contribution (in addition to other people's) fosters

Feedback 5-F

1. assistant (for an educational organization) needs
2. designs (of the house) show
3. engineer (of the firm) recommends
4. wiring (in these houses) does meet
5. truck (with two sets) (of dual rear wheels) is built
6. articles (in our local paper) are
7. serum (for the new virus) is

8. prisons (in the state) need
9. hotels (in Atlantic City) offer
10. assistant (at County Memorial Hospital) is

Feedback 5-G

1. Employees (of the plant) are
2. Clearness (in oral and written communications) is
3. objections (to the proposal) seem
4. pieces (of the equipment) need
5. skill (in dictation) appears
6. rooms are
7. drawing (together with his schematics) was submitted
8. charts were
9. nurses record
10. reporter (because of training and experience) reports

Feedback 5-H

1. Each (of the managers) grades
2. One (of the experiments) was
3. All (of our repair work) is
4. one (of my drawings) is
5. Some (of these errors) are
6. few (of the books) were
7. Everybody (in these cities) pays
8. None (of the supervisors) approves
9. Everyone is
10. Neither (of us) works

Feedback 5-I

1. Each (of the administrative assistants) types
2. Neither (of the house plans) has
3. Most (of the information) has
4. Everybody (at the hotel) likes
5. All (of the work) was
6. few (of the pine trees) have
7. Some (of the switches) need
8. Neither (of the newspapers) prints
9. One (of the accounts) shows
10. Each (of the truck drivers) owns

Feedback 5-J

1. Both (of those supervisors) advise
2. auditors (at the state agency) were
3. crate (of strawberries) is

4. trucks (on our highways) have
5. Each (of the computer operators) was
6. technicians (in the lab) recognize
7. One (of the students) is
8. Neither (of the detectives) chooses
9. doctor (in addition to a nurse) makes
10. roof (along with the chimney) needs

Feedback 5-K

1. box nor crates were
2. Sam or father is
3. supplies nor book has
4. proprietorship and trade are
5. Fred nor George has or wants
6. Engineering and architecture involve
7. Randy, his roommate, and his brother have
8. employees or employer is
9. college nor school has or hires
10. Monday or Tuesday appears

Feedback 5-L

1. rancher nor farmer specializes or tries
2. hammering and sawing were
3. green or blue absorbs
4. pick-up nor vans were
5. Energy and empathy help
6. Land, sea or air is
7. assistant nor stenographer accepts and takes
8. Science and technology help
9. type and topography are
10. pension and security offer

Feedback 5-M

1. computers, calculators are (On the table)
2. drawings are (for the motel)
3. burners were (In the lab)
4. forms are (Near the filing cabinet)
5. room is (At the end) (of the hall) (for special meetings)
6. reports were (on the desk)
7. reason is (in written form) (for accepting the proposal)
8. row is (Beside the new lab) (of chairs)
9. men are (for the job)
10. reports, results are

Feedback 5-N

1. printouts were (for the systems analyst)
2. games are (In the spring schedule)
3. styles are
4. display is (on the table) (of computers)
5. desk, center are (Near the end) (of the hall)
6. temperature, pressure were
7. specifications are (for this transmission)
8. styles are (of business letters)
9. architect, surveyor do research (of this lot)
10. switch is (behind the door) (for all the lights)

Feedback 5-O

Subjects are in italics, and verbs are in bold.

Once the *committee* of executives and marketing staff **meets** and **decides** which five candidates' *credentials* best **match** the needs of the company, *scheduling* of interviews **is** necessary. *All* of the committee members **are** required to be present for the planning meetings to formulate the questions and for the interviews. The two new *members* of the staff *and* the first *vice president* **are** excited to be part of the process. *Neither* the other staff members *nor* the *president* **is** as excited, but they are aware of the importance of this process.

Feedback 5-P

Subjects are in italics, and verbs are in bold.

There **are** many *advantages* to attending a community college. First, a *student* who **chooses** a community college usually **finds** that the community college **offers** a variety of programs, degrees, certificates, and transfer options. Second, almost *everyone* in the United States **has** access to a local community college. Furthermore, *neither* the parents *nor* the *student* **accrues** a large debt paying for the community college courses since *they* **are** often quite affordable. Even though *economics* **is** often the reason many *students* **choose** to attend a community college, *convenienceand* a *variety* of degree options **are** also benefits of studying locally.

MODULE 6

Pronouns

Objective: In this module, you will learn how to avoid the misuse of pronouns.

Upon completion of this module, you will be able:

- To identify correct forms of personal pronouns for various uses in the sentence.
- To apply six rules governing pronoun–antecedent agreement in number.

A **pronoun** is a word used in the place of a noun. In other words, a pronoun is a substitute for a noun. This module deals with what are called personal pronouns. You will study the forms and uses of the three types listed on this page: subject pronouns, object pronouns, and possessive pronouns.

SUBJECT PRONOUNS. Used as subjects or subject complements

	SINGULAR	PLURAL
1st person (speaking)	I	we
2nd person (spoken to)	you	you
3rd person (spoken of)	he	they
	she	
	it	

OBJECT PRONOUNS. Used as direct or indirect objects of action verbs or of prepositions

	SINGULAR	PLURAL
1st person (speaking)	me	us
2nd person (spoken to)	you	you
3rd person (spoken of)	him	them
	her	
	it	

POSSESSIVE PRONOUNS. Used to show ownership

	SINGULAR	PLURAL
1st person (speaking)	my (mine)	our (ours)
2nd person (spoken to)	your (yours)	your (yours)
3rd person (spoken of)	his (his)	their (theirs)
	her (hers)	
	its (its)	

Note that no apostrophe is used with a possessive pronoun. **It's** is a contraction for **it is. Who's** is a contraction for **who is. There's** is a contraction for **there is.**

DIAGNOSTIC EXERCISE

Choose the correct pronoun.

1. For Dennis, Amy and (me/I), the solution was simple.
2. They plan to visit (he/him) and (I/me) when they are on the Eastern shore.

3. The second team is clearly stronger than (we/us).
4. Each of the nurses is completing (their/his) internship at the hospital.
5. A student must check to make sure all of (their/her) paperwork for financial aid is filed in time.
6. Neither the nurses nor the doctor could find (their/her) stethoscope.
7. Our boss told me that the promotion was between you and (me/I).
8. Executives of companies should be responsible for (their/his or her) actions.
9. Most of the keyboards need (its/their) wires replaced.
10. Part of the report based (its/their) conclusions on the research that was completed last year.

PART I: PRONOUNS AS SUBJECTS

- When the subject of a sentence is a pronoun, use the subject form of the pronoun. You already know how to identify the subject of a sentence. In the sentences below, the subject is in bold type.

I applied for the job.
You are in line for promotion.
He got a raise.
She uses good judgment.
It was put in the file.
We drive to work together.
He and I were assigned to the project.
Don and she planned the program.
They attended a sales meeting.

- In addition to being used as the subject of an independent clause (a sentence), the subject pronoun is also used as the subject of a dependent clause. You will remember that a clause (independent or dependent) has a subject and a verb. The dependent clause signals are in italics, and the subjects of the dependent clauses are in bold type.

After **I** applied for the job, I was called for an interview.
The letter was retyped *before* **it** was put in the file.
The banker ***who*** handles our account is ill today.

NOTE The clause signals *who, which,* and *that* can be used both as signal and subject of a dependent clause.

ACTIVITY 6-A: Subject Pronouns

Underline the subject pronoun that is correct for the sentence.

1. (He/Him) arrived early for his interview.
2. Mary and (he/him) came together.
3. Have you and (she/her) had a vacation?

4. David and (me/I) usually work together.
5. In my opinion, (we/us) gave the best answers.
6. (They/Them) have made good progress.
7. To tell the truth, (she/her) made too many mistakes.
8. (We/Us), the consumers, will test the new product.
9. (She and I) (Her and me) are the advisers.
10. Are you and (him/he) going to the convention?

Check your responses in Feedback 6-A at the end of this module. If your responses were correct, proceed to Part II. If you missed any, review the subject pronouns and then do Activity 6-B.

ACTIVITY 6-B: Subject Pronouns

Underline the correct pronoun form.

1. Mr. Newton and (she/her) worked late at the office.
2. After Julia and (she/her) left, the office was closed.
3. What are you and (he/him) going to do about the deficit?
4. Kate and (I/me) attended the conference.
5. On the other hand, (he/him) and Brett did not attend.
6. For our benefit, Michael and (he/him) will explain the new product.
7. (She and I) (Her and me) took the patient to the operating room.
8. Are you and (they/them) writing the report together?
9. How are you and (he/him) getting to the meeting?
10. Did Jimmy and (she/her) leave early?

Check your responses in Feedback 6-B at the end of this module. If your responses were correct, proceed to Part II. If you missed any, review before continuing.

PART II: PRONOUNS AS SUBJECT COMPLEMENTS

In Module 1, you learned that the verb **to be** is a linking verb. Some of its forms are **am, is, are, was, were, has been, have been, may be, might be, can be, could be, want to be,** and **like to be.** When the word following the **be** verb is a noun or pronoun, it is called the **subject complement**.

- The subject complement renames the subject; therefore, if it is a pronoun, it must be a subject pronoun.

Subject—Linking Verb—Subject Complement
S—LV—SC

Jane is she. (**She** stands for Jane; **she** = Jane)

Treat the linking verb as an equal sign. In mathematics, what is on one side of the equal sign must equal what is on the other side of the equal sign. You can reverse the order without changing the meaning.

Subject = Subject Complement

In the examples below, the subject complement is in bold type.

The caller was **I.** (I was the caller. [**I** = caller])

Was the chairman **he?** (The chairman was he. [**he** = chairman])

The girl who took the message was **she.** (She was the girl who took the message. [**she** = girl])

The new supervisors are **she** and **I.** (She and I are the new supervisors. [**she** and **I** = supervisors])

The graduates were **they.** (They were the graduates. [**they** = graduates])

The judges should have been **we.** (We should have been the judges. [**we** = judges])

- The subject complement may also be part of a dependent clause.

He thought that the *caller* was **I.** (**I** was the caller.)

The committee will not be effective unless the *chairman* is **he.** (**He** is the chairman.)

ACTIVITY 6-C: Subject Complement Pronouns

Underline the correct pronoun form.

1. The new boss is (he/him).
2. The one who called was (me/I).
3. I don't think that it was (her/she).
4. Could it have been (him/he)?
5. It was probably Dan or (me/I).
6. It was (I/me) who saw the accident.
7. The consumers are you and (me/I).
8. Was it (him/he) who took first prize?
9. The winner should have been (she/her).
10. The candidates were John and (I/me).

Check your responses in Feedback 6-C at the end of this module. If your responses were correct, proceed to Part III. If you missed any, review Part II; then do Activity 6-D.

ACTIVITY 6-D: Subject Complement Pronouns

Underline the correct pronoun form.

1. The winner of the award was (he/him).
2. The person who called for an appointment was (she/her).
3. I don't know if it was (he/him).
4. Do you suppose it could have been (they/them)?
5. It was probably (I/me) who made the error.
6. It was (we/us) who solved the problem.
7. The best customers are you and (I/me).
8. Was it (he/him) who designed the house?
9. The new technician we hired yesterday was (she/her).
10. The applicants for the job were you and (he/him).

Check your responses in Feedback 6-D at the end of this module. If your responses were correct, proceed to Part III. If you missed any, review before continuing.

PART III: PRONOUNS AS DIRECT OBJECTS

An action verb, you will remember from Module 1, shows what the subject is doing—it shows an action. The noun or pronoun that receives that action is called the **direct object.** In other words, the direct object answers the question "what?" or "whom?" after an action verb.

- When a direct object is a pronoun, it must be the **object pronoun** form (see the list at the beginning of this module).

Subject—Action Verb—Direct Object
S—AV—DO

She hastily called **me.** (Called whom? Answer: **me** [object pronoun])

I know **him.** (Know whom? Answer: **him** [object pronoun])

I thanked **her** and **him.** (Thanked whom? Answer: **her** and **him** [object pronouns])

Maureen invited **us.** (Invited whom? Answer: **us** [object pronoun])

Janelle missed **them.** (Missed whom? Answer: **them** [object pronoun])

Randy hit **it.** (Hit what? Answer: **it** [object pronoun])

ACTIVITY 6-E: Object Pronouns

Underline the correct pronoun form.

1. Tell the supervisor and (him/he) what your job is.
2. Do not bother the technician and (me/I).
3. Do you remember (him and me) (he and I) from the conference?
4. Peggy will take (she and I) (her and me) to the meeting.
5. They will send you and (me/I) to the interview.
6. Tell (him/he) to finish the report by Thursday.
7. Do you know (her/she) from work?
8. Mr. Clark asked (me/I) to speak at the next seminar.
9. He will send (him/he) the dimensions of the rooms.
10. Have you told (they/them) about the project?

Check your responses in Feedback 6-E at the end of this module. If your responses were correct, proceed to Part IV. If you missed any, review Part III and do Activity 6-F.

ACTIVITY 6-F: Object Pronouns

Underline the correct pronoun form.

1. Call the receptionist and (I/me) when you have finished.
2. Did you ask the doctor and (she/her) to give you the report?
3. You should remember (he and she) (him and her) from last year's meeting.
4. Matthew will drive Paula and (she/her) to the appointment.
5. The company will call Betsy and (I/me) for an interview.
6. Tell Mr. Watson and (he/him) about the audit.
7. Do you know Ellen and (she/her) through your business?
8. Mrs. Delano required Collins and (I/me) to write an agenda.
9. Dr. Insley sent Harry and (she/her) the X-ray report.
10. We will see Innis and (they/them) at the board meeting.

Check your responses in Feedback 6-F at the end of this module. If your responses were correct, proceed to Part IV. If you missed any, review before continuing.

PART IV: PRONOUNS AS OBJECTS OF PREPOSITIONS

You will recall that a prepositional phrase consists of a preposition, its object, and any modifier of the object.

- If the object of the preposition is a pronoun, it must be in the object form (You may wish to review the list of prepositions in Module 3 Part I).

  from me
  with him
  beside her
  around us
  among them
  above it
  for you
  between you and me
  to him and her

  The ticket agent took the money **from me.**
  Jack sat down **beside her.**
  Here is a package **for you.**

- When there is more than one object of a preposition, *each pronoun is in the object form.* It would be incorrect to say **between you and I** or **to he and she.** Repeat the preposition in your mind as a test.

  between you and me (between you and between me)
  to him and her (to him and to her)
  for John and him (for John and for him)

ACTIVITY 6-G: Object Pronouns

Underline the correct pronoun form.

1. How long did you talk to (they/them)?
2. I sent the memo to (she/her).
3. She left her estate to (us/we).
4. He stood between you and (I/me).
5. Bill worked for Mr. Handy and (him/he) for ten years.
6. Give the report to (he and I) (him and me).
7. Between (you and I) (you and me), we can finish the work by tomorrow.
8. The yearly bonus was shared among Tom and (they/them).
9. Tell the boss about the secretary and (he/him).
10. At the conference, I sat beside (he and she) (him and her).

Check your responses in Feedback 6-G at the end of this module. If your responses were correct, proceed to Part V. If you missed any, review Part IV and then do Activity 6-H.

ACTIVITY 6-H: Object Pronouns

Underline the correct pronoun form.

1. How long have you been employed by Mr. Brown and (he/him)?
2. The letter was written to (he and I) (him and me).
3. The government awarded the contract to (she and I) (her and me).
4. The nurse waited in line between (you and I) (you and me).
5. Joseph worked for (he and I) (him and me) for the summer.
6. Give the microscopes to (she and I) (her and me).
7. Between (you and I) (you and me), this is a difficult job.
8. The company profits were shared by (they and I) (them and me).
9. Ask the doctor about (she and they) (her and them).
10. In the workshop, she sat beside (him and me) (he and I).

Check your responses in Feedback 6-H at the end of this module. If your responses were correct, proceed to Part V. If you missed any, review before continuing.

PART V: POSSESSIVE PRONOUNS

Used as Adjectives Modifying Nouns

The possessive form of a noun is used as an adjective to modify a noun; for example, *Mary's book,* the *city's streets,* a *day's work.*

- When a pronoun is substituted for a possessive noun, the possessive form of the pronoun must be used. Refer to the list of possessive pronouns at the beginning of this module.

John's report	His report
The workers' lunch hour	Their lunch hour

NOTE Possessive nouns have apostrophes. However, possessive pronouns never have apostrophes.

Its (possessive of **it**):	**Its** tail was caught in the door.
It's (contraction of **it is**):	**It's** cold in the building.

Like all adjectives, possessive pronouns modify specific nouns.

Howard took **my** paper.	**Its** fur is warm.
Your uniform is torn.	**Our** building is brick.
His calculator is new.	**Their** plane runs well.
Her report was lost.	

Used as Adjectives Modifying Gerunds

A **gerund** is a verb form ending in **-ing** used as a noun. Examples: *playing, walking, running, swimming, working.*

In the sentences below, each gerund is in bold type. Do you see that each one functions as a noun in that particular sentence?

> **Walking** is good exercise. (Subject)
> My favorite sport is **swimming.** (Subject complement)
> Today is a good day for **sleeping.** (Object of preposition)
> Of all the leisure activities, I prefer **fishing.** (Direct object)

Now consider the sentences below. In front of each gerund there is a possessive pronoun modifying the gerund. This is because gerunds act like nouns, and possessive pronouns act like adjectives.

> **His playing** has improved. (*Not* Him playing)
> We always enjoy **his playing.** (*Not* him playing)
> **His passing** is incredibly smooth. (*Not* Him passing)
> We love to watch **his passing.** (*Not* him passing)
> The doctor objected to **my eating** candy. (*Not* me eating)
> **Your speaking** to them aroused concern. (*Not* You speaking)
> **His arriving** late became a problem. (*Not* Him arriving)

Used as Subjects, Objects, and Complements

Sometimes a pronoun is used alone to replace both the possessive pronoun and the noun that it modifies. This can be done when it is clear what noun is being referred to. In this case, a special form of the possessive pronoun is used: **mine, yours, theirs,** etc. These forms are shown in parentheses in the list of possessive pronouns at the beginning of this module.

> The tractor with the new battery is **mine. Yours** has no oil.
> That folder was **hers. Ours** is on the desk.
> My computer is broken, so I used **theirs.**

Notice in the examples above that these possessive pronouns can function as subjects, as subject complements, and as direct objects.

ACTIVITY 6-1: Possessive Pronouns

Underline the form that is correct for the sentence.

1. No one could understand (him/his) forgetting to write the report.
2. After (their/them) talking to us, we decided to test the product again.
3. Did he approve of (you/your) writing the report?

4. The new calculator is (hers/her's).
5. Do you object to (my/me) being at the meeting?
6. (Its/It's) keys make the keyboard easy to use.
7. My desk is located opposite (your's/yours).
8. The foreman agreed to (us/our) taking the early shift.
9. (Him/His) leaving the room caused much concern.
10. (Theirs/Their's/There's) is in the drawer.

Check your responses in Feedback 6-I at the end of this module. If your responses were correct, proceed to Part VI. If you missed any, review Part V and then do Activity 6-J.

ACTIVITY 6-J: Possessive Pronouns

Underline the form that is correct for the sentence.

1. Everyone approved of (him/his) being hired for the job.
2. Before (them/their) coming into the building, the meeting began.
3. The boss did not approve of (me/my) recording the telephone conversation.
4. (His/Him) being late was annoying.
5. The old thermometer is (hers/her's).
6. (It's/Its) motor was running smoothly.
7. (Theirs/Their's/There's) fell off the desk.
8. The memo was not mailed because (it's/its) not legible.
9. (Theirs/Their's/There's) no reason for this error.
10. The new office is (yours/your's).

Check your responses in Feedback 6-J at the end of this module. If your responses were correct, proceed to Part VI. If you missed any, review before continuing.

PART VI: PRONOUN RULES

Here are some additional guides that will help you to choose the correct pronoun.

Rule 1. *When two pronouns are joined by a conjunction, take each pronoun separately to determine the correct one to use.* In the following sentences, which forms are correct?

Mail the portfolio to (him or I) (him or me).
(She and I) (Her and I) will be out of town.

The personnel manager selected (them and her) (them and she).
The boss talked to (you and me) (you and I).

To help you choose, try each pronoun by itself. You would not say, "Mail the portfolio to I," for example. Here is how to decide in the above sentences.

Mail the portfolio to **him.** Mail the portfolio to **me.** (Mail the portfolio to **him or me.**)

She will be out of town. **I** will be out of town. (**She and I** will be out of town.)

The personnel manager selected **them.** The personnel manager selected **her.** (The personnel manager selected **them and her.**)

The boss talked to **you.** The boss talked to **me.** (The boss talked to **you and me.**)

Rule 2. *When a pronoun and a noun are joined by a conjunction, try dropping the noun to determine which pronoun to use.* Which of the following sets are correct?

(He and the boss) (Him and the boss) planned the presentation.
The receptionist directed (the guests and her) (the guests and she) to the exhibit.
The foreman had a talk with (the supervisor and I) (the supervisor and me).

When you try the pronoun without the noun, it becomes easy to select the right pronoun for the sentence.

He [and the boss] planned the presentation.
The receptionist directed [the guests and] **her.**
The foreman had a talk with [the supervisor and] **me.**

Rule 3. *When using* **than** *or* **as** *in a comparison, complete the sentence in your mind to determine which pronoun to use.*

The captain played better than **he.** (than he played)
Are you as tall as **she?** (as she is)
He is nicer to Jan than **me.** (than he is to me)
He is nicer to Jan than **I.** (than I am)

Rule 4. *When a pronoun is next to the noun it refers to in apposition, omit the noun to decide on the correct pronoun.* (Remember that an appositive renames a noun or pronoun.) How would you choose the correct form in the following sentences?

(We mechanics) (Us mechanics) service our own vehicles.
The instructor greeted (us new students) (we new students).
Give the cards to (us members) (we members).

To help you determine which form to use, omit the noun. You would not say, "Us service our vehicles," "The instructor greeted we," or "Give the cards to we." Here are the correct responses:

We [mechanics] service our own vehicles.
The instructor greeted **us** [new students].
Give the cards to **us** [members].

Rule 5. *Do not substitute reflexive pronouns* (**myself, himself, yourself,** etc.) *for subject or object pronouns.*

WRONG: Mr. Samson gave the two best computers to my good friend and **myself.**
CORRECT: Mr. Samson gave the two best computers to my good friend and **me.**
WRONG: My boss, my assistant, and **myself** will go.
CORRECT: My boss, my assistant, and **I** will go.

The reflexive pronouns are used for emphasis and with so-called reflexive verbs where the action of the verb is done by and to the same subject. They must be used in conjunction with another noun or pronoun to be reflexive.

EMPHASIS	REFLEXIVE ACTION
I **myself** intend to join.	She cut **herself** accidentally.
He did the job **himself.**	I dusted **myself** off.
You **yourself** are to blame.	Ask **yourselves** the same question.
We wrote the report **ourselves.**	The lights burned **themselves** out.

NOTE Never use "hisself" or "theirselves." They are not standard English words although you may sometimes hear them spoken.

ACTIVITY 6-K: Pronoun Rules

Underline the correct pronoun form.

1. Mail the report to (him and I) (him and me).
2. (Her and I) (She and I) will be late for our interview.
3. The assistant asked (them and her) (they and she) for the letters.
4. (Him and the nurse) (He and the nurse) filled in the patient's chart.
5. The receptionist showed (the speaker and her) (the speaker and she) to the main office.
6. He types better than (she/her).
7. (Us nurses) (We nurses) registered early for the seminar.

8. The new building pleased (us employees) (we employees).
9. She gave instructions to my colleague and (myself/me).
10. He accidentally hit (himself/hisself) with the hammer.

Check your responses in Feedback 6-K at the end of this module. If your responses were correct, proceed to Part VII. If you missed any, review Part VI and then do Activity 6-L.

ACTIVITY 6-L: Pronoun Rules

Underline the correct pronoun form.

1. Send the report to (she and I) (her and me).
2. (He and I) (Him and me) will look at the ledger tonight.
3. The radiologist asked (them and her) (they and she) to do the test again.
4. (Her and the supervisor) (She and the supervisor) felt the conference was profitable.
5. The receptionist showed the (patient and I) (patient and me) to the private room.
6. He programs a computer faster than (I/me).
7. (Us technicians) (We technicians) take a break at noon.
8. The design was sent to (we architects) (us architects).
9. The directions were given by the foreman and (myself/me/I).
10. The worker cut (himself/hisself) on the sharp metal.

Check your responses in Feedback 6-L at the end of this module. If your responses were correct, proceed to Part VII. If you missed any, review before continuing.

PART VII: PRONOUN–ANTECEDENT AGREEMENT

Every pronoun must first be preceded by the use of a noun, or you will have a pronoun reference problem. The noun a pronoun stands for is called its **antecedent.** When you use a pronoun, you must make sure it agrees with its antecedent, or you will create a shift in number, often called a pronoun agreement problem. The following six rules will help you.

Rule 1. *A pronoun must agree in number with its antecedent.* If the antecedent is singular (meaning one), the pronoun also is singular. If the antecedent is plural (more than one), the pronoun must be plural.

> **An assistant** should write **his** (or **her**) own letters. (Singular)
> **Assistants** should write **their** own letters. (Plural)

Rule 2. *Use a plural pronoun to refer to two singular antecedents joined by* **and.**

> **Cathy** and her **friend** bought **their** train tickets.

Rule 3. *When the antecedent consists of two words in a* **neither . . . nor** *or* **either . . . or** *construction, the pronoun agrees in number with the second word, the word closer to the pronoun.*

> *Neither* the **nurse** *nor* the **doctor** wore **his** surgical mask.
> *Either* **Mrs. Moore** *or* the **assistants** have performed **their** jobs.
> *Neither* the **nurses** *nor* the **doctors** wore **their** surgical masks.
> *Either* the **assistants** *or* **Mrs. Moore** has performed **her** job.

Rule 4. *The following indefinite pronouns are singular. They require a singular personal pronoun and a singular verb.*

SINGULAR			
each	one	everybody	someone
anyone	everyone	nobody	either
anybody	no one	somebody	neither

> **Everyone** is working at **his** desk.
> **Each** of the waiters is at **his** station.
> **Neither** of the applicants brought **her** resumé.

Rule 5. *The following indefinite pronouns are plural; when used as antecedents, they take a plural pronoun.*

PLURAL			
both	few	many	several

> **Both** of the engineers brought **their** lunches.
> **Few** of the bullets found **their** target.
> **Many** of the students forgot **their** rulers.

Rule 6. *The following indefinite pronouns may be singular or plural.* The object of the preposition that usually follows them determines whether they are to be treated as singular or plural.

SINGULAR OR PLURAL			
all	none	half	most
any	some	part	

PLURAL	SINGULAR
All of the patients liked **their** rooms.	**All** of the equipment is in **its** last year of usefulness.
None of the books had **their** pages torn.	**None** of the appreciation was relayed to **its** recipient.
Half of the soybeans rotted in **their** bins.	**Half** of the crop lost **its** leaves to worms.

NOTE Avoid sexist language in your writing by choosing plural pronouns when possible, by eliminating gender reference, or by using a specific gender when there is no question of the composition of the group.

All employees were instructed to give **their** permits at the gate.

The administration ordered all employees to display parking permits on vehicles.

Each of the waitresses picked up **her** orders for the shift.

ACTIVITY 6-M: Pronoun Agreement

Underline the correct pronoun.

1. Workers should perform (his/their) own duties.
2. All of the administrative assistants wished (she/they) could type as fast as Marcia.
3. The foreman is good at (his/their) jobs.
4. Neither Ted nor Tom received (his/their) bonus.
5. Neither the foreman nor the supervisors took (his/their) vacation.
6. Everybody was happy when (he/they) saw the bonus check.
7. Part of the letters need (its/their) headings reprinted.
8. Several of the technicians brought (his/their) instruments.
9. Either the ledger or the account book lost (its/their) cover.
10. The Dilly Dally Company likes (their/its) employees to be punctual.

Check your responses in Feedback 6-M at the end of this module. If your responses were correct, proceed to Activity 6-O. If you missed any, review Part VII and then do Activity 6-N.

ACTIVITY 6-N: Pronoun Agreement

Underline the correct pronoun.

1. Accountants should do (his/their) own calculations.
2. Everyone wants (her/their) job to be exciting.

3. Neither debit nor credit was posted in (its/their) proper column.
4. Either the accountant or the bookkeepers left (her/their) books in the office.
5. Everyone brought (his/their) own sets of figures.
6. Neither of the accountants did (her/their) share of the work.
7. Some of the bookkeepers brought (his/their) books to the session.
8. None of the accounts were in (its/their) original folder.
9. Few accountants could give (his/their) explanation of the deficit.
10. No one believed in (his/their) own responsibility.

Check your responses in Feedback 6-N at the end of this module. If your responses were correct, proceed to Activity 6-O. If you missed any, review before continuing.

ACTIVITY 6-O: **Pronoun Review**

Choose the correct pronoun.

1. Everybody should know (his, their) own special skills.
2. Most of the account showed (its, their) profits clearly.
3. The company president and (she, her) made the policy decision.
4. (He and I, Him and me) will check with the biotechnology department.
5. Are you and (she, her) going to attend the conference?
6. The newly hired respiratory technician is (she, her).
7. The best draftsmen are (he and I, him and me).
8. Call the nurse and (he, him) about the meeting.
9. Did you ask (he and she, him and her) to go to the conference?
10. Between you and (I, me), a raise would be preferable to increased benefits.
11. Give the award to (he and she, him and her).
12. The reaction was caused by (him, his) giving the shot too soon after other medication.
13. (You, Your) driving to work in snow could be dangerous.
14. (We, Us) computer programmers have a monthly staff meeting.
15. Everyone filled out (his, their) request for reimbursement.

Check your responses in Feedback 6-O at the end of this module.

ACTIVITY 6-P: **Editing Practice**

Edit pronouns as needed in the following paragraph.

A committee of Margaret Chandler, Joseph Redmond, and myself has been appointed to prepare a proposal for sharing sick leave among we employees. Our research so far has involved us investigating practices of other large agencies in the state. Margaret was more ambitious than Joe and me, so we were surprised at what she discovered. She convinced Joe and I that we should analyze what other agencies are currently practicing so that our policy can reflect the best of all of them. Each state seems to have it's own version of sick leave policy. Some companies let the employees theirselves donate to a Sick Bank. For Margaret, Joe, and I to be successful, we will have to convince management officials that the beneficiaries will ultimately be them.

Check your responses in Feedback 6-P at the end of this module.

ACTIVITY 6-Q: Editing Practice

Edit pronouns as needed in the following paragraph.

Beginning college students often find theirselves frustrated because of their hectic schedules. They often are torn between many commitments and interests, and instructors expect they to manage their own time and meet deadlines. Them scheduling meetings and conferences with instructors can also be difficult since the instructors are often as busy as them. For instructors and they to find a mutually convenient time to meet often requires a lot of planning and arranging. When attending college, a student must carefully prioritize their time so that they get the most out of the experience.

Check your responses in Feedback 6-Q at the end of this module.

DIAGNOSTIC FEEDBACK

Choose the correct pronoun.

1. For Dennis, Amy and (<u>me</u>/I), the solution was simple.
2. They plan to visit (he/<u>him</u>) and (I/<u>me</u>) when they are on the Eastern shore.
3. The second team is clearly stronger than (<u>we</u>/us).
4. Each of the nurses is completing (their/<u>his</u>) internship at the hospital.
5. A student must check to make sure all of (their/<u>her</u>) paperwork for financial aid is filed in time.
6. Neither the nurses nor the doctor could find (their/<u>her</u>) stethoscope.
7. Our boss told me that the promotion was between you and (<u>me</u>/I).
8. Executives of companies should be responsible for (<u>their</u>/his or her) actions.
9. Most of the keyboards need (its/<u>their</u>) wires replaced.
10. Part of the report based (<u>its</u>/their) conclusions on the research that was completed last year.

FEEDBACK FOR MODULE 6

Feedback 6-A

1. He
2. he
3. she
4. I
5. we
6. They
7. she
8. We
9. She and I
10. he

Feedback 6-B

1. she (she worked)
2. she (she left)
3. he (you are going, he is going)
4. I (I attended)
5. he (he did attend)
6. he (he will explain)
7. She and I (She took, I took)
8. they (are you and they writing)
9. he (you and he are getting)
10. she (Jimmy and she did leave)

Feedback 6-C

1. he (The boss = he. He = the boss.)
2. I (The one . . . = I. I = the one . . .)
3. she (. . . it = she. She = it.)
4. he (. . . it = he. He = it.)
5. I (It = I. I = it.)
6. I (It = I. I = it.)
7. I (Consumers = you and I. You and I = consumers.)
8. he (It = he. He = it.)
9. she (Winner = she. She = winner.)
10. I (Candidates = John and I. John and I = candidates.)

Feedback 6-D

1. he (Winner = he. He = winner.)
2. she (person = she. She = person.)
3. he (It = he. He = it.)
4. they (It = they. They = it.)
5. I (It = I. I = it.)
6. we (It = we. We = it.)
7. I (customers = you and I. You and I = customers.)
8. he (It = he. He = it.)
9. she (Technician = she. She = secretary.)
10. he (Applicants = you and he. You and he = applicants.)

Feedback 6-E

1. him (tell him)
2. me (bother me)
3. him and me (remember him, remember me)

4. her and me (take her, take me)
5. me (send me)
6. him (tell him)
7. her (know her)
8. me (asked me)
9. him (send him)
10. them (told them)

Feedback 6-F

1. me (call me)
2. her (ask her)
3. him and her (remember him, remember her)
4. her (drive her)
5. me (call me)
6. him (tell him)
7. her (know her)
8. me (required me)
9. her (sent her)
10. them (see them)

Feedback 6-G

1. them (to them)
2. her (to her)
3. us (to us)
4. me (between you, between me)
5. him (for Mr. Handy, for him)
6. him and me (to him, to me)
7. you and me (between you, between me)
8. them (among Tom, among them)
9. him (about secretary, about him)
10. him and her (beside him, beside her)

Feedback 6-H

1. him (by Mr. Brown, by him)
2. him and me (to him, to me)
3. her and me (to her, to me)
4. you and me (between you, between me)
5. him and me (for him, for me)
6. her and me (to her, to me)
7. you and me (between you, between me)
8. them and me (by them, by me)
9. her and them (about her, about them)
10. him and me (beside him, beside me)

Feedback 6-I

1. his (his *forgetting*)
2. their (their *talking*)
3. your (your *writing*)
4. hers (possessive pronoun)
5. my (my *being*)
6. Its (its *keys*)
7. yours (possessive pronoun)
8. our (our *taking*)
9. His (His *leaving*)
10. Theirs (possessive pronoun)

Feedback 6-J

1. his (his *being* hired)
2. their (their *coming*)
3. my (my *recording*)
4. His (His *being*)
5. hers (possessive pronoun)
6. Its (Its *motor*)
7. Theirs (possessive pronoun)
8. it's (it is)
9. There's (There is)
10. yours (possessive pronoun)

Feedback 6-K

1. him and me (*to him, to me*)
2. She and I (*She will be late, I will be late*)
3. them and her (*asked them, asked her*)
4. He and the nurse (*He filled in, the nurse filled in*)
5. the speaker and her (*showed the speaker, showed her*)
6. she (*than she types*)
7. We nurses (*We registered*)
8. us employees (*pleased us*)
9. me (*to me*)
10. himself ("hisself" is not a word)

Feedback 6-L

1. her and me (*to her, to me*)
2. He and I (*He will look, I will look*)
3. them and her (*asked them, asked her*)
4. She and the supervisor (*She felt, the supervisor felt*)
5. patient and me (*showed the patient, showed me*)
6. I (*than I do*)

7. We technicians (*we take*)
8. us architects (*to us*)
9. me (*by me*)
10. himself ("hisself" is not a word)

Feedback 6-M

1. their (*Workers,* plural)
2. they (*all,* plural)
3. his (*foreman,* singular)
4. his (Ted nor *Tom,* singular)
5. their (*supervisors,* plural)
6. he (*everybody,* singular)
7. their (part of the *letters,* plural)
8. their (*several,* plural)
9. its (*book,* singular)
10. its (*Company,* singular)

Feedback 6-N

1. their (*accountants,* plural)
2. her (*everyone,* singular)
3. its (debit nor *credit,* singular)
4. their (accountant or *bookkeepers,* plural)
5. his (*everyone,* singular)
6. her (*neither,* singular)
7. their (*bookkeepers,* plural)
8. their (*accounts,* plural)
9. their (*accountants,* plural)
10. his (*no one,* singular)

Feedback 6-O

1. his
2. its
3. she
4. He and I
5. she
6. she
7. he and I
8. him
9. him and her
10. me
11. him and her
12. his
13. Your
14. We
15. his

Feedback 6-P

Corrected pronouns are in italics. This is a suggested corrected version. If you have different corrections, check with your instructor.

A committee of Margaret Chandler, Joseph Redmond, and *me* has been appointed to prepare a proposal for sharing sick leave among *us* employees. Our research so far has involved our investigating practices of other large agencies in the state. Margaret was more ambitious than Joe and *I,* so we were surprised what she discovered. She convinced Joe and *me* that we should analyze what other agencies are currently practicing so that our policy can reflect the best of all of them. Each state seems to have *its* own version of sick leave policy. Some companies let the employees *themselves* donate to a Sick Bank. For Margaret, Joe, and *me* to be successful, we will have to convince management officials that the beneficiaries will ultimately be *they*.

Feedback 6-Q

Corrected pronouns are in italics. This is a suggested corrected version. If you have different corrections, check with your instructor.

Beginning college students often find *themselves* frustrated because of their hectic schedules. They often are torn between many commitments and interests, and instructors expect *them* to manage their own time and meet deadlines. *Their* scheduling meetings and conferences with instructors can also be difficult since the instructors are often as busy as *they*. For instructors and *them* to find a mutually convenient time to meet often requires a lot of planning and arranging. When attending college, students must carefully prioritize their time so that they get the most out of the experience.

MODULE 7

Sentence Patterns

Objective: In this module, you will learn to identify and write clauses correctly.

Upon completion of this module, you will be able:

- To identify independent clauses.
- To identify dependent clauses.
- To recognize appropriate clause connectors.
- To recognize and to punctuate clauses correctly.

Like a sentence, a **clause** is a group of words that has a subject and a verb. However, as you will soon see, not all clauses are full sentences.

In the following sentences, the clauses are enclosed in parentheses. Notice that each group of words in parentheses has its own subject and verb. Therefore, each group is a clause.

S V S V
(He is the man) (who saw the accident.)

S V S V V
(I called him), but (he did not return my call.)

There are two kinds of clauses: independent and dependent. We will look at each type separately.

DIAGNOSTIC EXERCISE

Circle each dependent clause signal and underline the dependent clause twice. Underline each independent clause once.

1. Because he took six courses this semester, he decided to reduce his hours at work.
2. Although she has two victories, she is not favored to win the contest tonight.
3. We delayed the shipment so that we can make room for the products.
4. She is more organized than I am.
5. The manager reduced the numbers of available overtime hours because the company has caught up with demand.

Circle and label each transition or dependent clause signal.

1. We did not have time to break for lunch; consequently, we all went home hungry.
2. He declined the job offer because it did not have good benefits.
3. She agreed to complete the final tasks since she is the most detail oriented on our team.
4. Finally, we completed the project without any setbacks.
5. Before we can come to any conclusions, we have to examine the data.

PART I: INDEPENDENT CLAUSES

An **independent clause** (also called a major or main clause) is a clause that expresses a complete thought and can stand alone as a sentence. In the following examples, the independent clauses are underlined.

S V

The jury will announce its verdict soon.

S V S V

The directors objected, and the president resigned.

S V S V

Our sales manager spends lavishly; she has an unlimited expense account.

S V

After leaving the office, Cheryl was exhausted.

NOTE The introductory phrase is part of the independent clause.

Two or more independent clauses can be connected within a sentence in several ways.

Pattern 1. Two independent clauses (IC) joined by a coordinate conjunction (cc) take a comma before the conjunction. The pattern looks like this:

PUNCTUATION PATTERN 1

IC, cc IC.

Independent clauses can be connected by a **coordinate conjunction.** A **conjunction** is a connecting word. **Coordinate conjunctions** join words or groups of words of the same order or rank—for instance, two subjects, two verbs, two prepositional phrases, two verbal phrases, or two independent clauses.

COORDINATE CONJUNCTIONS

and	for	so
but	or	yet
	nor	

Here's an acronym to help you remember the seven coordinate conjunctions:

FANBOYS: *f*or, *a*nd, *n*or, *b*ut, *o*r, *y*et, *s*o.

S V S V

The design was completed, **but** the contractor reneged on the deal.

S V S V

We must arrive early, **for** the supervisor begins at 7 a.m.

NOTE When **for** is used as a coordinate conjunction, it has the same meaning as **because.** Remember that **for** is also a preposition with a totally different meaning: *I have a present for you.*

Pattern 2. Independent clauses can be joined by a **semicolon.** Use a semicolon to connect two *closely related* independent clauses. In this pattern, the semicolon takes the place of a coordinate conjunction.

S V S V

He gets the difficult assignments; he can handle them easily.

NOTE Use the semicolon sparingly, mainly for stylistic purposes. If the clauses are not closely related, it is better to use a period and separate them into independent sentences.

PUNCTUATION PATTERN 2

IC; IC.

Pattern 3. Independent clauses can be joined by a **semicolon and a transitional expression.**

Transitional expressions are connectors that show some kind of relationship between the clauses. The most common ones are listed below:

TRANSITIONAL EXPRESSIONS

accordingly	in fact
also	moreover
besides	namely
consequently	nevertheless
finally	next
for example	of course
for instance	on the other hand

furthermore
however
in addition
in conclusion
otherwise
still
then*
therefore
thus

* *Then* requires a semicolon only; it does not have to be followed by a comma.

PUNCTUATION PATTERN 3

IC; trans, IC.

❑ ***Punctuation Tip:***

- The transitional expression that joins two independent clauses should be preceded by a semicolon and followed by a comma. Note that the transitional expression is not a part of either independent clause.
- Another correct way of punctuating these sentences would be to use a period at the end of the first independent clause and begin a new sentence with the transitional expression.
- Note the difference in capitalization when using a semicolon versus a period with the transitional device.

We are expected to work overtime. **Therefore,** we should get a higher salary.
The design was completed. **However,** the contractor reneged on the deal.

PART II: DEPENDENT CLAUSES

A **dependent clause** (also called a subordinate clause) does not express a complete thought and, therefore, cannot stand alone. The following clauses are dependent and incomplete:

after Jones took charge
because there are defects in its basic structure
that we submitted last week

A dependent clause, as its name implies, must be supported by an independent clause. Otherwise, it is a fragment. A dependent clause usually adds detail to or completes the meaning of the independent clause.

In the following examples, the dependent clauses are underlined twice. Note that dependent clauses can occur at the beginning, in the middle, or at the end of a sentence.

Pattern 4.

PUNCTUATION PATTERN 4

DC, IC.

❑ ***Punctuation Tip:***

- When a dependent clause (DC) is at the beginning of a sentence, a comma is placed after it.
- When a dependent clause is at the end of a sentence, no comma is necessary between the independent and dependent clauses.

S V
After Jones took charge, he doubled sales.

Pattern 5.

PUNCTUATION PATTERN 5

IC DC.

The bridge is weak because there are defects in its basic structure.

Pattern 6. When a dependent clause comes in the *middle* of or splits an independent clause, the punctuation varies. For a full discussion of essential and nonessential punctuation, see Module 8. For now, the emphasis will only be on dependent clauses that come at the beginning or end of a sentence.

It is important to be able to identify dependent clauses so that you do not make the error of writing fragments instead of full sentences. Dependent clauses can be spotted easily because they are always introduced by a signal word such as the following:

DEPENDENT CLAUSE SIGNALS

after*	how	unless	which
although	if	until*	while
as*	once	what	who
as if	since*	whatever	whoever
as long as	so that	when	whom
as soon as	than	whenever	whomever

because	that	where	whose
before*	though	wherever	why
even though			

*The starred words may be used as prepositions but only when followed by an object. When used as clause signals, the starred words are followed by a subject and a verb. Compare the examples below.

PREPOSITIONAL PHRASE	CLAUSE
after the meeting	**after** the meeting was over
until noon	**until** the noon bell rings

Remember that these clause signals are *the first word of* the dependent clause, not connectors between two independent clauses. The signals suggest that answers to certain questions must be included in the sentences. Look at the following examples.

Because John was overqualified for the job
After Jeanine asked a most insulting question
Although Mrs. Walsh was an expert in math

These fragments would lead you to ask: What happened because John was overqualified? What happened after Jeanine asked a most insulting question? What happened although Mrs. Walsh was an expert in math?

Note also that if you remove the signal words—**because, after,** and **although**—from the fragments, you have independent clauses:

John was overqualified for the job.
Jeanine asked a most insulting question.
Mrs. Walsh was an expert in math.

Let these three items be your criteria for identifying a **dependent clause:**

1. Clause Signal
2. Subject
3. Verb

If a group of words contains a subject and verb but has no clause signal, it is considered an independent clause.

S V
The president knows why the company went bankrupt.

The president knows is an independent clause since it does not have a clause signal.

Sometimes what appears to be an independent clause does not make sense by itself. For example:

I heard that you were in town.

I heard does not seem to make a complete thought by itself. However, grammatically, it is an independent clause: It has a subject and a verb, and it is not introduced by a clause signal.

Some clause signals can serve as the subjects of dependent clauses as well as the signal words. These are **who, which, that, whoever,** and **whatever.**

DEPENDENT CLAUSE
S V
The man (who is discouraged easily) does not make a successful salesman.

clause signal as subject of dependent clause

DEPENDENT CLAUSE
S V
The advertisement (that drew the greatest response) was designed by an intern.

clause signal as subject of dependent clause

ACTIVITY 7-A: Clauses

Circle each dependent clause signal and draw two lines under each dependent clause. If a sentence has no dependent clause, do not mark it.

1. Keyboarding is useful.
2. The draftsman who completes his drawing first will be excused.
3. He acted as if he knew the correct procedure.
4. The draftsmen conferred early this morning.
5. They decided to accept the plan that was less complicated.
6. She called us when she knew the proper procedure.
7. Because he was in Baton Rouge, he attended the seminar.
8. He studied so much that he became exhausted.
9. We stayed in the meeting until the final session ended.
10. The boy who is sitting in the lobby is my son.

Check your responses in Feedback 7-A at the end of this module. If your responses were correct, proceed to Activity 7-C. If you missed any, review Part II and then do Activity 7-B.

ACTIVITY 7-B: Clauses

Circle the clause signals that introduce dependent clauses if the sentence has one.

1. The problem that most technicians faced was lack of trained personnel.
2. A man is a good worker when he is willing to do his share.

3. As computers have become more widespread, many working hours have been saved.
4. Mr. Steel studied the instructions before he began the project.
5. Although Mrs. Brown had a quorum, she delayed the meeting.
6. The conclusions must be accepted and implemented.
7. Since he entered the data into the computer this morning, he could give Tom the information before noon.
8. The repairs that Mr. Marvel made have been added to the bill.
9. Mr. Barnidge sent the memo when the conference was canceled.
10. She is very efficient, so she always meets the daily deadlines.

Check your responses in Feedback 7-B at the end of this module. If your responses were correct, proceed to Activity 7-C. If you missed any clause signals, review the list of dependent clause signal words and then proceed to Activity 7-C.

ACTIVITY 7-C: Clauses

Draw one line under each independent clause and two lines under each dependent clause. Circle each dependent clause signal.

1. Because the interview was important, she planned carefully.
2. This is the building that the draftsmen designed.
3. When the job is finished, we shall return to our families.
4. We looked for an employee who needed a summer job.
5. If you do well, you will be promoted.
6. It was shown that she really was a dedicated doctor.
7. When you send the bill, the company will write you a check.
8. He knew that female engineers have excellent job opportunities.
9. He had the skill although he failed to use it.
10. As I started the machine, he walked out.

Check your answers in Feedback 7-C at the end of this module. If you missed any, review Parts I and II.

PART III: APPROPRIATE CLAUSE CONNECTORS

Now that you can identify independent and dependent clauses, you will be presented with the three types of clause connectors that you worked with in Part II: *coordinate conjunctions, transitional expressions,* and *dependent clause signals.* Here you will learn how to choose the clause connector that is correct grammatically and that conveys the meaning you intend.

Coordinate Conjunctions

First let's review what you already know about coordinate conjunctions. Coordinate conjunctions join two independent clauses. They can also join two or more nouns, verbs, dependent clauses, etc. However, they do not connect an independent and a dependent clause. The sentence pattern (IC, cc IC.) is used for joining two independent clauses by means of a coordinate conjunction. This is an important pattern for you to master in your own writing. To use it properly, you should memorize and distinguish the meanings of the seven coordinate conjunctions: **and, but, yet, or, nor, for,** and **so.**

Consider the meaning of each coordinate conjunction as it is used in a sentence.

1. **And** is used to show addition. It connects items of similar qualities.

   The economy was good, **and** the new business thrived.

2. **But** and **yet** are used interchangeably to show contrast between ideas.

   She could type rapidly, **but** she could not do Excel spreadsheets.
   The wind was brisk, **yet** the day seemed mild.

3. **Or** and **nor** are used to show a choice.

   The old beakers can be used in the experiment, **or** the lab can purchase new ones.

   Nor indicates a negative choice between items. It means "not either one" is chosen. Notice that using nor requires using a helping verb like **did** or **will** right after it.

   The architect did not draw the plans to scale, nor did he use correct symbols.

4. **For** introduces a reason or explanation. Do not confuse it with the preposition **for,** which has a variety of other meanings.

   The architect did not draw the plans to scale, **for** he did not have the proper instruments.

5. **So** indicates a result.

   The architect did not draw the plans to scale, **so** his drawings were rejected.

Transitional Expressions

When a transitional expression is used to join two independent clauses, the transitional expression is preceded by a semicolon and followed by a comma (IC; trans, IC.). This pattern can add variety to your sentence structure;

however, it is important to know the meaning of the various transitional expressions in order to use them effectively.

In Part I, you were given a partial list of the more common transitional expressions. Here is a more complete list, grouped according to usage.

TRANSITIONAL EXPRESSIONS

Indicating Result
apparently
consequently
for this (that) reason
accordingly
therefore
thus
hence

Indicating Purpose
for this purpose
in order to do this
to this end
with this in mind
with this in view

Indicating Place
beyond
here
nearby
opposite
there
to the left (right)
in particular
namely
specifically

Indicating Contrast
however
in contrast
in spite of this
nevertheless
notwithstanding
on the contrary

Indicating Concession
at any rate
at least

Indicating Examples
for example
for instance
to illustrate

Indicating Emphasis
above all
certainly
indeed
in fact
in short
in truth
really
obviously
of course

Indicating End
in conclusion
on the whole
to summarize
on the other hand
still

Indicating Time
afterward
earlier
at the same time
in the meantime
later
meanwhile
simultaneously

Indicating Similarity
likewise
similarly

Indicating Addition
again
also
besides
equally important
finally
first, second, etc.
further
furthermore
in addition
in the first place
moreover
next
then
too

Indicating Details
especially
to enumerate
soon
then
first, second, next

Indicating Order of Importance
first, second, etc.
primarily
most importantly
next
finally

The following examples show how some of these bridging devices are used. Study them so that you will be able to incorporate these devices into your own writing, thereby adding more variety to your sentences.

> The architect worked his way through college; **consequently,** he was very conservative with his money. (Since the second independent clause is a result of the first, the clauses are connected with a transitional expression that indicates result, such as **consequently.**)
>
> The architect worked his way through college; **for this purpose,** he had to give up many social activities. (Here the transitional expression **for this purpose** shows that the first clause has stated a purpose and the second clause tells what the architect did because of his purpose.)
>
> The architect worked his way through college; **likewise,** his sister had a job while in school. (The transitional expression **likewise** indicates an idea in the second clause that is similar to the first.)
>
> The architect worked his way through college; **however,** he never had a full-time job until after graduation. (The transitional expression **however** shows that the second clause is an idea that contrasts with the first.)
>
> The architect worked his way through college; **specifically,** he held jobs as a cook, a sales clerk, and a draftsman. (The transitional expression **specifically** indicates that details will follow.)
>
> The architect worked his way through college; **at least,** he was industrious if not brilliant. (The transitional expression **at least** indicates a concession that this architect had drive, which some might consider less important than genius.)

These examples should give you an idea of how some of the transitional expressions on the list may be used to connect independent clauses. In most of the categories (except *time* and *place*), the expressions may be used interchangeably. Once you know what meaning you wish to convey, you can select the most appropriate word or phrase to use.

Notice how each transitional expression affects the meaning of the following series of sentences:

> The company made proper guarantees; **therefore,** the contract was accepted.
>
> The company made proper guarantees; **however,** the contract was not accepted.
>
> The company made proper guarantees; **afterward,** the contract was accepted.
>
> The company made proper guarantees; **in fact,** the contract was accepted.

The company made proper guarantees; **finally,** the contract was accepted.

The company made proper guarantees; **at any rate,** the contract was accepted.

Dependent Clause Signals

You learned earlier that a dependent clause can come at the beginning, in the middle, or at the end of a sentence and that it is introduced by a clause signal. Remember that a dependent clause signal, unlike a coordinating conjunction or a transitional expression, is actually a part of the clause and makes the clause an incomplete thought. You are already familiar with the dependent clause signals; here they are grouped according to use.

DEPENDENT CLAUSE SIGNALS

Indicating Time	as soon as	until
after	before	when
as	once	whenever
as long as	since	while
Indicating Place	*Indicating Result*	*Adjective Clause Signals (referring to specific nouns)*
where	as	
wherever	because	
	how	that
Indicating Contrast	since	what
although	so that	whatever
even though		which
though	*Indicating Condition*	who
	as if	whoever
Indicating Comparison	if	whom
as	unless	whomever
than	why	whose

Here are some sentences showing the correct use of dependent clause signals. Study the sentences so that you will be able to use these signals properly in your own sentences.

The nurse was qualified for a job in pediatrics **when** she graduated from DTCC. (The clause signal **when** indicates a time relationship.)

The nurse was qualified for a job in pediatrics **wherever** she wanted to work. (The clause signal **wherever** indicates place.)

The nurse was qualified for a job in pediatrics **although** she was placed in the geriatrics ward. (The clause signal **although** indicates a contrasting idea.)

The nurse is better qualified for a job in pediatrics **than** she is in geriatrics. (The clause signal **than** indicates comparison.)

Because the nurse was qualified for a job in pediatrics, she was hired immediately after graduation. (The clause signal **because** indicates result.)

If the nurse is qualified for a job in pediatrics, she will be hired immediately after graduation. (The clause signal **if** indicates condition.)

The nurse **who** is qualified for a job in pediatrics will be hired immediately after graduation. (The clause signal **who** introduces an adjective clause modifying the noun nurse. The entire clause acts as an adjective. An adjective clause is always next to the noun it modifies.)

The nurse was qualified for a job **which** was in pediatrics. (The clause signal **which** introduces an adjective clause which modifies the noun job.)

These examples should give you an idea of how some of the clause signals on the list are used to introduce dependent clauses. Decide on the meaning that you want your dependent clause to convey; then select an appropriate word from the proper group to begin the dependent clause.

You can change the meaning or emphasis of the sentence by changing the clause signal. Notice how the clause signals below give different meanings to the following sentence: **The office manager made out the payroll; he paid the taxes.**

The office manager made out the payroll **after** he paid the taxes.

The office manager made out the payroll **before** he paid the taxes.

The officer manager made out the payroll **because** he wanted to pay the taxes.

The officer manager **who** made out the payroll also paid the taxes.

The office manager made out the payroll **as soon as** he paid the taxes.

Although the office manager made out the payroll, he did not pay the taxes.

ACTIVITY 7-D: Review of Clauses

Circle each dependent clause signal and underline the dependent clause twice. Underline each independent clause once.

1. When we drove into the parking lot, we were given a space near the building.
2. The window overlooked the construction site, and we could see the experienced workers in their hard hats.
3. He always chose to perform those tasks that were most interesting to him.
4. Taking six weeks of sick leave was helpful; the compensation that he received was fair.
5. The emphasis by employers on accuracy, neatness, and initiative is to be expected by job applicants.
6. The receptionist who sits next to the telephone is responsible for taking all messages.
7. Because modern machinery can function unattended, the unemployment rate may increase.
8. Of course, the union members and business people will have to agree on the proposal.
9. The DuPont Company runs three shifts; otherwise, it does not get the necessary work completed on time.
10. Modes of transportation that have proved to be cost efficient should be subsidized by the federal government.

Check your responses in Feedback 7-D at the end of this module.

ACTIVITY 7-E: **Editing Practice**

Rewrite the following short, choppy paragraph combining ideas and using a variety of clauses and connecting devices as discussed in this module. Make sure you use a combination of dependent clauses, compound sentences, and transitional devices.

Most word processing programs have a feature called readability. You should use it. It checks reading levels of written work. Some students write short sentences. A readability will point this out. A good readability is at least tenth grade level. Readability depends on two features. One is sentence length. Sentences that are short bore readers. They also lack connection of ideas. Writers should connect ideas for readers. Readability also measures length of words. Heavy use of one or two syllable words will result in a low readability. The best way to raise a readability is to combine ideas using clause signals, transitions, and coordinate conjunctions. The readability on this piece is sixth grade. The average length per sentence is 7.5 words. Try not to write like this. Good writers should hear choppiness. Read your work out loud.

See a sample of a revision employing various sentence combining techniques of this paragraph in Feedback 7-E. You may want to check yours with your instructor.

ACTIVITY 7-F: Editing Practice

Rewrite the following short, choppy paragraph combining ideas and using a variety of clauses and connecting devices. Make sure you use a combination of dependent clauses, compound sentences and transitional devices.

A job interview is often an intimidating experience. Job seekers can improve their confidence by taking some time to carefully plan for the appointment. They should make sure that they have directions. They should know approximately how long it will take them to get to the interview location. They can even take a trial run before the day when the interview is scheduled. They should also thoughtfully plan their outfit choice. They should choose something that is appropriate for the work environment where they will be visiting for the interview. It is also important for job seekers to anticipate what kinds of questions will be asked of them. They should take some time to think about the answers that they might give. Preparing for an interview does take time and thought. Careful attention to detail just may pay off with a job.

See a sample of a revision employing various sentence combining techniques of this paragraph in Feedback 7-F. You may want to check yours with your instructor.

DIAGNOSTIC FEEDBACK

Circle each dependent clause signal and underline the dependent clause twice. Underline each independent clause once.

1. **Because he took six courses this semester,** he decided to reduce his hours at work.
2. **Although she has two victories,** she is not favored to win the contest tonight.
3. We delayed the shipment **so that we can make room for the products.**
4. She is more organized **than I am.**
5. The manager reduced the numbers of available overtime hours **because the company has caught up with demand.**

Circle and label each transition or dependent clause signal.

1. We did not have time to break for lunch; consequently, we all went home hungry. (transition)
2. He declined the job offer because it did not have good benefits. (DC)

3. She agreed to complete the final tasks since she is the most detail oriented on our team. (DC)
4. Finally, we completed the project without any setbacks. (transition)
5. Before we can come to any conclusions, we have to examine the data. (DC)

FEEDBACK FOR MODULE 7

Feedback 7-A

1. (None)
2. who completes his drawing first
3. as if he knew the correct procedure
4. (None)
5. that was less complicated
6. when she knew the proper procedure
7. Because he was in Baton Rouge
8. that he became exhausted
9. until the final session ended
10. who is sitting in the lobby

Feedback 7-B

1. that
2. when
3. As
4. before
5. Although
6. (None)
7. Since
8. that
9. when
10. (None)

Feedback 7-C

1. Because the interview was important, she planned carefully.
2. This is the building that the draftsman designed.
3. When the job is finished, we shall return to our families.
4. We looked for an employee who needed a summer job.
5. If you do well, you will be promoted.
6. It was shown that she really was a dedicated doctor.
7. When you send the bill, the company will write you a check.

8. He knew (that) female engineers have excellent job opportunities.
9. He had the skill (although) he failed to use it.
10. (As) I started the machine, he walked out.

Feedback 7-D

1. (When) we drove into the parking lot, we were given a space near the building.
2. The window overlooked the construction site, and we could see the experienced workers in their hard hats.
3. He always chose to perform those tasks (that) were most interesting to him.
4. Taking six weeks of sick leave was helpful; the compensation (that) he received was fair.
5. The emphasis by employers on accuracy, neatness, and initiative is to be expected by job applicants.
6. The receptionist (who) sits next to the telephone is responsible for taking all messages.
7. (Because) modern machinery can function unattended, the unemployment rate may increase.
8. Of course, the union members and business people will have to agree on the proposal.
9. The DuPont Company runs three shifts; otherwise, it does not get the necessary work completed on time.
10. Modes of transportation (that) have proved to be cost-efficient should be subsidized by the federal government.

Feedback 7-E

Major revisions are shown in italics.

Most word processing programs have a feature called readability *which you should use because it checks reading levels of written work. If students write short sentences, a readability will point this out.* A good readability, *which is at least tenth grade level,* depends on two features. One is sentence length. *Sentences that are short bore readers; in addition, they lack connection of ideas. While writers should connect ideas for readers, a readability also measures length of words. Heavy use of one or two syllable words will result in a low readability; however, the best way to raise a readability is to combine ideas using clause signals, transitions, and coordinate conjunctions. The readability on this piece is sixth grade, and the average length per sentence is 7.5 words, so you should try not to write like this. Good writers should hear choppiness, so read your work out loud.*

NOTE The new average length per sentence is 16.4 words. The readability went up to 7.8, but it is still low because of the use of one and two syllable words. When you have choppiness, work on combining sentences. Change the number of syllables of words only if necessary. Frequently, shorter words are the best words to use.

Feedback 7-F

Since a job interview is often an intimidating experience, job seekers can improve their confidence by taking some time to carefully plan for the appointment. First, they should make sure that they have directions, and they should know approximately how long it will take them to get to the interview location; furthermore, they can even take a trial run before the day when the interview is scheduled. They should also thoughtfully plan their outfit choice, and they should choose something that is appropriate for the work environment where they will be visiting for the interview. Of course, it is also important for job seekers to anticipate what kinds of questions will be asked of them and to take some time to think about the answers they might give. Preparing for an interview does take time and thought, but careful attention to detail just may pay off with a job.

NOTE The readability improved to 12.0 (unedited paragraph: 8.2); average words per sentence improved to 29.8 (Unedited paragraph: 12.9).

MODULE 8

Punctuation

Objective: This module is designed to help you in the three main areas in which students have trouble with punctuation.

Upon completion of this module, you will be able:

- To identify the basic patterns of punctuation.
- To write sentences using the punctuation patterns correctly.
- To apply five basic comma rules for correct sentence construction.

DIAGNOSTIC EXERCISE

Add commas where necessary.

1. The renovations will include updates to the labs classrooms offices and kitchen facilities.
2. The costly time-consuming repairs have set the project back four months.
3. Taking time to carefully plan a report is one of the most important things you can do when writing.
4. Because the project has been delayed the profits have dwindled considerably.
5. We plan to leave for the conference when our boss returns from lunch.
6. The editor reviewed the corrections and she approved the book for publishing.
7. We plan of course to update the calendar immediately.
8. The man who wrote the program for eBay is now a billionaire.
9. Accepting a gift from the book vendor the instructor violated ethical standards.
10. The most recent edition of our book which is scheduled to be published next month contains extra practice exercises.

PART I: BASIC SENTENCE PUNCTUATION PATTERNS

Review and memorize the basic sentence patterns listed below. Using them as models will help you to punctuate your own sentences.

PATTERN ABBREVIATIONS*		EXAMPLES
Pattern 1	IC, cc IC.	My boss warned me about being late, but he didn't fire me.
Pattern 2	IC; IC.	My boss warned me about being late; he didn't fire me.
Pattern 3	IC; trans, IC.	My boss warned me about being late; however, he didn't fire me.
Pattern 4	DC, IC.	Although my boss warned me about being late, he didn't fire me.
Pattern 5	IC DC.	My boss didn't fire me although he warned me about being late.

*KEY TO ABBREVIATIONS

IC: Independent Clause (has a subject and a verb and can stand alone).

DC: Dependent Clause (is introduced by a signal word and followed by a subject–verb unit). See list of dependent clause signals following.

cc: Coordinate Conjunction (all seven in list following).

trans: Transitional Expression (see list of the most common ones following; see index for a more complete list).

DEPENDENT CLAUSE SIGNALS			COORDINATE CONJUNCTIONS	COMMON TRANSITIONAL EXPRESSIONS	
Patterns 4–5			Pattern 1	Pattern 3	
after	once	whenever	and	accordingly	in conclusion
although	since	where	but	also	in fact
as	so that	wherever	for	besides	namely
as if	than	which	nor	consequently	nevertheless
as long as	that	while	or	finally	of course
as soon as	though	who	so	for example	on the other hand
because	unless	whoever	yet	for instance	then
before	until	whom		furthermore	therefore
even though	what	whomever		however	thus
how	whatever	whose			
if	when	why			

Pattern 1: IC, cc IC. Two independent clauses (sentences) joined by a coordinating conjunction should have a comma before the conjunction.

Pattern 2: IC; IC. Two closely-related independent clauses (two sentences) can be separated by a semicolon for stylistic purposes. Use a semicolon only if a period works as well.

Pattern 3: IC; trans, IC. If you use a transitional expression to connect two independent clauses, you can use a semicolon before and a comma after the transitional expression. It would also be correct to use a period in place of the semicolon.

Pattern 4: DC, IC. If you introduce the sentence with a dependent clause, the clause, not just the signal, should be separated from the independent clause by a comma.

Pattern 5: IC DC. If the dependent clause comes at the end of the sentence, typically no comma is used between the clauses.

To help you remember these five punctuation patterns, here they are again with illustrations.

Punctuation Patterns

IC, cc IC. (Two independent clauses joined by a coordinate conjunction)

My boss telephoned me	,	but	I wasn't home.

IC; IC. (Two independent clauses joined by a semicolon)

My boss telephoned me	;	I wasn't home.

IC; trans, IC. (Two independent clauses joined by a transitional expression)

My boss telephoned me	;	however	,	I wasn't home.

DC, IC. (A dependent clause followed by an independent clause)

When	my boss telephoned me	,	I wasn't home.

IC DC. (A independent clause followed by an dependent clause)

My boss telephoned me	when	I wasn't home.

ACTIVITY 8-A: Punctuation Patterns

Write the five basic sentence patterns *from memory.*

Pattern 1 ______________________________

Pattern 2 ______________________________

Pattern 3 ______________________________

Pattern 4 ______________________________

Pattern 5 ______________________________

Check your responses in Feedback 8-A at the end of this module. If you missed any, review until you can write the patterns from memory.

ACTIVITY 8-B: Sentence Punctuation Patterns

Take the following paired sentences, and run each pair through the five patterns.

A. It rained on Friday. The construction crew didn't work.

Pattern 1 ______________________________

Pattern 2 ______________________________

Pattern 3 ______________________________

Pattern 4 ______________________________

Pattern 5 ______________________________

B. The blueprint machine was broken. The building plans weren't ready for the client.

Pattern 1 ______________________________

Pattern 2 ______________________________

Pattern 3 ______________________________

Pattern 4 ______________________________

Pattern 5 ______________________________

C. I kept a good record of my expenses for the year. I was ready for the accountant to do my taxes.

Pattern 1 ______________________________

Pattern 2 ______________________________

Pattern 3 ______________________________

Pattern 4 ______________________________

Pattern 5 ______________________________

Check your responses in Feedback 8-B at the end of this module. Then proceed to Activity 8-C.

ACTIVITY 8-C: Sentence Punctuation Patterns

Identify the pattern in each of the following sentences. Write the pattern abbreviation to the left of the sentence.

_______ 1. If we advertise in newspapers, our business will certainly increase.

_______ 2. He became very nervous as he read the contract.

_______ 3. Mr. Nyton should support company policy, or he should resign.

_______ 4. Some policies pay on disability; others pay on death.

_______ 5. She tried to improve sales; to illustrate, she called on more customers.

_______ 6. Mr. Wook showed his disapproval when he heard the bad report.

_______ 7. The money was allocated by the legislature, but the hospital received none of it.

_______ 8. The bridge is located in this county; in fact, it is only 6 miles from here.

_______ 9. Employment did not increase; the company experienced a slump.

_______ 10. He put his valuables into the office safe; however, the building burned down.

Check your responses in Feedback 8-C at the end of this module. If your responses were correct, proceed to Part II. If you missed any, review before continuing.

PART II: OTHER BASIC COMMA RULES

You saw where the comma is required in sentence patterns 1, 3, and 4. In addition, there are several other rules to remember about where and when to use a comma. These rules will help you to avoid common punctuation errors in your writing. There are other rules for comma use, but the ones that follow frequently occur in business and technical writing.

Rule 1. *Use a comma to separate three or more words, phrases, or clauses in a series.*

Words in a series

The hotel manager required her employees to be *neat, clean,* and *efficient.*

Phrases in a series

The hotel agreed *to host the conference, to provide for all meals,* and *to plan the closing banquet.*

Clauses in a series

The manager gave instructions on *how a bed is made, how a bathroom is cleaned,* and *how the heating system is regulated.*

In some publications, you may see items in a series without a comma before the **and** preceding the last item. This can sometimes cause confusion.

The City Council elected a president, vice-president, secretary and treasurer.

Were three or four officers elected? Without the comma after the word *secretary,* it is not clear whether one person holds the combined office of secretary and treasurer or whether there are four officeholders. Placing the comma after *secretary* indicates clearly that there are four officers. To be sure your sentences are clear, it is wise to use the comma before the **and** in a series.

The City Council elected a president, vice-president, secretary, and treasurer.

If there were only three officers, *secretary-treasurer* would probably be hyphenated.

The County Council elected a president, vice-president, and secretary-treasurer.

Sometimes each item in a series is joined by **and.** In this case, the commas are unnecessary.

The sisters spent the afternoon shopping and visiting relatives and delivering packages.

Rule 2. *Use a comma to separate items in dates and addresses.*

Dates: Use a comma to set off the day of the week, the day of the month, and the year, and also after the year when it is not the end of the sentence. Do not use a comma between the month and the day.

The first meeting will be held on Tuesday, May 5, at the high school.

The financial statement was mailed on March 13, 2008, in the late afternoon.

It rained on Monday, August 20, 2008, before the crop was harvested.

❑ ***Punctuation Tip:***

No commas are needed when only the month and the year are used.

The tropical storms of July 2004 were very severe.

Addresses: Consider the street number and street name as one item and the state and zip code as one item. Each additional item is followed by a comma.

The branch office address is 20125 Seashore Highway, Georgetown, DE 19947, a location which is near the home office.

His new business address is 958 Ridge Road, Hayes, KS, which is in the northern part of the state.

Portland, Oregon, is the site of the new factory.

Deliver the package to John Newton, Room 602, 29292 Ocean Drive, Ocean City, MD 21842.

❑ ***Punctuation Tip:***

No comma is used between the state and the zip code.

Rule 3. *Use a comma to separate coordinate adjectives (two or more adjectives preceding the same noun or pronoun).*

The **long, involved** court case cost the company $200,000 in fees and fines.

In this example, **long** and **involved** are coordinate adjectives because they both describe the court case. Compare the sentence above with the following:

Many of the wares in Williamsburg reflect authentic colonial design.

In this sentence *authentic* and *colonial* do not both describe *design. Authentic* describes *colonial.* Thus, the meaning is *authentic colonial,* not *authentic design.* In this case, do not use a comma.

There are two tests you can apply to tell if adjectives are coordinate:

1. *Coordinate adjectives sound correct when joined by* **and.**
   the long **and** involved court case (*Right*)
   the authentic **and** colonial design (*Wrong*)
2. *Coordinate adjectives can be reversed and still sound right.*
   the **involved, long** court case (*Right*)
   the **colonial authentic** building (*Wrong*)

See how these tests apply:

the **quick, efficient** secretary (*Use comma—quick and* efficient secretary)
a **bright red** tractor (*No comma—not bright* and *red tractor*)
a **scorching, sarcastic** book review (*Use comma—scorching and . . .* sarcastic book)
a **floral patterned** dress (*No comma—not floral and patterned* dress)

ACTIVITY 8-D: Comma Rules

Insert commas where necessary.

1. The Society for the Advancement of Management elected a chairman historian secretary and treasurer.
2. The journalist expects to interview the celebrity to take pictures and to write the feature article by Monday.
3. The next conference will be held on Friday January 12 2008 in Room 100.
4. The police officers will send condolence cards to Mrs. Jerome Gray 201 Olympia Drive Seattle Washington 90105 preferably by noon Friday.
5. The patient considerate nurse listened to the sick man's problems.
6. The brand new computer will soon be in operation.
7. The social worker spoke to the group on alcoholic services educational opportunities and job seminars.
8. The supervisors and the assembly line worker and the secretaries were all impressed with the presentation.
9. The technician reported that the television had been struck by lightning that the main tube was ruined and that it would cost $50 to fix it.
10. Contributions are being accepted at the main headquarters in Peoria Illinois.

Check your responses in Feedback 8-D at the end of this module. If your responses were correct, proceed to Rule 4. If you missed any, review Rules 1, 2, and 3 and then do Activity 8-E.

ACTIVITY 8-E: Comma Rules

Insert commas where necessary.

1. The law office hired a secretary a bookkeeper and an accountant. (three employees)
2. A community college enables a student to get an education to qualify for a good job and to be a contributing member of society.
3. The last meeting was held on Monday June 12 2008 at 2 P.M.
4. The new office building will be located at 4123 First Avenue Salisbury MD 21801 behind the old factory.
5. The skillful clever architect designed an interesting building.
6. A dull gray building is an eyesore.
7. The architect and the builder and the interior decorator planned the facility.
8. Seminars were held in the conference room in the gym and in the theater.
9. The student nurses received instructions in how to administer artificial respiration how to use the CPR technique and how to take blood pressure.
10. The new supplies will arrive on December 2 2008 on the afternoon train.

Check your responses in Feedback 8-E at the end of this module. Then proceed to Rule 4.

Rule 4. *Use commas to set off certain introductory words and phrases.*

- *One-word expressions at the beginning of a sentence should be set off.*

  Oh, did the report come in?
  Yes, I read it yesterday.

- *Introductory, descriptive verbal phrases must be set off by a comma.*

  Hearing his name called, he turned around.
  Hurt by the fall, the lineman sat stunned.

- *Introductory words or phrases that might be misread are set off with a comma.*

  After smoking, the nurse returned to the patient.
  To John, Henry was a good friend.
  By 2010, 450 students were enrolled.

Rule 5. *Use commas to set off interrupters.*

Interrupters are words or phrases that come in the middle of a sentence; that is, the word or phrase comes somewhere after the first word or before the last word in the sentence. Interrupting expressions are not essential, and, therefore, they are set off with a pair of commas, one before and after the word or phrase. Interrupters do, however, add emphasis or additional detail to the main idea of the sentence.

Emphasis

Some interrupters are used to add emphasis to a statement.

- **Parenthetic elements,** such as **therefore, however, moreover, on the other hand,** and so on, fall into this category. You may notice that these words also fall into the category of transitional expressions. They are transitional expressions when they come at the beginning of the second sentence of a pair of related sentences. They are interrupters when they occur in the middle of one independent clause.

  Transitional expression

  The bid for the construction job was submitted late; **consequently,** the local company did not get the job.

  Parenthetical expression

  The local company, **consequently,** did not get the job.

One helpful way to check for a parenthetic element is to see if you can change its position in the sentence to the beginning, middle, or end. If the meaning is not affected, the word or phrase can be classified as a parenthetic expression.

- Another technique used for emphasis is the **negative expression.** It can be easily recognized because it is formed by using some form of the words *no* or *not.* These expressions frequently come in the middle or end of a sentence and require the use of a comma or a pair of commas.

  The balance sheet was correct, **wasn't it?**

  Your letter, **not mine,** was chosen for the company report.

- **Direct address** adds emphasis to a sentence because you speak directly to a person, not about the person. It works like an interrupter when it occurs in the middle of a sentence, but, like parenthetical expressions, direct address can occur almost anywhere in the sentence. Therefore, it should be set off with a comma or a pair of commas.

  We know, *Mr. Lord,* that your CIS course is the best in the state.

  Mary, would you retype this letter?

  Mail it today, *John.*

Additional Detail

Interrupters are also used to add more detail to a sentence.

- Expressions like **such as** and **especially** indicate that more detail is coming.

  Computer supplies, **such as printer paper, cartridges, and pads,** are located in the storage closet.

  Your figures, **especially the most recent ones,** are startling.

- **Appositives,** which are words, phrases, or clauses that rename or give added information about a noun or pronoun immediately preceding them, should be set off with commas.

  Ms. Smith, **the Agri-Business advisor,** has an extensive background in agriculture.

  The company president, **a graduate in accounting,** spoke about the company's assets.

- *A single-word appositive,* usually a name, is not set off with commas to avoid confusion with direct address.

  His sister **Cindy** is studying to be a nurse practitioner.

ACTIVITY 8-F: **Comma Rules**

Supply commas where necessary. Circle transitional expressions/interrupters and determine if there are two sentences or one.

1. Mr. Jones meets with his class accordingly three times a week.
2. The communications student writes well doesn't she?
3. Yes Ms. Winter will speak to the secretaries.
4. Tom seldom however answers the instructor's question in class.
5. Seeing her employer June asked for a raise.
6. Giving the receptionist her paycheck the lawyer said that it was time for her to go to the bank.
7. The employer said that the memo however was hard to read.
8. Taking his time he writes letters well.
9. Most of the time however he is late for class.
10. The student a chemistry major wrote the lab report.

Check your responses in Feedback 8-F at the end of this module. If your responses were correct, proceed to Activity 8-H. If you missed any, do Activity 8-G.

ACTIVITY 8-G: **Comma Rules**

Supply commas where necessary.

1. Miss Jones will you please send a memo to all departments about the meeting.

2. The new lab technician a graduate of the local community college is doing all the blood samples.
3. Many times however the computer is not being used.
4. The new nursing program is very popular with the students isn't it?
5. Graduating with a business degree they will all have jobs.
6. The representative from DELL therefore will interview the graduates on June 24.
7. The floor supervisor Elizabeth Fleming has posted the schedule for next week on the bulletin board.
8. According to the freight department our shipment should be here by June 1.
9. To begin with the cafeteria is very busy at that time.
10. Did you write the memo Miss Earlson?

Check your responses in Feedback 8-G at the end of this module. Then proceed to essential and nonessential adjective clauses.

Essential and Nonessential Adjective Clauses

Adjective clauses, which begin with the words **who, which,** or **that,** can be essential or nonessential (also known as restrictive or nonrestrictive). A nonessential clause works like an interrupter because it adds detail or emphasis to the sentence and is not necessary to the meaning of the sentence core. These clauses are set off from the rest of the sentence by commas. Essential clauses, on the other hand, are necessary for meaning; therefore, they are not separated from the rest of the sentence by commas.

One way to tell the difference between the two types of clauses is to ask yourself, "Do I need the clause to IDENTIFY the noun preceding it?" If your answer is "Yes," then the clause is **essential,** and no commas are used to set it off. If your answer is "No," then the clause is **nonessential** and is set off with commas.

NOTE THAT clauses are ALWAYS essential (No commas).
WHICH clauses are USUALLY nonessential (Use commas).
WHO clauses can be either (Apply the identity tip).

- NONESSENTIAL CLAUSES

The driver of the second car, **who was also from Baltimore,** presented his license.

Computer skills, **which can be updated through evening classes,** are critical in the workforce.

The president summoned Ms. Birch, **who spoke fluent Spanish.**

In the sentences above, the boldface adjective clause is not necessary to IDENTIFY the driver, computer skills, or Ms. Birch; consequently, commas are needed.

- ESSENTIAL CLAUSES

He is the man **who was elected to City Council.**
The computer **that Henry was using** is broken.

These clauses are essential because one begins with **that,** and the other is needed to **IDENTIFY** which man was elected to City Council.

> **NOTE** Proper nouns are frequently followed by nonessential clauses. Common nouns are usually followed by essential clauses.

Special Problems with Essential and Nonessential Wording

You can now see that punctuation of wording that comes in the middle of a sentence depends on whether it is essential or nonessential. When dealing with essential and nonessential wording, the use of commas can change the meaning of a sentence. Consider the following examples:

The order forms, which are green, are kept on the top shelf. (All order forms are green, and they are kept on the top shelf.)
The order forms which are green are kept on the top shelf. (Only the green order forms are kept on the top shelf. Other order forms may be kept elsewhere.)

You can also now reconsider Pattern 5, IC DC. If the DC happens to be a nonessential adjective clause, then that clause must be separated from the dependent clause by a comma.

The president summoned Ms. Birch, who spoke fluent Spanish.

ACTIVITY 8-H: Punctuating Essential and Nonessential Clauses

Punctuate the following sentences where necessary.

1. The Mayor who happened to favor the new shopping mall met in closed session with the City Council.
2. The person whose knowledge of the market is up-to-date is most likely to make the sale.
3. Anything which can be done to save energy should be suggested.
4. Fred Henry whose technical expertise was well known in the company was assigned the task of drafting the report.
5. The pharmaceutical company's representative who was familiar to each of the doctors in the clinic rarely had to wait ten minutes to get an appointment.

6. The person who invented photocopiers changed office routines dramatically.
7. Dr. Angela Sims who organized the reconstruction of the Indian village used many volunteers at the site.
8. Your supervisor whose experience should have qualified her for the task decided you would be better at working with new trainees.
9. The employer who sets high standards gets better performance on the job.
10. Mrs. Roberts who spoke at the assistants' conference gave the audience some excellent guidelines on office procedures.

Check your responses in Feedback 8-H at the end of this module. If your responses were correct, proceed to Activity 8-J. If you missed any, review and do Activity 8-I.

ACTIVITY 8-I: Punctuating Essential and Nonessential Clauses

Punctuate the following sentences where necessary.

1. The Space Shuttle astronauts who were recognized by only a few workers toured the plant yesterday.
2. Safety programs which were started in the past year are superior to previous programs.
3. The trainer bandaged the horse's injured leg which still showed some swelling.
4. Groundbreaking for the newest factory which will be located on the north side of town is scheduled for Thursday at 10 A.M.
5. The Three Mile Island reactors which caused a national panic have been thoroughly checked by the engineers.
6. On Wednesday which is usually his day off Chuck works on his antique cars.
7. Long distance charges that are over three minutes are closely monitored in the front office.
8. The person who worked on the newest soybean hybrids spoke to the horticulture class yesterday.
9. The chief technician who drove his new car today was in a very good mood.
10. The office assistant who answers the phone is extremely valuable to a boss.

Check your responses in Feedback 8-I at the end of this module. If your responses were correct, proceed to Activity 8-J. If you missed any, review before continuing.

ACTIVITY 8-J: Review of Punctuation Patterns and Rules

Punctuate the following sentences correctly. In the space provided, identify the patterns or rules used.

Patterns: IC, cc IC. IC; IC. IC; trans, IC. DC, IC. IC DC.
Rules: series, date, address, coord. adj., interr., intro. word or phrase (specify one-word, verbal, or misreading).

_______ 1. The students took their texts and notebooks to class apparently they expected a review before the test.

_______ 2. However we are not requiring the civil engineers to participate in the experiment.

_______ 3. Arriving late for the meeting the reporter had to sit in the back of the room.

_______ 4. The famous murder trial in Emporia Virginia on March 28 1952 drew a large crowd.

_______ 5. Agri-Business is an interesting technology isn't it?

_______ 6. Yes Mrs. Grant it was an informative field trip.

_______ 7. Many students in data processing have information that they have to feed into the computer.

_______ 8. Auditing an Accounting course dealing with the extrnal audit process is necessary for anyone who wants to become a CPA.

_______ 9. The tall slender student was interested only in his technology and his job.

_______ 10. The biology instructor too gave a difficult assignment.

_______ 11. When we asked for a motel room the manager said that there were no vacancies.

_______ 12. To succeed in sales in 2008 500 new people must increase their accounts.

_______ 13. He told his supervisor the correct answer apparently to the question.

_______ 14. His address is 214 College Avenue Philadelphia PA 21069 a prosperous business area.

_______ 15. He spoke to the construction builders there was a flaw in the weather-stripping.

Check your responses in Feedback 8-J at the end of this module.

ACTIVITY 8-K: Editing Practice

Insert commas where needed for sentence patterns and those rules discussed in this module.

Commas are without a doubt the most difficult troublesome area of proofreading for many writing students. Most students have to "unlearn" many of their lifelong habits concerning punctuation. For example commas are used for structural purposes not for pauses. The area most students have trouble with is the comma used for introductory elements like transitional phrases prepositional phrases and certain kinds of words or phrases used frequently at the beginning of a sentence. Then there are the interrupters phrases that come somewhere in the middle of a sentence. Sometimes these elements get commas and sometimes unfortunately they do not. The punctuation depends on whether there is emphasis detail or special stylistic purposes. In September 2009 the Society for Chronic Comma Users of 417 Lexington Avenue New York, NY 20012 will meet to devise a campaign to help writers become aware of problems with commas coming from arbitrary punctuation habits.

Check your responses in Feedback 8-K at the end of this module.

ACTIVITY 8-L: Editing Practice

Insert commas where needed for sentence patterns and those rules discussed in this module.

When writing a research report students must document cited material carefully so that they avoid plagiarizing their sources. It is important for students to know that statistics results of surveys quotations and paraphrased ideas must be cited. In fact students must also cite information gleaned from personal communications and audio-visual materials. Their own ideas and conclusions however do not need documentation. Thorough conscientious college students always take care to cite information when writing a documented report since plagiarism is equivalent to stealing ideas and it can ruin their reputation.

Check your responses in Feedback 8-L at the end of this module.

DIAGNOSTIC FEEDBACK

Add commas where necessary.

1. The renovations will include updates to the labs, classrooms, offices, and kitchen facilities.
2. The costly, time-consuming repairs have set the project back four months.

3. Taking time to carefully plan a report is one of the most important things you can do when writing.
4. Because the project has been delayed, the profits have dwindled considerably.
5. We plan to leave for the conference when our boss returns from lunch.
6. The editor reviewed the corrections, and she approved the book for publishing.
7. We plan, of course, to update the calendar immediately.
8. The man who wrote the program for eBay is now a billionaire.
9. Accepting a gift from the book vendor, the instructor violated ethical standards.
10. The most recent edition of our book, which is scheduled to be published next month, contains extra practice exercises.

FEEDBACK FOR MODULE 8

Feedback 8-A

Pattern 1: IC, cc IC.
Pattern 2: IC; IC.
Pattern 3: IC; trans, IC.
Pattern 4: DC, IC.
Pattern 5: IC DC.

Feedback 8-B

A. 1. It rained on Friday, and (so) the construction crew didn't work.
2. It rained on Friday; the construction crew didn't work.
3. It rained on Friday; therefore (as a result), the construction crew didn't work.
4. Because (Since) it rained on Friday, the construction crew didn't work.
5. The construction crew didn't work on Friday because (since) it rained.

B. 1. The blueprint machine was broken, and (so) the building plans weren't ready for the client.
2. The blueprint machine was broken; the building plans weren't ready for the client.
3. The blueprint machine was broken; consequently (therefore), the building plans weren't ready for the client.
4. Because (Since) the blueprint machine was broken, the building plans weren't ready for the client.
5. The building plans weren't ready for the client because (since) the blueprint machine was broken.

C. 1. I kept a good record of my expenses for the year, and (so) I was ready for the accountant to do my taxes.
2. I kept a good record of my expenses for the year; I was ready for the accountant to do my taxes.

3. I kept a good record of my expenses for the year; thus (therefore, consequently), I was ready for the accountant to do my taxes.
4. Since (Because) I kept a good record of my expenses for the year, I was ready for the accountant to do my taxes.
5. I was ready for the accountant to do my taxes since (because) I kept a good record of my expenses for the year.

Feedback 8-C

1. DC, IC.
2. IC DC.
3. IC, cc IC.
4. IC; IC.
5. IC; trans, IC.
6. IC DC.
7. IC, cc IC.
8. ICIC; trans, IC.
9. IC; IC.
10. IC; trans, IC.

Feedback 8-D

1. chairman, historian, secretary, and treasurer.
2. to interview the celebrity, to take pictures, and to write the feature article by Monday
3. Friday, January 12, 2008, in Room 100.
4. Mrs. Jerome Gray, 201 Olympia Drive, Seattle, Washington 90105, preferably by noon Friday
5. patient, considerate
6. (No commas)
7. alcoholic services, educational opportunities, and job seminars
8. (No commas)
9. that the television had been struck by lightning, that the main tube was ruined, and that it would cost $50 to fix it
10. Peoria, Illinois

Feedback 8-E

1. secretary, a bookkeeper, and an accountant
2. education, to qualify . . . job, and to be . . .
3. Monday, June 12, 2008, at 2 P.M.
4. 4123 First Avenue, Salisbury, MD 21801, behind . . .
5. skillful, clever architect
6. (No commas)
7. (No commas)
8. room, . . . gym, . . .
9. respiration, . . . technique, . . .
10. January 2, 2008, on the afternoon train.

Feedback 8-F

1. class, accordingly, (one sentence)
2. well, doesn't she?

3. Yes, Ms. Winter
4. seldom, however, (one sentence)
5. employer,
6. paycheck,
7. memo, however, (one sentence)
8. time,
9. time, however, (one sentence)
10. student, a chemistry major,

Feedback 8-G

1. Miss Jones, will
2. technician, . . . college,
3. times, however,
4. students, isn't it?
5. degree, they
6. DELL, therefore,
7. supervisor, Elizabeth Fleming,
8. department, our
9. To begin with,
10. memo, Miss Earlson?

Feedback 8-H

1. The Mayor, who happened to favor the new shopping mall, met in closed session with the City Council.
2. No changes
3. No changes
4. Fred Henry, whose technical expertise was well known in the company, was assigned the task of drafting the report.
5. The pharmaceutical company's representative, who was familiar to each of the doctors in the clinic, rarely had to wait ten minutes to get an appointment.
6. No changes
7. Dr. Angela Sims, who organized the reconstruction of the Indian village, used many volunteers at the site.
8. Your supervisor, whose experience should have qualified her for the task, decided you would be better at working with new trainees.
9. No changes
10. Miss Roberts, who spoke at the assistants' conference, gave the audience some excellent guidelines on office procedures.

Feedback 8-I

1. The Space Shuttle astronauts, who were recognized by only a few workers, toured the plant yesterday.
2. No changes

3. The trainer bandaged the horse's injured leg, which still showed some swelling.
4. Groundbreaking for the newest factory, which will be located on the north side of town, is scheduled for Thursday at 10 A.M.
5. The Three Mile Island reactors, which caused a national panic, have been thoroughly checked by the engineers.
6. On Wednesday, which is usually his day off, Chuck works on his antique cars.
7. No changes
8. No changes
9. The chief technician, who drove his new car today, was in a very good mood.
10. No changes

Feedback 8-J

1. class; apparently, *IC; trans, IC*
2. However, *intro. Word*
3. Arriving late for the meeting, *intro. phrase (verbal)*
4. Emporia, Virginia, on March 28, 1952, *address, date*
5. technology, isn't it? *interr. (neg. expr.)*
6. Yes, Mrs. Grant, *interr. (dir. add.)*
7. (no comma) *IC DC*
8. Auditing, a course dealing with the external audit process, *interr.*
9. tall, slender *coord. adj.*
10. instructor, too, *interr. (paren. elem.)*
11. room, *DC, IC*
12. To succeed in sales in 2008, *intro. phrase (verbal, misreading)*
13. answer, apparently, *interr. (paren. elem.)*
14. College Avenue, Philadelphia, PA 21069, *address*
15. builders; *IC; IC*

Feedback 8-K

Commas are, without a doubt, the most difficult, troublesome area of proofreading for many writing students. Most students have to "unlearn" many of their lifelong habits concerning punctuation. For example, commas are used for structural purposes, not for pauses. The area most students have trouble with is the comma used for introductory elements like transitional phrases, prepositional phrases, and certain kinds of words or phrases used frequently at the beginning of a sentence. Then there are the interrupters, phrases that come somewhere in the middle of a sentence. Sometimes, these elements get commas, and sometimes, unfortunately, they do not. The punctuation depends on whether there is emphasis, detail, or special stylistic purposes. In September 2009, the Society for Chronic Comma Users of 417 Lexington Avenue, New York, NY 20012, will meet to devise a campaign to help writers become aware of problems with commas coming from arbitrary punctuation habits.

Feedback 8-L

When writing a research report, students must document cited material carefully so that they avoid plagiarizing their sources. It is important for students to know that statistics, results of surveys, quotations, and paraphrased ideas must be cited. In fact, students must also cite information gleaned from personal communications and audio-visual materials. Their own ideas and conclusions, however, do not need documentation. Thorough, conscientious college students always take care to cite information when writing a documented report since plagiarism is equivalent to stealing ideas, and it can ruin their reputation.

MODULE 9

Fragments and Run-Ons

Objective: This module is devoted to a punctuation problem that deserves special attention. It will help you to identify and correct two types of errors.

Upon completion of this module, you will be able:

- To identify and to correct fragments of sentences.
- To identify run-on sentences and to punctuate them for clarity.

In conversation, fragments and run-ons go unnoticed and are quite acceptable. In writing, however, fragments and run-ons must be avoided because they are incorrect and can result in misinterpretation of your intended meaning. Therefore, it is important to be able to recognize these errors and learn how to correct them.

A **fragment** is an incomplete sentence. **Run-ons** are two or more sentence units that have been run together as one sentence. Before taking up each of these types of errors, you need to know what a sentence is.

A **sentence** is a group of words that has a subject and a verb and expresses a complete thought. An independent clause is a whole sentence. A sentence contains at least one independent clause. It can be very brief, consisting only of the S–V unit, or it can be amplified with modifiers. In an imperative sentence (command), only the verb is stated; the subject *you* is understood but not stated. For example, in the sentence *Close the file,* the understood subject is *you.*

SUBJECT	VERB
Draftsmen	design.
Secretaries	type.
Technicians	test.
He	spoke.
(You—understood)	Run!

A sentence may be very short, containing only a subject and a verb, or it may be longer, with many modifiers and clauses. Whether long or short, a sentence must have the two requirements mentioned: subject and verb in an independent clause. Remember, a sentence contains at least one independent clause (IC), which is not introduced by a clause signal. It may, of course, also contain one or more dependent clauses (DC), which are introduced by a clause signal.

As I came to work, I saw the accident.
DC — As I came to work; IC — I saw the accident

Below are examples of IC sentences with modifiers.

Our draftsmen are designing many new products.
An efficient secretary types with speed and accuracy.
The technicians have tested all the specimens carefully.
He spoke with me for about an hour.
Run to the window quickly.

DIAGNOSTIC EXERCISE

Label as a fragment or run-on, and correct the all errors in wording and punctuation to eliminate all fragments and run-ons in the following paragraph.

1. _____ The students who take too many classes and who can't keep up with their work.
2. _____ We reviewed the recommended changes and then we updated the catalog.
3. _____ Because we cannot afford a larger apartment in this section of the city.
4. _____ The lab where the virus was identified and where the cure was developed.
5. _____ The attorneys filed the briefs late consequently the case was dismissed.
6. _____ The notes written by the caseworker were illegible so they were deemed inadmissible as evidence.
7. _____ The technician who handles the sick animals when they have to be quarantined.
8. _____ Writing the proposal and estimating the cost with all of the information we have been given.
9. _____ Write the summary report based on the article don't forget to use a memo heading.
10. _____ She purchased the equipment but she did not get a receipt.

PART I: FRAGMENTS

After having learned to recognize a complete sentence, you should be able to identify a fragment (which is only a part of a sentence) and not fall into the trap of punctuating a fragment as though it were a sentence. Here are the six types of fragments that are likely to cause problems. As you can see, there are several ways of turning fragments into sentences.

FRAGMENT 1: A Dependent Clause

PROBLEM: after the farmer cleared his field

SOLUTION: *Add an independent clause.*
After the farmer cleared his field, he planted corn.

FRAGMENT 2: A Prepositional Phrase

PROBLEM: throughout his report

SOLUTION: *Add an independent clause.*
There were numerous errors throughout his report.

FRAGMENT 3: A Verbal Phrase

PROBLEM: typing the letter for the saleswoman

SOLUTION: A. *Change the verbal into a verb and add a subject.*
Jane was typing the letter for the saleswoman.

B. *Add an independent clause.*
Typing the letter for the saleswoman, Jane was quick and efficient.

FRAGMENT 4: A Subject

PROBLEM: the engineers at the chemical plant

SOLUTION: *Add a verb.*
The engineers at the chemical plant were on strike. (or) The engineers were at the chemical plant.

FRAGMENT 5: A Verb

PROBLEM: took his temperature

SOLUTION: *Add a subject.*
The nurse took his temperature.

FRAGMENT 6: Other Phrases

PROBLEM: such as memos and reports

SOLUTION: *Add an independent clause.*
The assistant typed business correspondence, such as memos and reports.

NOTE One good way to spot fragments is to read *out loud* from the bottom up in your paper; that is, read the last sentence, then the next to last sentence, and so on so that you are reading out of context.

ACTIVITY 9-A: Fragments

Rewrite any fragments to make sentences; if the sentence is complete, write OK.

1. The car stopping too quickly.
2. The financial statement indicated a profit.
3. The farmer in the barn with the cows.
4. Cleaned and adjusted by the mechanic.
5. Ambulances raced toward the accident.
6. Thundering and lightning in the west.
7. On the drawing an octagonal window.
8. Several college students surveying the field.
9. The timer rang.
10. Seeming more concerned about his reactions than his answers.

Check your responses in Feedback 9-A at the end of this module. If your responses were correct, proceed to Part II. If you missed any, do Activity 9-B.

ACTIVITY 9-B: Fragments

Rewrite any fragments to make sentences; if the sentence is complete, write OK.

1. Entered into the computer.
2. Sally's first patient in the recovery room.
3. Lime spreads evenly on a calm day.
4. While the engine was running rapidly.
5. During the investigation on Tuesday.
6. Drew an alternative plan that met specifications.
7. Smiling pleasantly, the receptionist, Miss Harrington.
8. Reestablished an obscure benchmark after researching the boundaries of adjoining lands.
9. Somewhere between the motor and the transmitter.
10. It is good business to be considerate.

Check your responses in Feedback 9-B at the end of this module. If your responses were correct, proceed to Part II. If you missed any, review Part I.

PART II: RUN-ONS

Run-on sentences are two or more independent clauses written together as one sentence. All run-ons result from errors in punctuation.

Below are some common methods used to avoid run-on sentences.

(a) Sentence ______ .	Sentence ______ .	IC. IC.
(b) Sentence ______ ;	sentence ______ .	IC; IC.
(c) Sentence ______ ,	conjunction sentence ______ .	IC, cc IC.
(d) Sentence ______ ;	transition, sentence ______ .	IC; trans, IC.
(e) One sentence ______	with a compound verb ______ .	IC (cv).

There are five common types of punctuation errors that result in run-on sentences. The following list shows you how to correct each of these run-ons into one of the patterns indicated above:

RUN-ON 1: Two independent clauses with no punctuation between them

PROBLEM: The foreman made up the payroll he issued the work orders for the crew.

SOLUTION: A. *Make two sentences* (IC. IC.).
The foreman made up the payroll. He issued the work orders for the crew.

B. *Use a semicolon when the ideas are closely related* (IC; IC).
The foreman made up the payroll; he issued the work orders for the crew.

RUN-ON 2: Two independent clauses separated by a comma, not a period (known as a comma splice)

PROBLEM: The foreman made up the payroll, he issued the work orders for the crew.

SOLUTION: A. *Make two sentences* (IC. IC.).
The foreman made up the payroll. He issued the work orders for the crew.

B. *Use a semicolon* (IC; IC.).
The foreman made up the payroll; he issued the work orders for the crew.

RUN-ON 3: Two independent clauses and a conjunction without a comma

PROBLEM: The foreman made up the payroll and he issued the work orders for the crew.

SOLUTION: A. *Use a comma before the conjunction* (IC, cc IC.).
The foreman made up the payroll, and he issued the work orders for the crew.

B. *Rewrite with a compound verb* (IC with cv).
For a discussion of compound verbs, see Module 5, Part V.
The foreman made up the payroll and issued the work orders for the crew.

RUN-ON 4: Two independent clauses joined by a transitional expression with no punctuation

PROBLEM: The foreman made up the payroll furthermore he issued the work orders for the crew.

SOLUTION: A. *Use a semicolon and a comma* (IC; trans, IC.).
The foreman made up the payroll; furthermore, he issued the work orders for the crew.

B. *Make two sentences* (IC. IC.).
The foreman made up the payroll. Furthermore, he issued the work orders for the crew.

Remember that words such as **however, therefore,** and **furthermore** are sometimes interrupters appearing in the middle of one sentence rather than transitional words connecting two sentences. The following sentence has an interrupter in the middle.

The foreman, however, made up the payroll.

RUN-ON 5: Two independent clauses joined by a transitional expression with only commas

PROBLEM: The foreman made up the payroll, furthermore, he issued the work orders for the crew.

SOLUTION: A. *Use a semicolon and comma* (IC; trans, IC.).
The foreman made up the payroll; furthermore, he issued the work orders for the crew.

B. *Make two sentences* (IC. IC.).
The foreman made up the payroll. Furthermore, he issued the work orders for the crew.

The word **then** is a possible signal of a run-on. Usually, it is a transitional expression and, therefore, should be preceded by a semicolon or a period. Note also that you do not need to use a comma after **then.**

PROBLEM: The foreman made up the payroll, **then** he issued the work orders for the crew. (Run-on)

SOLUTION: A. The foreman made up the payroll; **then** he issued the work orders for the crew. (IC; trans. IC.)

B. The foreman made up the payroll. **Then** he issued the work orders for the crew. (IC. IC.)

ACTIVITY 9-C: Run-Ons

Punctuate any run-on sentences correctly in one of the five ways discussed previously. If a sentence is correctly punctuated, write OK after it.

1. The speaker on the subject of soil chemistry was famous, there was a large audience.
2. Contractors arrived early for the bid opening, they stayed late to ask about quotations.
3. The power source was a factor; established industries planned expansion of facilities.
4. The strike created a financial crisis, and the company applied for bankruptcy.
5. No clues were evident, a detective was assigned to the case.
6. Alcoholism is treated as a disease however it is not necessarily fatal.
7. You can save money by learning to rebuild your own engine, of course, you can always buy a rebuilt one.
8. All students learn to word process on computers others learn to program computers.
9. Under a heavy workload, an efficient administrative assistant learns to assign priorities; then she can complete the urgent tasks sooner.
10. In nearly every community, some people suffer from poverty their needs usually vary.

Check your responses in Feedback 9-C at the end of this module. If your responses were correct, proceed to Activity 9-E. If you missed any, review Part II; then do Activity 9-D.

ACTIVITY 9-D: Run-Ons

Correct any run-ons. If a sentence is correctly punctuated, mark it OK.

1. Most fertilizer companies employ truck drivers and warehouse workers on a part-time basis, moreover a few companies maintain these employees on a full-time schedule.
2. Years ago, trees were often used as benchmarks; today, more lasting objects are preferred.
3. Donna is a legal secretary, she makes an excellent salary.
4. Most managers in large corporations prepare financial statements they are seldom involved in detailed accounting procedures.
5. Designing the building to specifications requires more consultation with the client than constructing the building on its site.
6. Servicing electrical motors and appliances is his vocation, designing electrical equipment is his hobby.
7. Many laborers develop low blood pressure, nevertheless they are able to continue working.
8. As an undercover agent, she was outstanding; as a traffic regulator, she was incompetent.
9. He works as an automobile mechanic during the week, and he rebuilds antique cars on weekends.
10. Some restaurants are exclusive, most cater to a wider clientele.

Check your responses in Feedback 9-D at the end of this module. If your responses were correct, proceed to Activity 9-E. If you missed any, review Part II before continuing.

ACTIVITY 9-E: Fragments and Run-Ons

In the space provided, identify the following items as F (fragment), R (run-on), or S (sentence). Correct each item that is not a sentence.

______ 1. The conference speaker was famous, there was a large audience.

______ 2. The executive having received the memo.

______ 3. She was invited to be a guest speaker at the safety meeting, the main topic was fire prevention.

______ 4. Of course, you can always find employees in the coffee shop you can also meet them in the lounge.

_______ 5. Coming in for a cup of coffee between appointments.

_______ 6. In the late evening the building is deserted, however in the morning it is alive with activity.

_______ 7. Only technicians who have served an internship will be hired.

_______ 8. Working in an air-conditioned office which has plush carpeting.

_______ 9. His strong point being his skill in electronics.

_______ 10. Architecture is an exciting field you can use your creative talents fully.

Check your responses in Feedback 9-E at the end of this module. If you missed any, do Activity 9-F.

ACTIVITY 9-F: **Fragments and Run-Ons**

In the space provided, identify the following items as F (fragment), R (run-on), or S (sentence). Correct each item that is not a sentence.

_______ 1. The hospital was large, it had a new south wing added last year.

_______ 2. The receptionist having taken a coffee break.

_______ 3. The electronics specialist was called in to look at the spectrophotometer, it was not registering properly.

_______ 4. In my opinion, the nurses should ask for a higher salary; furthermore, they deserve added benefits.

_______ 5. The contractor building the new airport facility.

_______ 6. After the meeting, the group went to the new restaurant it had a reputation for good food.

_______ 7. Lab assistants who have experience are being hired.

_______ 8. The architect who won the award for his design.

_______ 9. Such as her desire to get a better job.

_______ 10. Nursing is a rewarding career one can help many people as a nurse.

Check your responses in Feedback 9-F at the end of this module. If your responses were correct, proceed to Activity 9-G. If you missed any, review before continuing.

ACTIVITY 9-G: Editing Practice

Correct all errors in wording and punctuation to eliminate all fragments and runs-ons in the following paragraph.

An excellent way to learn about new subjects and to meet new people is to take adult education classes, many colleges, high schools, and adult education centers offer them. Such courses attract different kinds of people who share common interests, for example, students, office workers, teachers, and business people can enroll in courses to update their skills and to expand their horizons in their free time. Cooking and photography classes bringing people together interested in forming local clubs and learning new techniques. Although adult ed centers offer cultural activities, such as day trips to museums, theater, and local and national historic sites. These classes clearly enrich the students' lives and they can improve themselves and meet new acquaintances.

Check your responses in Feedback 9-G at the end of this module.

ACTIVITY 9-H: Editing Practice

Correct all errors in wording and punctuation to eliminate all fragments and run-ons in the following paragraph.

Many technical careers require effective communication skills because people who choose technical careers often have to communicate with diverse audiences for example, police officers communicate with attorneys, fellow law enforcement officials, and also the general public. Furthermore nurses must communicate with doctors, other health professionals, and also patients and their families. Who often do not understand medical terminology and whose ability to focus may be limited because of being ill or emotionally drained. Computer and automotive technicians often find themselves having to explain difficult concepts to lay people as well and they must remember to use different vocabulary depending to whom they are speaking. Since they are often relaying ideas to people of different levels of expertise it is important for those in technical careers to consider their audience when writing and speaking and to adjust their communication as applicable.

Check your responses in Feedback 9-H at the end of this module.

DIAGNOSTIC FEEDBACK

Label as a fragment or run-on, and correct the all errors in wording and punctuation to eliminate all fragments and run-ons in the following paragraph.

1. __F___The students who take too many classes and who can't keep up with their work.
   Example of one way to fix this fragment: eliminate the second "who"—The students who take too many classes can't keep up with their work.
2. __RO___We reviewed the recommended changes, and then we updated the catalog.
3. __F___Because we cannot afford a larger apartment in this section of the city.
   Example of one way to fix this fragment: eliminate "Because"—We cannot afford a larger apartment in this section of the city.
4. __F___The lab where the virus was identified and where the cure was developed.
   Example of one way to fix this fragment: add the verb "is"—The lab is where the virus was identified and where the cure was developed.
5. __RO___The attorneys filed the briefs late; consequently, the case was dismissed.
6. __RO____The notes written by the caseworker were illegible, so they were deemed inadmissible as evidence.
7. __F____The technician who handles the sick animals when they have to be quarantined.
   Example of one way to fix this fragment: eliminate "who"—The technician handles the sick animals when they have to be quarantined.
8. __F___Writing the proposal and estimating the cost with all of the information we have been given.
   Example of one way to fix this fragment: add a subject and helping verb—We are writing the proposal and estimating the cost with all of the information we have been given.
9. __RO___Write the summary report based on the article; don't forget to use a memo heading.
10. ___RO__She purchased the equipment, but she did not get a receipt.

FEEDBACK FOR MODULE 9

Feedback 9-A

There is more than one possible correct answer. If your answers differ from the feedback, check them with your instructor.

1. The car was stopping too quickly; (*or*) stopped.
2. OK

3. The farmer in the barn with the cows is my brother. (*or*) The farmer was in the barn with the cows.
4. The engine was cleaned and adjusted by the mechanic.
5. OK
6. We noticed thundering and lightning in the west. (*or*) It was thundering and lightning in the west.
7. On the drawing, an octagonal window is drawn near the corner.
8. Several college students were surveying the field.
9. OK
10. The supervisor seemed more concerned about his reactions than his answers.

Feedback 9-B

There is more than one possible correct answer. If your answers differ from the feedback, check them with your instructor.

1. The account was entered into the computer.
2. Sally's first patient in the recovery room had a kidney removed.
3. OK
4. While the engine was running rapidly, he shifted into third gear.
5. A fingerprint expert was summoned during the investigation on Tuesday.
6. The architect drew an alternative plan that met specifications.
7. Smiling pleasantly, the receptionist, Miss Harrington, guided us to our destination.
8. The surveyors reestablished an obscure benchmark after researching the boundaries of adjoining lands.
9. The problem was located somewhere between the motor and the transmitter.
10. OK

Feedback 9-C

There is more than one possible correct answer. If your answers differ from the feedback, check them with your instructor.

1. famous; (*or*) famous. There
2. opening; (*or*) opening. They (*or*) contractors arrived early . . . and stayed late . . .
3. OK
4. OK
5. evident; (*or*) evident. A
6. disease; however, (*or*) disease. However,
7. engine; (*or*) engine. Of course,
8. computers; (*or*) computers. Others
9. OK
10. poverty; (*or*) poverty. Their

Feedback 9-D

There is more than one possible correct answer. If your answers differ from the feedback, check them with your instructor.

1. basis; moreover, (*or*) basis. Moreover,
2. OK
3. secretary; (*or*) secretary. She (*or*) Donna is . . . and makes . . .
4. statements; (*or*) statements. They
5. OK
6. vocation; (*or*) vocation. Designing
7. pressure; nevertheless, (*or*) pressure. Nevertheless,
8. OK
9. OK
10. exclusive; (*or*) exclusive. Most

Feedback 9-E

There is more than one possible correct answer. If your answers differ from the feedback, check them with your instructor.

1. R famous; (*or*) famous. there
2. F The executive, having received the memo, wrote a response. (*or*) The executive received the memo.
3. R meeting; (*or*) meeting. The
4. R Of course, you can always find . . . and also meet . . . (*or*) . . . shop. You . . .
5. F The boss came in for a cup . . . (*or*) Coming in . . . appointments, the boss relaxed.
6. R deserted; however, (*or*) deserted. However
7. S
8. F She was working . . . (*or*) Working . . . carpeting, she was happy with her job.
9. F His strong point was his skill in electronics. (*or*) His strong point being his skill in electronics, he was hired immediately.
10. R field; (*or*) field. You (*or*) field, and

Feedback 9-F

There is more than one possible correct answer. If your answers differ from the feedback, check them with your instructor.

1. R large; (*or*) large. It (*or*) large and had . . .
2. F The receptionist, having taken a coffee break, went back to work. (*or*) The receptionist took a coffee break.
3. R spectrophotometer; (*or*) spectrophotometer. It
4. S
5. F The contractor was building the new airport facility.
6. R restaurant; it (*or*) restaurant. It
7. S
8. F The architect won the award for his design. (*or*) The architect who won the award for the design was trained at the technical college.
9. F She held many hopes for the future, such as her desire to get a better job.
10. R career; one (*or*) career. One

Feedback 9-G

This is a suggested revision. There are other options. If you have any questions about your editing, check with your instructor.

An excellent way to learn about new subjects and to meet new people is to take adult education classes. Many colleges, high schools, and adult education centers offer them. Such courses attract different kinds of people who share common interests. For example, students, office workers, teachers, and business people can enroll in courses to update their skills and to expand their horizons in their free time. Cooking and photography classes bring people together interested in forming local clubs and learning new techniques. Although adult ed centers offer cultural activities, such as day trips to museums, theater, and local and national historic sites, there could be a slight charge for these events. Continuing education classes clearly enrich the students' lives, and they can improve themselves and meet new acquaintances.

Feedback 9-H

This is a suggested revision. There are other options. If you have any questions about your editing, check with your instructor.

Many technical careers require effective communication skills because people who choose technical careers often have to communicate with diverse audiences; for example, police officers communicate with attorneys, fellow law enforcement officials, and also the general public. Furthermore, nurses must communicate with doctors, other health professionals, and also patients and their families who often do not understand medical terminology and whose ability to focus may be limited because of being ill or emotionally drained. Computer and automotive technicians often find themselves having to explain difficult concepts to lay people as well, and they must remember to use different vocabulary depending to whom they are speaking. Since they are often relaying ideas to people of different levels of expertise, it is important for those in technical careers to consider their audience when writing and speaking and to adjust their communication as applicable.

MODULE 10

Paragraph Writing

Objective: This module provides the fundamentals of paragraph writing.

Upon completion of this module, you will be able:

- To choose an appropriate topic for a paragraph.
- To construct a topic sentence with a controlling idea.
- To outline a coherent paragraph.
- To write a cohesive reasons paragraph.
- To write a cohesive reasons and examples paragraph.
- To write a cohesive pro and con paragraph.
- To write a cohesive process paragraph.

DIAGNOSTIC EXERCISE

Label the subject, the controlling idea, and all of the transitional phrases in the following paragraph.

When composing a report, students should spend 25% of their time organizing their ideas and planning the report. By spending time before writing, students are more likely to have a coherent organizational plan. In fact, careful planning can help the students identify and eliminate unrelated ideas. Furthermore, taking time to plan can test the students' report idea or thesis to make sure that they have enough information for the scope of the report. Of course, part of the planning process should include taking time to analyze the audience and make sure that the format and vocabulary are appropriate. Many students don't realize that spending some thoughtful time before writing can actually make the report writing process more efficient.

PART I: INTRODUCTION

Writing is not just a matter of correct grammar. Good writing results from careful planning, thoughtful revising, and precise proofreading. Look at some of these techniques as they apply to composing a paragraph.

Writing an effective paragraph—one that is completely developed and within the right range of development—takes planning. Many paragraphs are too short and, therefore, do not cover a topic well enough. Some paragraphs are too long because of repetition or wordiness. Other paragraphs are oversimplified and do not really say anything. It is not an easy job to create a detailed, well-developed paragraph.

Of greater importance, the paragraph is an effective writing technique used in business and desired by managers who must deal with large amounts of written correspondence. Writing on the job must, therefore, be as precise and as clear and concise as possible. The important thing to remember is that you should never sacrifice clarity for brevity. By learning methods of planning, designing, and developing paragraphs, you can be an asset on the job when you must deal with written correspondence.

The paragraph format can be found in many areas of business and technical writing. Often, a memo (memorandum) is paragraph length. You will frequently be asked to summarize or to prepare abstracts of lengthier correspondence. In cases of multiparagraph formats, such as business letters and reports, a well-constructed paragraph can be very useful in helping focus thoughts and ideas so that they can be easily and readily absorbed by the reader. Proposals and requests are often limited to paragraph length. Therefore, you can see that the paragraph is not only a good way to learn writing techniques but also a most effective tool on the job.

PART II: THE PARAGRAPH

What is a paragraph? You will probably remember being taught that a **paragraph** is a group of related sentences about one idea. Structurally, a paragraph is a group of sentences consisting of a topic sentence, sentences of development (called the body), and a concluding sentence. The paragraph can exist alone in many cases, but it is commonly used to separate longer papers into shorter segments of thought. Whether the paragraph exists as a unit on its own or is part of a larger whole depends on the amount of detail that is needed to explain your purpose. In report and letter writing, you will use sequences of paragraphs to form reports and business letters.

One of the most frequent questions writing students ask is, "How long should the paragraph be?" Obviously, there is no one correct answer, but there are certain guidelines for length and development. Certainly, you will want to choose a subject you know something about. The more you know about the subject, the more you can select and share with your readers. Another consideration is to avoid repetition. Sometimes a paragraph looks lengthy but is actually saying the same thing over and over. Some writers combine all their ideas into one or two longer sentences. Others use a series of short sentences, each containing one idea. Since sentence formation will have a definite effect on length, you should separate all your ideas in the planning process and then make choices about whether to combine them as you write a rough draft. At a minimum, a paragraph should contain one topic sentence, at least three sentences of development, and a concluding sentence. The content and length of these will be determined by your own writing style. Your aim in writing is to think through your idea and say as much as you can without repeating yourself. In this way, your writing will be more interesting because of the development, more persuasive because of the support you include for your opinion, and more successful in achieving its goal because it provides a thorough explanation instead of a superficial overview.

Here is a sample paragraph:

Topic sentence	There are several advantages to fast food restaurants.
Body	First of all, their big draw is the time saved. Customers can walk in the door, walk up to the counter, place an order, and have their lunch in a matter of minutes. If customers prefer to remain in their car, they can go through the drive-in window and eat in the automobile. The quality of the food is consistent; people can learn which items on the menu suit them and which ones they can count on. Best of all, the prices are usually unbeatable.
Concluding sentence	Consequently, fast food restaurants are attracting more and more customers.

Now that you have an overview of the paragraph, examine its elements carefully.

PART III: CONSTRUCTING THE TOPIC SENTENCE

Perhaps the most important sentence in the paragraph, and, therefore, the one that deserves a lot of attention, is the topic sentence. The **topic sentence** establishes the purpose of the paragraph by stating the main or controlling idea about a certain subject. The topic sentence consists of two parts: the *subject* and the *controlling idea.* Both must be carefully chosen if your paragraph is to be successful.

> *Subject* (S)—what you are talking about (not necessarily the grammatical subject of the sentence)
>
> *Controlling Idea* (CI)—what you say about the subject (often with an opinion)

For example, note the subjects and controlling ideas marked in the following topic sentences.

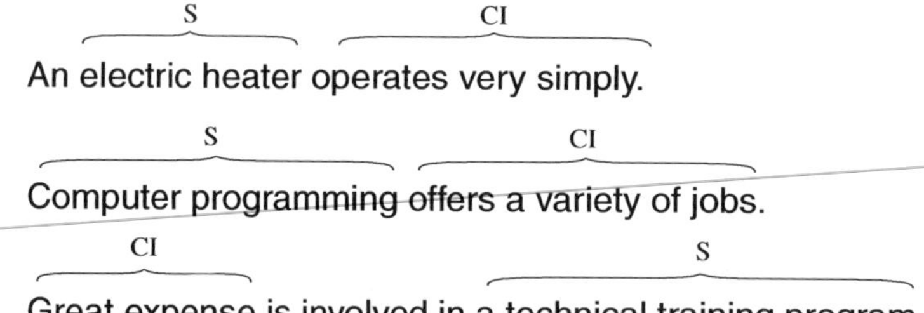
S
CI
An electric heater operates very simply.
S
CI
Computer programming offers a variety of jobs.
CI
S
Great expense is involved in a technical training program.

As you can see from these examples, the subject indicates generally what the paragraph will deal with, whereas the controlling idea indicates specifically the direction the supporting sentences will take.

Because of its importance to your reader in establishing your purpose, the topic sentence works best as the first sentence in the paragraph. Thoughtfully composed, the topic sentence will be the key to your selection of supporting ideas in the body of the paragraph. Finally, the topic sentence will help you decide how to conclude the paragraph when you have presented all the details.

PART IV: CHOOSING A SUBJECT

Because the paragraph is a relatively short piece of writing, it should deal with only one subject. Even so, you must be careful to select a subject that will be narrow enough to be covered in eight to ten sentences at most. Not all subjects will lend themselves for discussion at that length. *Proper Telephone Techniques in Business* is one subject that you could develop in a single paragraph. However, *The History of the Telephone* would probably be better suited to a longer paper because of the extensive detail needed. When you choose a subject for a paragraph, one of the first steps is to narrow the scope to paragraph length. Look at the following examples:

BROAD SUBJECT	MULTIPARAGRAPH LENGTH	PARAGRAPH LENGTH
Beach	Employment Opportunities at the Beach	Problems of Working at a Resort Hotel
Working	Getting a Job	Self-employment
Public Speaking	Oral Communication Course	Benefits of Being Videotaped in a Speaking Course

In essence, what you should strive for in selecting your subject is to choose one you know a lot about so that you can narrow it to a number of precise areas. Visualize slicing a pie:

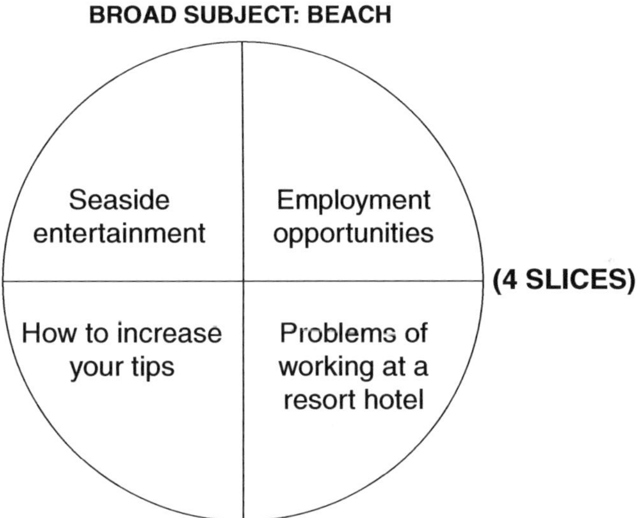

From your final topics, you can choose the slice you feel comfortable with or have the ideas to support. Surprisingly enough, sometimes the points you want to stress in the body of a paper will fall into place once you have narrowed the topic. Writers often reveal that once this decision is made, the rest of the paragraph is easy.

You can see why this very first step in selecting the subject of your paragraph is so critical. When you write, take the time to think before you actually write. Examine and explore options. Instead of jumping right in and writing a paragraph, try jotting down different approaches toward a subject. With some careful planning, the final product can be much more effective and appealing. Why not make the final product one you are proud of because of the thought and consideration you have put into it?

ACTIVITY 10-A: Narrowing the Subject

Narrow the following broad subjects, making them suitable for a paragraph.

Broad Subject	Paragraph Length
1. Technical Training	________________
2. Jobs	________________
3. Business	________________
4. Books	________________
5. Computer Information Systems	________________
6. College	________________
7. Automobiles	________________
8. Newspapers	________________
9. Communication	________________
10. Politics	________________

Check your responses with your instructor. Then proceed to Part V.

PART V: CHOOSING A CONTROLLING IDEA

Once you have decided on a subject (for example, the Peer Counseling Program), you are ready to convert it into a topic sentence by choosing the controlling idea. The controlling idea is the main statement you wish to make about your subject.

> The Peer Counseling Program at Delaware Technical and Community College *has many advantages.*

By adding the second half to the original subject, you can make a statement about the subject. Now you can select information that will support the idea of "advantages." These ideas will become the body of your paragraph. Practice identifying the subject and controlling idea by completing Activity 10-B.

ACTIVITY 10-B: **Subject and Controlling Idea**

Bracket and label the subject (S) and controlling idea (CI) in the following topic sentences.

1. A gasoline carburetor functions better at night.
2. The coastal area offers many recreational activities.
3. What is engineering?
4. Architecture interests me.
5. Shortages of materials today have seriously affected many companies.

Check your responses in Feedback 10-B at the end of this module. If your responses were correct, proceed to "Focusing the Topic Sentence." If you missed any, do Activity 10-C.

ACTIVITY 10-C: **Subject and Controlling Idea**

Bracket and label the subject (S) and controlling idea (CI).

1. Most homeowners need a well-equipped toolbox for repair jobs.
2. Courtesy pays off in improved job relations.
3. Assembling parts without first reading instructions promises disaster.
4. Safety rules are established for a purpose.
5. Certain qualities of an applicant are observed in a job interview.

Check your responses in Feedback 10-C at the end of this module. If you missed any, review before proceeding to "Focusing the Topic Sentence."

Focusing the Topic Sentence

The next step in constructing a paragraph is to determine whether the topic sentence is well focused, too broad, or too narrow. In writing a topic sentence, you must take into consideration whether it is for a paragraph or a longer paper. In this module, confine your thinking to writing topic sentences that are logical in scope—neither too broad nor too narrow—for a paragraph.

Examine the following sentences:

The computer has a color monitor. (Too narrow)
Computers have changed greatly over the last two decades. (Too broad)
A home computer can perform several helpful functions. (Well focused)
CPR stands for cardiopulmonary resuscitation. (Too narrow)
Scientists and doctors have developed many life-saving techniques. (Too broad)
CPR (cardiopulmonary resuscitation) involves several basic steps. (Well focused)

Remember that a paragraph is a relatively small unit of writing. Therefore, you should have a controlling idea that is narrow enough to be supported well in a few sentences. If your CI is too broad, it may take many, many paragraphs, maybe pages and pages, to develop it adequately. Say your assignment is to write a paragraph on the broad subject of social security. Here are two possible topic sentences (TS) that would narrow the subject properly. The CI is underlined.

At the current rate, social security payments are not sufficient to meet the needs of the elderly. (*This TS could be supported by giving examples of normal expenses the elderly face.*)
Some people are concerned that the social security fund may go broke before they draw retirement benefits. (*This TS could be supported by citing the questionable methods being used to administer the program today.*)

The controlling idea is the key to a unified paragraph. If your CI is too broad, as in "Social security is bad," or too narrow, as in "A radio station plays music," it will not help you develop a unified paragraph. One thing to consider at this point is choice of words for the controlling idea. Words such as "nice," "interesting," and "bad" are usually ineffective because they lack specific meaning. Words like "bad" can be confusing because they can also be slang. If you are at a loss for a good word to use as your controlling idea, you may want to consult a thesaurus or a dictionary for synonyms. If you start with a logical, well-focused CI, then the supporting statements will flow naturally, and your paragraph will be unified.

ACTIVITY 10-D: Subject and Controlling Idea

In each group of sentences, one sentence is too broad (TB), one is too narrow (TN), and one is well focused (WF). Label them accordingly.

Group 1

_____ a. Poultry production is increasing.

_____ b. Poultry production is increasing in our area.

_____ c. Poultry production originated in our area.

Group 2

_____ a. The telephone is on the desk.

_____ b. The telephone provides a vehicle for good public relations.

_____ c. The telephone is convenient.

Group 3

_____ a. Computer Information Systems offers many career opportunities.

_____ b. Computer Information Systems is a technology.

_____ c. Many careers are available to today's graduate.

Group 4

_____ a. Compact automobiles are the most economical vehicles.

_____ b. Compact automobiles are more economical to operate than larger cars.

_____ c. Compact automobiles are small.

Check your responses in Feedback 10-D at the end of this module. If your responses were correct, proceed to Part VI. If you missed any, do Activity 10-E.

ACTIVITY 10-E: Subject and Controlling Idea

In each group of sentences, one sentence is too broad (TB), one is too narrow (TN), and one is well focused (WF). Label them accordingly.

Group 1

_____ a. The engineer went to work.

_____ b. Engineering is an important field.

_____ c. An architectural engineer performs a variety of jobs.

Group 2

_____ a. A good nurse should possess specific qualities.

_____ b. Nursing is an art.

_____ c. The nurse took the patient's temperature.

Group 3

_____ a. There is going to be a great need for fuel in the future.

_____ b. A source of energy is oil.

_____ c. The use of nuclear energy has many dangerous aspects.

Group 4

_____ a. Nutrition is important.

_____ b. A dietician uses nutritional guidelines to plan a well-balanced meal.

_____ c. The dietician prepared the menu for the evening meal.

Check your responses in Feedback 10-E. If you missed any, review before proceeding to Part VI.

PART VI: WRITING THE CONCLUDING SENTENCE

A paragraph has three main parts—the topic sentence, the body, and the concluding sentence. For the paragraph to function as a unit, you must end it properly to let your reader know that you have finished your discussion. The best way to conclude your paragraph is to remind the reader of what you originally set out to do. You may want to restate the main idea of the topic sentence using different wording to avoid repetition. If the paragraph has at least three main points of discussion, you may want to use a summary technique to conclude.

Consider the following examples:

TOPIC SENTENCE:	Exercise routines should be carefully planned for best results.
RESTATEMENT TYPE CONCLUDING SENTENCE:	Therefore, exercise can be beneficial if some basic guidelines are followed.
SUMMARY TYPE CONCLUDING SENTENCE:	As you can see, proper supervision, good eating habits, and strict routines can produce excellent outcomes for the exercise enthusiast.

ACTIVITY 10-F: Writing a Topic Sentence and a Concluding Sentence

Write a topic sentence and a concluding sentence for each of the following paragraphs.

Topic Sentence: ____

____

Students can enroll in business or computer information systems. In addition, there are careers available in the medical area, such as nursing and lab technology. Engineering is another broad field including wastewater and drafting.

Concluding Sentence: ____

Topic Sentence: ____

____

First, you must choose a subject. Next, you should narrow the subject so that you can deal with it in a paragraph. Then you need to construct a topic sentence that contains a controlling idea which tells the reader how you plan to deal with the subject. Following that, you must supply sufficient facts, details, and examples to develop the body of the paragraph. Finally, you write a concluding sentence that restates the idea expressed in the topic sentence.

Concluding Sentence: ____

Topic Sentence: ____

____

Arrive for the interview early. Be certain that you are neatly and appropriately dressed. Take your cues from the interviewer. Give that person a firm handshake as you announce your name. Wait to be invited to have a seat. Answer questions completely yet briefly, always being honest in your replies. When the interviewer signals the close of the interview, be sure to thank the person for his or her time.

Concluding Sentence: ____

Check your responses with your instructor. Then proceed to Part VII.

PART VII: DEVELOPING UNITY

Unity means oneness. In writing, it has to do with combining ideas—facts, details, and examples—into an entity or a harmonious whole. You have been told that a paragraph is a group of *related* sentences. Each sentence must contribute to the support or proof of the controlling idea. A sentence that is related to the subject but not to the controlling idea destroys the unity of the paragraph.

To see how this happens, look at the sample paragraph. Its topic was *fast food restaurants.* Its controlling idea was *advantages.* A sentence such as the following would be related to the subject but not to the controlling idea and thus should be eliminated.

There are too many fast food restaurants in our town.

The main reason errors in unity occur is that many writers sit down and compose from their thoughts without taking the time to organize their ideas through the use of a plan or an outline. If you compose without planning, you run the risk of wandering off the topic or, more precisely, your controlling idea. If you do not make a habit of planning, commit yourself to start right now. You will be delighted with the improvement you will see in your writing.

In your writing, check each fact, detail, or example you include to see that it supports the controlling idea. After you jot down supporting ideas, look at each one in relation to the controlling idea. It is much easier to spot material that does not belong in a paragraph at this stage than after you have proofread your final product.

ACTIVITY 10-G: **Developing Unity**

In the following paragraphs, circle the controlling idea in the topic sentence and cross out any sentences that do not support it.

There are several definite guidelines to use in writing a resumé. It must be typed and only one page long. The Job Objective should be clearly defined. It should be noted that a resumé is the same as a data sheet. The wording should be as brief as possible, using phrases rather than complete sentences. References should not be included. The letter of application is used to ask for the job interview. Previous salaries should not be included. Neatness and appearance are extremely important. An effective resumé will be the result of following these principles.

You should make every effort to apply the basic punctuation rules to your writing. Do not forget to separate words in a series by using commas. Also, use commas to separate items in dates and addresses. Make sure your subjects and verbs agree. Coordinate adjectives provide another occasion to use the comma. In addition, commas are needed with interrupters and introductory words or phrases. Avoid using fragments in your writing. A review of the fundamentals of punctuation will improve your writing.

Check your responses in Feedback 10-G. Then do Activity 10-H.

ACTIVITY 10-H: Paragraph Unity

The following paragraph illustrates how sentences that do not support the controlling idea can destroy paragraph unity. See if you can spot the unrelated statements that should be eliminated. (In any paragraphs you write, be sure to avoid any statements that do not directly support the CI.) Read the paragraph and then fill in the blanks below it.

Topic Sentence: The county's technical colleges have a wide variety of curriculum offerings. (1) They are located in the county seat. (2) Students can find course offerings adapted to their aptitudes and interests. (3) For example, students who would like to own their own businesses can enroll in Business Administration. (4) In addition, they can play on the basketball team if they are sports-minded. (5) Another course offered is in the very popular field of Computer Information Systems. (6) For those interested in engineering, there are such technologies as drafting, wastewater, and mechanical. (7) One student who took two CAD courses obtained a job as a draftsman. (8) Other students may wish to pursue a career as an administrative assistant, a lab technician, a registered nurse, or a newspaper reporter. (9) They may also come to enjoy the social life. (10) As you can see from the wide variety of courses offered at technical colleges, there is something for everyone.

Subject: ____________________

CI: ____________________

Supporting Statements (give sentence numbers): ____________________

Unrelated Statements: ____________________

Concluding Statements: ____________________

Transitional Expressions: ____________________

____

____

____

Check your responses in Feedback 10-H at the end of this module. If your responses were correct, proceed to Part VIII. If not, review before continuing.

PART VIII: DEVELOPING COHERENCE

Coherence may look like a difficult concept because of its strange name. It is a crucial area in writing because it has to do with the logical connection between ideas. Unity is necessary because the sentences in the body of a paragraph must relate to the topic sentence. Coherence is directly related to the results you will achieve from your writing, for the overall impact will depend on the way you order or sequence ideas.

There are two basic approaches to coherence. The first one is called chronological and is used when time helps with sequencing. For example, sets of directions follow a chronological sequence since steps must be done in a certain order to achieve the correct result. Paragraphs using details of time, such as historical development, will use a chronological approach (see transitional expressions indicating time in Module 7).

The second type of sequencing ideas is a bit more complicated, for it is based on the order of importance. In paragraph development, your ideas should be sequenced from the most important to the least important or vice versa. In other words, put the most important ideas first or last. In technical writing, the preferred method is putting the most important idea first. This step in writing is best accomplished at the plan or outline stage (see transitional expressions indicating order of importance in Module 7).

Coherence is especially important in business and technical writing. In persuasive writing, your arguments must not only relate to the issue at hand but also be properly ordered so that the reader is able to follow your logic. Writing is a precise exercise; readers cannot know what you intend unless you state your meaning clearly and completely. This same notion is true for writing sets of directions. Following directions is not that easy, especially if the directions are oversimplified or major steps are overlooked.

Transitional Expressions

Transitional expressions are linking words and phrases that show relationships between two or more ideas. They are the glue that holds the parts together. If you do not use enough, the parts will fall apart; if you use too much, you will see the glue instead of the parts. Your goal should be to move smoothly from one sentence to the next so that the reader is unaware of the links that connect your ideas and unify the paragraph.

Transitional expressions can be used to emphasize organization and direction of thought. They may appear at the beginning, middle, or end of a sentence. Refer to Module 7 for a list of transitional expressions you can use in writing paragraphs.

ACTIVITY 10-1: Transition

Supply appropriate transitional expressions in the blanks. Remember that when writing actual paragraphs, it is not necessary to use a transitional expression for every sentence.

A police officer often has a thankless job. Most, whether right or wrong, do not appreciate being reprimanded. _________ very often in the process of breaking up an argument, the officer winds up being injured.

_________ even when the officer is simply doing his or her job, the officer is frequently criticized. _________, it is rare that the public shows gratitude to a police officer.

Check your responses with your instructor. Then proceed to Part IX.

PART IX: ORGANIZING AND WRITING A PARAGRAPH

You have mastered the first step in writing a unified paragraph by demonstrating your ability to write a topic sentence (TS) with a clear-cut subject (S) and controlling idea (CI). Your next step is to organize your paragraph by constructing an outline.

Making an outline need not be a complicated procedure. Simply jot down, in grocery list fashion, all ideas you can think of to give solid support to the controlling idea. It is preferable not to use complete sentences. Then write the concluding sentence (CS), which restates the topic sentence in different words. Here is how to construct an outline for a TS.

SAMPLE PARAGRAPH OUTLINE

TS	Using a computer for writing saves time.
Outline of ideas	1. Setting margins and tabs simply 2. Typing faster with no carriage returns 3. Using helpful features such as underlining or highlighting 4. Revising easily 5. Checking spelling 6. Saving work on diskette (more efficient storage)
CS	It is easy to see that writing with a computer has many advantages over a typewriter or a pad and pencil.

The outline makes your job easier because you think out the paragraph before you begin writing it. If your ideas are out of order or one doesn't really support your CI, you can reorganize or eliminate at the beginning. As your paragraphs become more complex, the outline will be even more helpful in organizing than in this simple topic. Constructing the outline is a critical step because it forces you to plan your paragraph from the beginning.

ANOTHER SAMPLE PARAGRAPH OUTLINE

TS	The use of cruise control in an automobile is beneficial on long trips for several reasons.
Outline	1. Maintain regular speed 2. Save gasoline 3. Have no threat from highway patrol 4. Feel less tired and more alert during trip 5. Feel more rested at destination
CS	Consequently, it would be beneficial to use cruise control on a long trip.

After writing a topic sentence and jotting down all the points you can think of to support it, you then write a concluding sentence. This skeleton provides the basis for your paragraph. To put flesh on the skeleton, you will need to expand the phrases listed as points in your outline. Each point may or may not be a separate sentence. You will want to use transitional expressions to tie the thoughts together. Also, you should try to vary your sentence patterns.

ACTIVITY 10-J: Writing an Outline

On your own paper, construct a simple outline with a topic sentence related to your field of study. List five supporting ideas and then add a concluding sentence. Check your outline with your instructor. Then proceed to Part X.

PART X: THE REASONS PARAGRAPH

There are many different types of paragraphs. Four that are most commonly used by technicians are presented in Parts X–XIII.

The first type of paragraph you will write is the paragraph supported by reasons. In a **reasons paragraph,** the controlling idea of the TS is usually a statement of opinion. The supporting statements must give reasons to verify that opinion.

Look back at the outline for "Cruise Control." What follows is a reasons paragraph developed from that outline. Note that the following paragraph is more expansive than its outline. Your writing should reflect college-level thinking with varied sentence structure.

Note the transitional words and phrases (in italics) that link the sentences smoothly.

The use of cruise control is beneficial on a long trip for several reasons. *First,* once cruising speed is reached, that speed is maintained; *as a result,* less gasoline is used. Assuming the cruise control is set at or below the legal speed limit, the highway patrol should pose no threat to the driver. Because drivers do not have to keep a foot on the gas pedal constantly, the leg and foot muscles are more relaxed, leaving drivers less tired and more alert during a trip. This *also* means drivers are more rested when they reach their destination. *Consequently,* it would be beneficial to use cruise control on a long trip.

In this paragraph, each sentence goes directly back to support the CI, beneficial for several reasons. There are no irrelevant sentences to destroy the unity of the paragraph. Also, transitional expressions tie the sentences together nicely.

ACTIVITY 10-K: Reasons Paragraph

Choose one of the topics listed and write a unified reasons paragraph with at least four supporting statements and a concluding sentence. Follow the procedures given below; write an outline and then the paragraph. If you are not inspired by any of these topic sentences, choose a subject to your liking.

Topics

1. Restrictions on inexperienced drivers have many benefits.
2. There is a great demand for electronics technicians.
3. Laws regulating the use of cell phones are necessary (or unnecessary).
4. Getting a technical education provides for a sound future.
5. Credit cards are beneficial (or harmful).

Procedures for Paragraph Writing

1. Construct outline as follows:
   Topic sentence
   (1) Reason
   (2) Reason
   (3) Reason
   (4) Reason
   Concluding sentence
2. Write a rough draft from the outline.
3. Proofread, using the following checklist:
   a. Spelling
   b. Punctuation (Module 8)
   c. Pronoun agreement (Module 6)
   d. Subject–verb agreement (Module 5)
   e. Fragments (Module 9)
   f. Apostrophe for possession (Module 4)
   g. Read your paragraph aloud to hear any omissions, incorrect verb endings, or awkward phrases.

4. Revise to improve unity through the use of transitional expressions (Module 7).
5. Word process final copy.
6. Hand it in to your instructor.

After completing the reasons paragraph, proceed to Part XI.

PART XI: THE REASONS AND EXAMPLES PARAGRAPH

A more advanced method of expanding a topic sentence is to use both reasons (major support) and examples (minor support). The **reasons and examples paragraph** is basically the same as the reasons paragraph, except that each reason is further developed or clarified by one or more examples.

Every *reason,* or *major supporting statement,* should be a direct and definite explanation of the controlling idea stated in the topic sentence. In other words, you should be able to draw a line from the major support to the CI.

SAMPLE OUTLINE FOR REASONS AND EXAMPLES PARAGRAPH

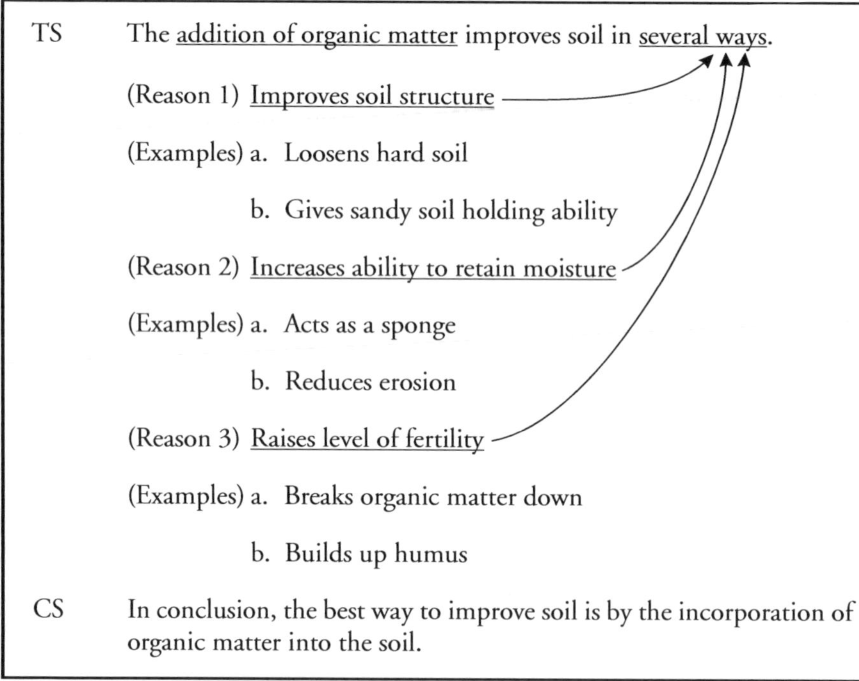

TS The addition of organic matter improves soil in several ways.
(Reason 1) Improves soil structure
(Examples) a. Loosens hard soil
b. Gives sandy soil holding ability
(Reason 2) Increases ability to retain moisture
(Examples) a. Acts as a sponge
b. Reduces erosion
(Reason 3) Raises level of fertility
(Examples) a. Breaks organic matter down
b. Builds up humus
CS In conclusion, the best way to improve soil is by the incorporation of organic matter into the soil.

Every *example,* or *minor supporting statement,* should explain its major statement in terms of the CI. You should be able to draw a line from the minor support to the major support.

Thus, you have a way to check yourself to see if every sentence supports the CI either directly or indirectly. If a sentence doesn't refer to the CI, you should eliminate it, or it will destroy your paragraph unity.

Notice how the major and minor supports work in the following paragraph on how the addition of organic matter improves soil.

ACTIVITY 10-L: Reasons and Examples Paragraph

Analyze the following paragraph according to the criteria following the paragraph. For reasons, examples, and conclusion, give the numbers of the appropriate sentences.

(TS) The addition of organic matter improves soil in several ways. (1) First of all, the addition of organic matter improves soil structure. (2) Organic matter loosens hard-packed clay soil. (3) It enables sandy soil to hold more water and nutrients. (4) Another benefit of a high level of organic matter in soil is an increased ability to retain water. (5) Organic matter acts as a sponge, soaking up rainwater and storing it. (6) As a result, erosion is reduced because water is absorbed by the soil and does not run off. (7) Also, as organic matter is broken down by soil organisms, the level of fertility is raised. (8) Humus, the residue of decay, is built up in the soil, providing plants with the nutrients for growth. (9) In conclusion, the best way to improve soil is by the incorporation of organic matter into the soil.

Subject: ______________________________

CI: ______________________________

Reasons: ____________ *Examples:* ____________ *Conclusion:* ____________

Transitional Expressions: ______________________________

____

Check your responses in Feedback 10-L at the end of this module. Then proceed to Activity 10-M.

ACTIVITY 10-M: Writing a Reasons and Examples Paragraph

Using one of your own topic sentences, write a paragraph supported by reasons and examples. Construct your outline similar to the one below.

Topic Sentence
(1) Reason (major)
  a. Example (minor)
  b. Example (minor)

(2) Reason (major)
  a. Example (minor)
  b. Example (minor)

(3) Reason (major)
  a. Example (minor)
  b. Example (minor)

Concluding Sentence

NOTE There is no magic number for the major reasons and their supporting examples. The important thing is to cover the subject thoroughly and accurately.

After outlining your paragraph, follow procedures given in Activity 10-K. After completing the reasons and examples paragraph, proceed to Part XII.

PART XII: THE PRO AND CON PARAGRAPH

The third type of paragraph in this module is the **pro and con paragraph.** In this type of paragraph, you develop two (or more) opposing ideas. You must mention both controlling ideas in the topic sentence, and you will need to use a compound CI to express the ideas. The central thought of the paragraph has two parts, and each part contrasts with the other. The contrasting idea may be stated, as in the first example, or implied, as in the second example.

A student may find that a weekend job (S) has its advantages as well as its disadvantages (CI). (stated)

In our society, there are many arguments concerning (CI) legalized abortion (S). (implied)

The concluding sentence of a pro and con paragraph does not take a stand but merely restates both sides of the issue.

The following paragraph illustrates the development of a compound CI. Note that the TS indicates divided opinion on an issue. Notice the italicized transitional expression of contrast, which notifies the reader when the writer shifts from explaining the desirable aspects of solar energy as a heat source (pro) to the less desirable (con). Also, notice that in the conclusion the writer remains objective, letting the reader make up his or her own mind. You should not take a stand in the conclusion.

SAMPLE OUTLINE

TS	Solar energy (S) as a heat source for homes has potential (CI), but there are some problems (CI) that need to be resolved.
	Pro 1. Unlimited resource 2. Nonpolluting energy 3. Resource not controlled by humans for profit
	Con 1. High construction cost of collection devices 2. Collection and storage not perfected 3. Collectors somewhat unsightly
CS	To sum up, using the sun's energy for home heating is an option that must be carefully considered.

SAMPLE PARAGRAPH

Solar energy as a heat source for homes has potential, but there are some problems that need to be resolved. Compared to other sources of energy, the sun is an unlimited, largely untapped reserve. Millions of nonpolluting units of energy are released every day. Also, the sun is a source of energy that no corporation or nation can gain control of and sell for profit. *On the other hand,* the high construction costs of solar collection devices can be an obstacle for many. In addition, collection and storage of that energy has not been perfected. A further drawback is that many people object to collectors perched on rooftops and clinging to the sides of buildings. To sum up, using the sun's energy for home heating is an option that must be carefully considered.

ACTIVITY 10-N: **Pro and Con Paragraph**

Study the following pro and con paragraph and then answer the questions following it.

In our society, there is little agreement on the merits of incarcerating (putting in prison) those who have committed crimes. One of the main arguments used by those who favor incarceration is that criminals must pay for their crimes; in other words, "an eye for an eye." They also feel that removing these offenders from society eliminates possible criminal activities by them for that period. In addition, these people believe that offenders should be exposed to a good rehabilitation program before they are released. Another argument advanced favoring imprisonment is that it curbs others when they see the possible consequences for similar acts. On the other hand, those with opposing viewpoints have strongly voiced arguments that some crimes, such as crimes of passion, are likely one-time offenses, and they question what imprisonment accomplishes. These same people also contend that the chances these crimes would be repeated are negligible. They further stress that rehabilitation programs are not only ineffective but also practically nonexistent in most institutions. Besides this, opponents fear that so-called correctional institutions can be teaching grounds for crime. Just as strongly, they challenge the idea that incarceration serves to deter others from crime. All in all, a meeting of the minds on this issue is yet to come.

What is the subject? ______________________________

What are the two CIs? ______________________________

What expression signals transition to opposing arguments?

____

List the supporting ideas briefly:

Pros	*Cons*
a. ____________	a. ____________
b. ____________	b. ____________
c. ____________	c. ____________
d. ____________	d. ____________
	e. ____________

Check your responses in Feedback 10-N at the end of this module. If you have any questions, check with your instructor. Then proceed to Activity 10-O.

ACTIVITY 10-O: Writing a Pro and Con Paragraph

Write a paragraph supported by the pro and con method. Construct your outline as follows:

Topic Sentence (with compound CI)
(1) Pro reasons:
  a.
  b.
  c.
(2) Con reasons:
  a.
  b.
  c.
Concluding Sentence

After writing an outline for your paragraph, follow the procedures given in Activity 10-K. After completing the pro and con paragraph, proceed to Part XIII.

PART XIII: THE PROCESS PARAGRAPH

The final type of paragraph you will learn to write is probably the most significant to you as a technician. This is the **process paragraph,** which explains how to do something or how something is done. The topic sentence is a statement of what process is to be explained. Supporting statements take the reader through the process, step by step. The concluding sentence restates the topic sentence in different words.

Following is one example of a process paragraph. Notice especially that numbers are used here to show transition from one point to another.

SAMPLE OUTLINE

TS The following procedure will greatly improve your ability to assist in artificial respiration during a respiratory arrest.

Preparation	Procedure
1. Position victim	1. Tilt head
2. Loosen clothing	2. Lift chin
3. Check mouth for objects	3. Open jaw
4. Pull tongue forward	4. Keep head back
	5. Pinch nostrils
	6. Take deep breath
	7. Place mouth over victim's
	8. Blow
	9. Repeat
	10. Watch for normal breathing

CS In conclusion, the knowledge and ability to perform the technique of artificial respiration properly could mean the difference between life and death.

SAMPLE PARAGRAPH

The following procedure will greatly improve your ability to assist in artificial respiration during a respiratory arrest.

Preparation

For optimum effectiveness, prepare the victim carefully:

1. Lay the victim on his or her back.
2. Prepare the victim for artificial respiration by helping loosen clothing around the neck, chest, and waist.
3. Be sure to check the mouth for false teeth, gum, or other objects that could block the flow of air.
4. Make certain that the victim's tongue is pulled forward before starting artificial respiration.

Procedure

Once the victim is in position, follow these steps to perform artificial respiration:

1. Tilt the head back as far as possible.
2. Make sure the chin is up so that the neck is stretched tight.
3. Insert your thumb between the victim's teeth; at the same time, pull the victim's lower jaw open.
4. Keep the victim's head pushed back.
5. Pinch the nostrils shut.
6. Open your mouth, and take a deep breath.
7. Place your mouth firmly over the victim's mouth.
8. Blow forcefully into the victim's mouth until you can see the chest rise.
9. Repeat this method every three or four seconds.
10. Normal breathing should start after not more than 15 minutes.

In conclusion, the knowledge and ability to perform artificial respiration properly could mean the difference between life and death.

Note how the details in the process paragraph can be enumerated, as in the previous example, or developed in conventional paragraph form, as follows. Choose the one that best suits your purpose.

SAMPLE PROCESS PARAGRAPH OUTLINE

TS Calculating the percent increase or decrease between this year's sales figures and last year's sales figures can be accomplished with a series of computations on an electronic calculator.

Preparation

1. Turn machine on.
2. Turn grand total key off.
3. Clear memory.
4. Set decimal at 2.

Procedure

1. Enter this year's sales.
2. Press plus key.
3. Enter last year's sales.
4. Press memory plus key.
5. Press minus key.
6. Press subtotal key.
7. Press divide key.
8. Press memory recall key.
9. Press percent key.

CS In conclusion, using an electronic calculator to find the percent increase or decrease can be quite simple if you follow the correct procedure.

ACTIVITY 10-P: Identifying S, CI, and Transitions

In the spaces provided, list the S, the CI, and at least five transitional expressions in the paragraph on calculating sales increases.

Sample (Conventional Format)

Calculating the percent of increase or decrease between this year's sales figures and last year's sales figures can be accomplished with a series of computations on an electronic calculator. Initially, make sure the machine is turned on. Also, be sure the grand total key is off and the memory key is cleared. Set the decimal indicator at two. The primary step in calculating the percent increase or decrease is to find the actual increase or decrease between this year's sales and last year's sales. First, enter this year's sales into the calculator; press the plus key. Then enter last year's sales into the calculator; press the memory key. Next, press the minus key and then the subtotal key. This figure is the actual increase or decrease between this year's and last year's sales. After that, press the divide key followed by the memory recall key. Finally, press the percent key. This figure is the percent of increase or decrease between this year's and last year's sales. In conclusion, using an electronic calculator to find the percent of increase or decrease can be quite simple if you follow the correct procedure.

Subject: ______________________________

CI: ______________________________

List transitions: ______________________________

____

Check your responses in Feedback 10-P at the end of this module. If you have any questions, check with your instructor. Then proceed to Activity 10-Q.

ACTIVITY 10-Q: Writing a Process Paragraph

Write a process paragraph in conventional or enumerated form. Construct your outline as follows:

Topic Sentence
Preparation (if applicable)
(1)
(2)
(3)
Procedure
(1)
(2)
(3)
Concluding Sentence

After constructing your outline, follow the procedure given in Activity 10-K.

ACTIVITY 10-R: Editing Practice

Label the subject, controlling idea, and all of the transitional phrases in the following paragraph.

Using text messaging abbreviations is inappropriate in professional communication, such as emails to instructors or supervisors, interoffice memos, and letters. However, much to the frustration of many employers and teachers, more and more students and new hires are letting this abbreviated language slip into more formal communications. In fact, many instructors are specifically addressing this issue with students in classes and preparing detailed policies that reject this kind of language. The problem seems to stem from the fact that many students spend more time writing with electronic communications, such as email and text messaging, than they spend writing reports for classes and, consequently, have formed the habit of using abbreviations and symbols in their written communications. While this kind of language may be necessary for efficient text messaging, it is sloppy and often inarticulate in reports and emails submitted to instructors, supervisors, and colleagues. For instance, these people may not be familiar with the abbreviations, so the message may not communicate effectively and may actually leave the reader confused. Furthermore, when readers feel as though a writer has not taken them into consideration when drafting communication, they can often become frustrated and even dismissive of the writer and the ideas put forth. In order to avoid confusing and awkward communication, students should not use text messaging abbreviations in their communication with teachers, co-workers, and especially with supervisors and potential employers.

Check your responses in Feedback 10-R at the end of this module.

DIAGNOSTIC FEEDBACK

Label the subject, the controlling idea, and all of the transitional phrases in the following paragraph.

<u>When composing a report, students should spend 25% of their time organizing their ideas and planning the report</u>. By spending time before writing, students are more likely to have a coherent organizational plan. <u>In fact</u>, careful planning can help the students identify and eliminate unrelated ideas. <u>Furthermore</u>, taking time to plan can test the students' report idea or thesis to make sure that they have enough information for the scope of the report. <u>Of course</u>, part of the planning process should include taking time to analyze the audience and make sure that the format and vocabulary are appropriate. Many students don't realize that spending some thoughtful time before writing can actually make the report writing process more efficient.

FEEDBACK FOR MODULE 10

Feedback 10-B

1. A gasoline carburetor functions better at night.

   S CI

2. The coastal area offers many recreational activities.

   CI S

3. What is engineering?

   S CI

4. Architecture interests me.

   S CI

5. Shortages of materials today have seriously affected many companies.

Feedback 10-C

   S CI

1. Most homeowners need a well-equipped toolbox for repair jobs.

   S CI

2. Courtesy pays off in improved job relations.

   S CI

3. Assembling parts without first reading instructions promises disaster.

   S CI

4. Safety rules are established for a purpose.

   S CI

5. Certain qualities of an applicant are observed in a job interview.

Feedback 10-D

Group 1	Group 2	Group 3	Group 4
(a) TB	(a) TN	(a) WF	(a) TB
(b) WF	(b) WF	(b) TN	(b) WF
(c) TN	(c) TB	(c) TB	(c) TN

Feedback 10-E

Group 1	Group 2	Group 3	Group 4
(a) TN	(a) WF	(a) TB	(a) TB
(b) TB	(b) TB	(b) TN	(b) WF
(c) WF	(c) TN	(c) WF	(c) TN

Feedback 10-G

There are several definite guidelines to use in writing a resumé. It must be typed and only one page long. The Job Objective should be clearly defined. ~~It should be noted that a resumé is the same as a data sheet~~. The wording should be as brief as possible, using phrases rather than complete sentences. References should not be included. ~~The letter of application is used to ask for the job interview~~. Previous salaries should not be included. Neatness and appearance are extremely important. An effective resumé will be the result of following these principles.

You should make every effort to apply the basic punctuation rules to your writing. Do not forget to separate words in a series by using commas. Also, use commas to separate items in dates and addresses. ~~Make sure your subjects and verbs agree~~. Coordinate adjectives provide another occasion to use the comma. In addition, commas are needed with interrupters and introductory words or phrases. ~~Avoid using fragments in your writing~~. A review of the fundamentals of punctuation will improve your writing.

Feedback 10-H

Subject: Technical colleges
CI: wide variety of curriculum offerings
Supporting: 2, 3, 5, 6, 8
Unrelated: 1, 4, 7, 9
Concluding: 10
Transitions: For example, In addition, Another, also

Feedback 10-L

Subject: Organic matter
CI: improves soil in several ways
Reasons: 1, 4, 7
Examples: 2, 3, 5, 6, 8
Conclusion: 9
Transitions: First of all, Another, As a result, Also, In conclusion

Feedback 10-N

Subject: Incarceration (imprisonment)
CIs: for and against (little agreement)
Transition: on the other hand

Pros

a. Criminals must pay for crimes.
b. Imprisonment prevents further crimes.
c. Criminals need rehabilitation.
d. Threat of prison curbs others.

Cons

a. Some crimes are one-time offenses.
b. Chances of repetition are negligible.
c. Rehabilitation programs are ineffective.
d. Prisons teach crime.
e. Incarceration does not deter others.

Feedback 10-P

Subject: Calculating percent of increase or decrease
CI: series of computations
Transitions: Initially, Also, First, Then, Next, After that, Finally, In conclusion

Feedback 10-R

Subject: Using text messaging abbreviations
Controlling idea: is inappropriate in professional communication,
Transitions: However, In fact, consequently, For instance, Furthermore

MODULE 11

Shifts

Objective: This module will help you to recognize and to correct various shifts or inconsistencies so that you may attain smoothness and clearness in your writing.

Upon completion of this module, you will be able:

- To identify and to correct inconsistencies in tense and voice of a verb.
- To identify and to correct shifts in two pronoun forms: person and number.

Your writing goal should be to develop your thoughts clearly and concisely so that they move easily from one sentence to the next. If you begin a sentence in one way and then change its flow, the reader becomes confused. To achieve smoothness and clearness, you must pay careful attention to being consistent in the use of voice, tense, person, and number.

One of the basic guidelines governing good writing is the concept of unity. Unity implies a sense of oneness. A good paper has one basic idea to develop. It has one point of view, and it should be presented in one tense. All of these factors support the idea of unity. In order to achieve unity, therefore, the writer must be familiar with the concept of **shifting,** for it is through shifting voice, tense, person, and number that unity is broken.

Shifts occur in verbs and pronouns. Shifts in voice and tense occur in verbs; shifts in person and number occur in pronouns. To check for shifts in your writing, you need only examine those two kinds of words: verbs (tense and voice) and pronouns (person and number).

Unity is important to good writing. Once shifts are identified, errors that contribute to breakdowns in unity can be avoided.

DIAGNOSTIC EXERCISE

Correct shifts in voice, tense, person, and number.

1. The adjunct instructor signed the contract, and it was submitted by the department chairperson.
2. Nurses have to calculate measurements, and you have to accurately administer medication.
3. A student should check with the financial aid office before withdrawing from a course, and they should also talk with their advisor.
4. The students filed a complaint, and it was investigated by the dean.
5. A police officer should have excellent communication skills, and they should also be able to stay calm under pressure.
6. An attorney spends a significant amount of their day writing reports, memos, and messages.
7. The council member made a motion, and it was seconded by the secretary.
8. Technicians are often detail-oriented, and you should also be able to analyze data.
9. The counselor started the victim advocacy group today, and next week started the drug and alcohol program.
10. The president of the college announced his retirement, and a scholarship has been established by him.

PART I: SHIFTS IN VOICE

Voice is a concept that is rather new to most writers. Voice determines if the subject of the sentence is performing or receiving the action of the verb. In active voice, the subject performs the action; in passive voice, the subject receives the action. Passive voice usually includes a prepositional phrase beginning with *by* to indicate the doer of the action. Another signal of the passive voice is a form of the helping verb *to be,* such as *is, am, are, was, were, been, being.*

V
ACTIVE: **He read** the manual. (In the **passive voice,** the subject is receiving the action of the verb.)

V
PASSIVE: **The manual was read** by him.

Look at some more examples to see how the voice of the verb can be changed.

ACTIVE VOICE

He wrote his report. (Subject *he* doing action of verb *wrote*)

The board approved the new pension plan. (Subject *board* doing action of verb *approved*)

Mr. Jones programmed the computer. (Subject *Mr. Jones* doing action of verb *programmed*)

PASSIVE VOICE

His report was written. (Subject *report* receiving action of verb *written*)

The new pension plan was approved by the board. (Subject *plan* receiving action of verb *approved*)

The computer was programmed by Mr. Jones. (Subject *computer* receiving action of verb *programmed*)

ACTIVE: John drove the car for inspection.

PASSIVE: The car was driven by John for inspection.

You probably have noticed that the sentences written in the active voice are more forceful than those written in the passive voice. Active verbs convey information with much more emphasis and vigor, and for that reason, they are preferred. Sentences in the active voice are less wordy and, therefore, more practical in business writing. Unlike the vague and sometimes weak passive voice, the active voice catches the subject in action.

If the active voice is preferred, why use the passive voice at all? The answer is that there are a few instances in which the passive voice is useful. Consider the following example:

An error in the account was made.

Here the passive voice is more diplomatic than the active because it shifts the emphasis from who made the error (which is not mentioned) to the fact that an error was made, thereby blaming no particular person. However, in most cases, you will want to use the active voice for emphasis and forcefulness. The passive voice can be used when the doer of the action is either unknown or unimportant.

NOTE Passive voice is not an error; it is simply not a preferred format.

The most important thing to remember about voice is that you should keep it consistent. If you start out a sentence in the active voice, all verbs in that sentence should be in the active voice. If, on the other hand, you begin a sentence in the passive voice, all verbs in that sentence should be in the passive voice.

In the following examples, the voice shifts from active to passive within one sentence. Notice how the shifts are corrected by changing the second verb from passive to active voice.

SHIFT: **Jason liked** (Active) journalism, but **agriculture was preferred** (Passive) by Keith.

CORRECTED: **Jason liked** (Active) journalism, but **Keith preferred** (Active) agriculture.

SHIFT: **Karen took** (Active) a course in nursing while a program in **data processing was pursued** (Passive) by Anita.

CORRECTED: **Karen took** (Active) a course in nursing while **Anita pursued** (Active) a program in data processing.

Note that the passive voice always has a helping verb which is a form of the verb **to be (is, am, are, was, were, been, being)**. However, forms of the verb **to be** are not always signals for the passive voice.

When these verbs are used alone as linking verbs (as explained in Module 1, Part II), they are not in the passive voice. (Another signal of the passive voice is the *by* phrase, as in *by Keith* and *by Anita.*)

Pete **was given** a job in accounting. *Was* is a helper for the main verb *given* (past participle of *give*). The verb is in the passive voice.

Pete **was** a good accountant. *Was* is the main verb; therefore, it is a linking verb—not in the passive voice.

To change a sentence from passive to active voice, follow these three steps:

1. Find the main verb (without the helper).
2. Ask the question *who* or *what* does (or did) the action of the verb.
3. Rewrite the sentence with the new subject doing the action of the verb. The old subject is now the direct object.

PASSIVE: Directions **are given** to the drivers by the transportation chief. (Main verb? *given* Who does the giving? *transportation chief*)
New sentence:
ACTIVE: The transportation chief gives directions to the drivers.
PASSIVE: The ads **were prepared** by the journalism students. (Main verb? *prepared* Who did the preparing? *journalism students*)
New sentence:
ACTIVE: The journalism students prepared the ads.
PASSIVE: The data **is selected** by computers. (Main verb? *selected* What does the selecting? *computers*)
New sentence:
ACTIVE: Computers select the data.

ACTIVITY 11-A: Voice

Underline the complete verbs in the following sentences. If the verb is in the active voice, write *active* in the blank; if the verb is in the passive voice, write *passive* in the blank. Change the sentences in passive voice to active voice.

1. The field trip was arranged by the supervisor. __________
2. The civil engineer surveyed the lot. __________
3. The Chicago Police Department hired one of our criminal justice students. __________
4. Very often the lab results are written by the lab technicians. __________
5. A very accurate story was written by the reporter. __________
6. The lab technician completed the blood test. __________
7. A report was written by her. __________
8. The prints were drawn by the architectural intern. __________
9. The company constructed the new plant. __________
10. The patient's temperature was taken by the CNA. __________

Check your responses in Feedback 11-A at the end of this module. If your responses were correct, proceed to Activity 11-C. If you missed any, review and then do Activity 11-B.

ACTIVITY 11-B: Voice

Underline the complete verbs in the following sentences. Identify the voice by writing *active* or *passive* in the blank. Change all passive voice sentences to active voice.

1. The nurse checked the patient's pulse. __________
2. The programs are written by the computer programmer. __________
3. Every morning the electrical engineer checks all the switches. __________
4. Faulty switches are repaired by the maintenance men. __________
5. The police investigated the murder. __________
6. The theft was reported by the shop owner. __________
7. The Criminalistics Unit was called in by the manager after the theft. __________
8. The supervisor scheduled the plant visitation. __________
9. The lot was surveyed by the civil engineer. __________
10. One of our graduates was hired by the Atlanta Police Department. __________

Check your responses in Feedback 11-B at the end of this module. If your responses were correct, proceed to Activity 11-C. If you missed any, review before continuing.

ACTIVITY 11-C: Voice

Correct any shift in voice by making sure both parts of the sentence are written in the same voice.

1. The lab technician completed the blood test, and a report was written by her.
2. Plans were drawn by the architectural intern, and his company constructed the new plant.
3. The nurse checked the patient's pulse, and his temperature was taken by the CNA.
4. The programs are usually written by the personnel in the computer room, but we write our own program when they are too busy.
5. Every morning the electrical engineer checks all the switches, and any that are faulty are repaired by the maintenance men.

6. As we came in on the bus, the factory was seen on the right.
7. Not enough attention is devoted to quality-control instruction; the company conducts seminars only once a year.
8. An apology was made by him when he saw the evidence.
9. The transformer was checked because the engineer had discovered a current shortage.
10. Instructions were received by mail and I typed the report.

Check your responses in Feedback 11-C at the end of this module. If your responses were correct, proceed to Activity 11-D. If you missed any, review before continuing.

ACTIVITY 11-D: Voice

Read the following paragraph and change all passive voice sentences to active voice.

Forestry rangers have a wide variety of responsibilities. One of their duties is to watch for forest fires. Also, as a preventive measure, trenches must be dug by them. In addition, trees must be marked for cutting. Sometimes, they have to supervise campgrounds. Diseased trees must be found. In short, forest rangers are kept busy by their many duties.

Check your responses in Feedback 11-D at the end of this module. If your responses were correct, proceed to Part II. If you missed any, review before continuing.

PART II: SHIFTS IN TENSE

Probably the easiest shift to locate is one in tense. Once the verb tense is established in the introduction, you should be sure to keep that tense throughout the paper. In business writing, most reports will occur in the present, past, or future tense. You must be careful to establish the tense and keep it throughout the report. In fact, shifts in tense are rare, so this is not a critical problem for most writers.

Tense means *time.* When you change time in a sentence or within a report without justification, you make a shift in tense. You might be talking about a past event and suddenly, for no reason, switch to the present.

John **started** on his new job yesterday. He **checked** his equipment and **begins** to work. (Shift in tense)

The first two verbs in this example—**started** and **checked**—are *past tense,* but the third verb—**begins**—is *present tense.* There are two ways to correct this inconsistency: Change all the verbs to past tense or change all the verbs to present tense.

SHIFT CORRECTED: John **started** on his new job yesterday. He **checked** his equipment and **began** to work. (*past tense*)

SHIFT CORRECTED: John **starts** on his new job. He **checks** his equipment and **begins** to work. (*present tense*)

Once you have set the time of the action, you should be consistent. This does not mean that you can never change tense. A shift in tense is logical if time words such as **today** (*present*), **yesterday** (*past*), **tomorrow** (*future*), and many other expressions of time are used. The verb tense must be consistent with the time expressed.

Yesterday, I **worked** on the computer. Today, I **am working** in the lab. Tomorrow, I **will take** the day off. (Acceptable shifts)

Here are some examples of inappropriate shifts in tense. Notice how the shifts are corrected by putting all verbs in the same tense.

SHIFT: Kendall **noted** (Past) the drop in secretarial students while Elizabeth **discusses** (Present) the increase in electronics students.

CORRECTED: Kendall **noted** (Past) the drop in secretarial students while Elizabeth **discussed** (Past) the increase in electronics students.

SHIFT: The architect **talks** (Present) to the prospective builder, **draws** (Present) the house plans, and then **consulted** (Past) the builder again.

CORRECTED: The architect **talks** (Present) to the prospective builder, **draws** (Present) the house plans, and then **consults** (Present) the builder again.

ACTIVITY 11-E: Tense

Underline any verb that is inconsistent in tense with the rest of the sentence. Write the correct form of the inconsistent verb.

1. The inspector will visit your plant Monday, and next week she visited my plant.
2. Finally, the salesman reaches his goal, and he won the award for being the top salesman.
3. We hurried to the board meeting, but nobody is there.
4. The arbitration board announced that it reaches agreement on the new contract.
5. The new assistant knows how to operate the word processor, but he did not know how to run the answering machine.
6. The carpenter began repairing the fence while the painter paints the walls.
7. The accountant checked the data, and then she writes the profit and loss statement.
8. The nurse checked the patient, and then she talks to the doctor.
9. After we ate lunch yesterday, the boss tells the employees about their new working hours.
10. When the weather gets better, I plan to have finished the job.

Check your responses in Feedback 11-E at the end of this module. If your responses were correct, proceed to Activity 11-G. If you missed any, review and then do Activity 11-F.

ACTIVITY 11-F: Tense

Underline any verb that is inconsistent in tense with the rest of the sentence. Write the correct form of the inconsistent verb.

1. The doctor visits the patients early in the morning; at night he made rounds again.
2. Finally, the architect finishes the drawing, and she won an award for the design.
3. The reporter hurried to the scene of the accident, but no one is there.
4. The committee notified the board of trustees that it reaches its decision at noon yesterday.
5. The receptionist greeted the callers while the assistant starts the meeting.
6. Before the journalist writes a story, she carefully checked the facts.
7. After the nurse took the patient's blood pressure, the doctor checks his heart.
8. Yesterday afternoon, the computer breaks down in the middle of a program.
9. I wanted to interview him tomorrow, but he cancels the appointment.
10. When summer comes, the farmers looked forward to better weather.

Check your responses in Feedback 11-F at the end of this module. If your responses were correct, proceed to Activity 11-G. If you missed any, review before continuing.

ACTIVITY 11-G: Tense

Read the following paragraph and correct any shifts in tense.

A field trip is a valuable experience for a student. For instance, a civil engineering student benefited from visiting various types of bridges. A nursing student learned a great deal from a trip to the hospital. In addition, an administrative assistant student will get helpful hints while he visited an office. On the whole, a relevant field trip enlightens a student.

Check your responses in Feedback 11-G at the end of this module. If your responses were correct, proceed to Part III. If you missed any, review before continuing.

PART III: SHIFTS IN PERSON

The most troublesome shift for the writer is the shift in **person** or **point of view.** At the organizational state of writing, you should determine the point of view and keep it consistent throughout the paper. There are three persons or points of view: **First person** is forms of **I** and **we** (**I, we, our, us, me,** etc.) and is used only for very personal writing. It is used in business in memos and letters only. **Second person** consists of forms of **you** (**you, your**) and is used only with procedures. Both of these points of view are used with very informal forms of writing.

Since most business writing is formal, **third person** is the preferred point of view. Third person basically consists of **all nouns** and **any pronoun that is not a form of I,we,** or **you** (**he, they, someone, one,** etc.) All writing has some form of third person in it since it is impossible to compose without nouns.

Point of view must be consistent throughout the paper. It is easy to maintain consistency within a sentence or even a single paragraph, but maintaining consistency throughout an entire report is rather difficult. Often shifts in person are easily overlooked because they do not sound awkward or incorrect while you are writing. The only way to avoid this error is to proofread for shifts in person or point of view. This should be one of the first steps in the revision process.

The structure or purpose of your report determines what point of view should be used. The controlling idea of your topic sentence, which determines the structure of the report, will also determine which point of view is appropriate. Consult the chart below to choose the point of view that you should use for a document. Then use your editing skills to proofread your draft to be sure you remain consistent.

TYPE/STRUCTURE OF WRITING	POINT OF VIEW	PRONOUNS/ NOUNS USED
Informal: letters, memos, personal narratives, stories	First person	I, me, my, mine, myself, we, us, our, ourselves
Informal: procedures (process), instructions	Second person	You, your, yourself, yourselves
Formal: exposition, argument	Third person	All nouns and pronouns except those listed above

Here are some examples of shifts in person. Notice how the shifts are corrected.

SHIFT: To be a good nurse, a **person** (3rd sing) needs to be alert. **You** (2nd) should continually be aware of what the patient is doing.

CORRECTED: To be a good nurse, a **person** (3rd sing) needs to be alert. **She** (3rd) should continually be aware of what **her** (3rd) patient is doing.

SHIFT: The **client** (3rd sing) will find these stores very convenient; **you** (2nd) cannot get the supplies **you** (2nd) need by mail.

CORRECTED: The **client** (3rd sing) will find these stores very convenient; **he** (3rd) cannot get the supplies **he** (3rd) needs by mail.

ACTIVITY 11-H: Person

Correct the shifts in person by writing the correct form of the inconsistent word. In some cases, the verb form may need to be changed as well.

1. Marty would like to know where you could find a good mechanic.
2. You prepared the bids that one must submit to get the contract.
3. The bookkeeper balanced out the account, which you must total every day.

4. They reported for work early each morning to find a place to park your car.
5. I broke my microscope; you always hurry to finish the experiment on time.
6. If one is to finish the program for the computer on time, you probably will have to work overtime.
7. You will receive your check from the comptroller after one completes the job.
8. Anyone can fill in the application if you concentrate.
9. Everybody should develop a resumé, which you need when applying for a job.
10. When the contractors finished with the shopping center project, you moved on to the next assignment—building a high-rise apartment.

Check your responses in Feedback 11-H at the end of this module. If your responses were correct, proceed to Activity 11-J. If you missed any, review Part III and do Activity 11-I.

ACTIVITY 11-I: Person

Correct the shifts in person by writing the correct form of the inconsistent word. In some cases, the verb form may need to be changed as well.

1. I asked the employment office where you could find an efficient assistant.
2. Mr. Blevins is doing the work you must do to qualify for the job promotion.
3. We checked the patients' charts, which you must look at every day.
4. His calculator was not working; therefore, you must check the warranty.
5. If one is to get paid for overtime, you first must work a 40-hour week.
6. You will get a raise as soon as one passes the competency examination.
7. Anyone can do the job correctly if you read the manual.
8. Everybody brought a stock portfolio, which you need to sit on the Stock Exchange.
9. When they completed the job assignment, you went on to the next task.
10. When a person goes for an interview, you should dress appropriately.

Check your responses in Feedback 11-I at the end of this module. If your responses were correct, proceed to Activity 11-J. If you missed any, review before continuing.

ACTIVITY 11-J: Person

Read the following paragraph and correct any shifts in person.

A personnel manager may try in several ways to upset a job applicant to see how you handle an awkward situation. You may offer the interviewee coffee but no cream or sugar. Another trick is for the interviewer to have the applicant stand awkwardly without offering a seat. It would be wise for a prospective employee to be aware of possible attempts to frustrate you.

Check your responses in Feedback 11-J at the end of this module. If your responses were correct, proceed to Part IV. If you missed any, review before continuing.

PART IV: SHIFTS IN NUMBER

Pronouns can present a problem with shifts. Whenever a pronoun is used, the noun to which it refers (its *antecedent*) should be double-checked for agreement. One area to check is that of number. This simply means making sure a plural pronoun is used to refer to a plural noun; likewise, a singular pronoun must be used for a singular noun. The indefinite pronouns are particularly troublesome here, so it is necessary to know which are singular and which are plural. See Module 6 on Pronoun Agreement for a list of these indefinite pronouns. In addition, collective nouns or group nouns, such as **committee** or **team,** take the singular pronoun **it** because they are usually used as singular nouns.

You can also confuse the meaning of your paragraph by making an unjustified shift in number. If you begin with a plural subject, every pronoun you subsequently use to refer to that subject should be plural; if you start with a singular noun, refer to it with a singular pronoun.

Here are some examples of shifts in number. Notice how the shifts are corrected.

Sing

SHIFT: Each **draftsman** has done a fine job designing the

Pl

new beach house. Not only have **they** worked well

Pl

together, but **they've** also produced some good

Pl

ideas. Furthermore, the **men** seem to have enjoyed

Pl

working on **their** project.

Pl

CORRECTED: All of the **draftsmen** have done a fine job designing

Pl

the new beachhouse. Not only have **they** worked well

Pl

together, but **they've** also produced some good

Pl

ideas. Furthermore, the **men** seem to have enjoyed

Pl

working on **their** project.

Sing Pl
SHIFT: Each electronics **student** was asked to bring in **their** old computer set to repair.

Sing Sing
CORRECTED: Each electronics **student** was asked to bring in **his** (or **her**) old computer to repair.

Collective nouns (such as **administration, association, club, committee, company, faculty, group, jury, organization, personnel, staff, team,** etc.) are considered singular when the group is thought of as a unit but are considered plural when the individual members of the group are stressed. Usually, collective nouns are singular.

Coll Pl
SHIFT: The **jury** deliberated three hours before **they** reached a verdict. (*Emphasizes members*)

Coll Sing
CORRECTED: The **jury** deliberated three hours before **it** reached a verdict. (*Acts as a unit*)

Pl
CORRECTED: The **members** of the jury deliberated three hours

Pl
before **they** reached a verdict.

Coll
SHIFT: The **Business and Professional Women's Club** is

Pl
holding **their** annual meeting soon.

Coll
CORRECTED: The **Business and Professional Women's Club** is

Sing
holding **its** annual meeting soon. (*Acts as a unit*)

Pl
CORRECTED: The **ladies** of the Business and Professional Women's

Pl
Club are holding **their** annual meeting soon.

NOTE A present tense verb can be a clue for the pronoun agreement. Notice how the verb in the last example agrees with both the subject and the ensuing pronoun.

You will recall from Module 6 that some indefinite pronouns, such as **all, any, some, part, most, none,** and **half,** can be singular or plural. Certain other indefinite pronouns, such as **anyone, everybody, each, either,** etc., are always singular. The indefinite pronouns **both, few, several,** and **many** are always plural.

ACTIVITY 11-K: Number

Underline any shift in number, and write the correct form above it. Circle the antecedent. Consider all collective nouns as singular. Change verb forms if necessary.

1. Colleges should encourage teaching methods other than the lecture. It should promote consideration of individualized instruction.
2. The accounting club agreed to elect their officers at the next meeting.
3. Businessmen build goodwill through advertising. He should set aside money in the budget for sales promotion.
4. Every one of the assistants was asked to retype their letters.
5. All of the nurses are wearing her new uniforms today.
6. The group discussed the problem and decided on their strategy.
7. The publishing company asked for the script. They wanted to publish the play.
8. We all know that my financial resources are devalued in time of depression.
9. A good accountant knows that neatness is important. In addition, they always strive for accuracy.
10. The archery team won the match yesterday. They were pleased at the victory.

Check your responses in Feedback 11-K at the end of this module. If your responses were correct, proceed to Activity 11-M. If you missed any, review and do Activity 11-L.

ACTIVITY 11-L: Number

Correct the shifts in number by writing the correct form of the inconsistent word. Consider all collective nouns as singular. Change verb forms if necessary.

1. Employment agencies should advertise job openings; furthermore, it should help match people to jobs.
2. The board of trustees agreed to announce their findings at the July meeting.
3. Salespersons attend conventions regularly. One must be away from home a great deal.
4. Every one of the flight attendants checked their schedule before going home.
5. Both of the architects displayed his new design in the showcase.

6. The group met to review their news articles.
7. The manufacturing company discussed their sales promotion with the new employees.
8. We are all aware that my sales decrease in summer.
9. A good waitress is conscious of personal appearance. They know how important first impressions are.
10. The college staff met to discuss the issue; they made an important decision.

Check your responses in Feedback 11-L at the end of this module. If your responses were correct, proceed to Activity 11-M. If you missed any, review before continuing.

ACTIVITY 11-M: Number

Read the following paragraph and correct any shifts in number.

Nurses have many jobs to perform during a typical day. He or she must check the patients' temperature and blood pressure at regular intervals. They should also ask patients if they are having any complications. Furthermore, a nurse must administer medication to their patients and enter the dosage on their charts. Truly, nurses have a busy schedule.

Check your responses in Feedback 11-M at the end of this module. If your responses were correct, proceed to Activity 11-N. If you missed any, review before continuing.

ACTIVITY 11-N: Review

Rewrite these sentences on your own paper to correct any shifts in voice, tense, person, or number. Check verbs (voice and tense) and pronouns (person and number).

1. The tour of the industry was planned by the public relations officer, and the group of engineers arrived at 9:00 A.M.
2. The tour guide was a petroleum engineer, and she takes the group around the plant.
3. The public relations officer planned the industrial tour, and they set up an itinerary for the group.
4. Anyone could participate in the tour if you wanted to.
5. The group took the tour; then there is a question-and-answer period.
6. The engineers seemed to enjoy the tour; you got a complete view of the plant's operation.
7. The engineers enjoyed the tour; a complete view of the plant's operation was gotten.

8. As the members of the group entered the processing room, large vats were seen by them.
9. After the tour was completed, the guide invites the group to have lunch.
10. Everyone should take advantage of such a tour if they would like to learn more about a company.

Check your responses in Feedback 11-N at the end of this module. If your responses were correct, proceed to Activity 11-O. If you missed any, review before continuing.

ACTIVITY 11-O: Review

Correct the unnecessary shifts in each of the following sentences. In the space provided, identify the type of shift (voice, tense, person, or number).

TENSE: The surveyor had remembered to bring his transit, but he forgets his clipboard.

The surveyor had remembered to bring his transit, but he had forgotten his clipboard.

______ 1. The salesman worked to meet his quota, and 10 new accounts were opened in one week.

____

____

______ 2. Bradford will repair the television, and Stillman helped him.

____

____

______ 3. We transported the tire to Indianapolis, and it has been charged to the manufacturer.

____

____

______ 4. Sue totaled the daily receipts, but several errors were made.

____

____

______ 5. Since Ross will retire at the conclusion of this project, no suggestions will be offered by him.

____

____

______ 6. The supervisor installed and tested the new equipment. Next month, it will be put into operation.

____

____

______ 7. The hotel manager made arrangements for the convention, and his assistant requests the confirmations.

____

____

______ 8. The computer has been programmed by Murphy, and he checked it for bugs yesterday.

____

____

______ 9. A police officer holds a very important job in the community. Many people depend on them for help.

____

____

______ 10. Because everyone works hard, you should take a midmorning break to relax.

____

____

______ 11. When the boss saw that an employee was sick, she was sent home to rest.

____

____

______ 12. Before I started to drive, my seat belt was fastened and the emergency brake released.

____

____

______ 13. A tourist can stop frequently if they drive their own car.

____

____

______ 14. A person does well in an interview if they prepare ahead of time.

____

____

______ 15. People should not trust rumors without checking for oneself.

____

____

Check your responses in Feedback 11-O at the end of this module. If you missed any, review.

ACTIVITY 11-P: Editing Practice

Edit the following paragraph for any shift problem. Eliminate all use of the passive voice.

Heightened security at airports should be welcomed by travelers. Despite the inconvenience, many of the measures provided the assurance that flights will be as safe as possible, and it will take off on time if passengers follow a few common sense guidelines. If you are traveling, pack sensibly and get to the airport well ahead of your flight. Travelers who keep themselves informed are appreciated by fellow passengers and airport personnel.

Check your responses in Feedback 11-P at the end of this module.

ACTIVITY 11-Q: Editing Practice

Edit the following paragraph for any shift problems. Eliminate all use of the passive voice.

Even though many students today have extensive experience sending email, some students do not understand the importance of format and clarity when sending electronic communication. Email had several nuances that make it different than oral communication; for instance, it is impossible for readers to interpret tone or get any other clues about the communication from nonverbal clues, such as the speaker's inflection, body language, and gestures. Many electronic communicators try to replace the lack of body language with icons that indicate laughing, rolling the eyes, and angry expressions, but these icons were woefully inadequate since not all readers are familiar with these symbols, and these pictures may be misinterpreted by them. Furthermore, some students do not understand the importance of using a subject line and signing your email, which is especially important in professional and educational communication since hundreds of email are received by some of these people on a daily basis. It is important for a student to approach their email with instructors and professional contacts much as you would approach a formal report or memo, by organizing their information carefully, keeping the message concise yet thorough, and considering the readers and then writing specifically to meet the needs and expectations of your audience.

Check your responses in Feedback 11-Q at the end of this module.

DIAGNOSTIC FEEDBACK

Correct shifts in voice, tense, person and number.

1. The adjunct instructor signed the contract, and the department chairperson submitted it.

2. Nurses have to calculate measurements, and they have to accurately administer medication.
3. Students should check with the financial aid office before withdrawing from a course, and they should also talk with their advisor.
4. The students filed a complaint; the dean investigated it.
5. Police officers should have excellent communication skills, and they should also be able to stay calm under pressure.
6. Attorneys spend a significant amount of their day writing reports, memos, and messages.
7. The council member made a motion, and the secretary seconded it.
8. Technicians are often detail-oriented, and they should also be able to analyze data.
9. The counselor started the victim advocacy group today and next week will start the drug and alcohol program.
10. The president of the college announced his retirement, and he established a scholarship.

FEEDBACK FOR MODULE 11

Feedback 11-A

1. was arranged (*passive*). The supervisor arranged the field trip.
2. surveyed (*active*)
3. hired (*active*)
4. are written (*passive*). Very often the lab technicians write the lab results.
5. was written (*passive*). The reporter wrote a very accurate story.
6. completed (*active*)
7. was written (*passive*). She wrote a report.
8. were drawn (*passive*). The architectural intern drew the prints.
9. constructed (*active*)
10. was taken (*passive*). The CNA took the patient's temperature.

Feedback 11-B

1. checked (*active*)
2. are written (*passive*). The computer programmer writes the programs.
3. checks (*active*)
4. are repaired (*passive*). The maintenance men repair the faulty switches.
5. investigated (*active*)
6. was reported (*passive*). The shop owner reported the theft.
7. was called (*passive*). After the theft, the manager called in the Criminalistics Unit.
8. scheduled (*active*)
9. was surveyed (*passive*). The civil engineer surveyed the lot.
10. was hired (*passive*). The Atlanta Police Department hired one of our graduates.

Feedback 11-C

All sentences are written in the active voice. If your responses differ, check with your instructor since there is more than one possible correct answer.

1. The lab technician completed the blood test, and she wrote a report.
2. The architectural intern drew the plans, and his company constructed the new plant.
3. The nurse checked the patient's pulse, and the CNA took his temperature.
4. The personnel in the computer room usually write the programs, but we write our own program when they are too busy.
5. Every morning the electrical engineer checks all the switches, and the maintenance men repair any that are faulty.
6. As we came in on the bus, we saw the factory on the right.
7. The company does not devote enough attention to quality-control instruction; it conducts seminars only once a year.
8. He made an apology when he saw the evidence.
9. The engineer checked the transformer because he had discovered a current shortage.
10. I received instructions by mail and typed the report.

Feedback 11-D

Forestry rangers have a wide variety of responsibilities. One of their duties is to watch for forest fires. Also, as a preventive measure, *they must dig* trenches. In addition, *they must mark* trees for cutting. Sometimes, they have to supervise campgrounds. *They must find* diseased trees. In short, the many duties of forest rangers keep them busy.

Feedback 11-E

Possible answers are shown. If your responses differ, check with your instructor.

1. The inspector *will visit* your plant Monday, and next week she *will visit* my plant.
2. Finally, the salesman *reached* his goal, and he *won* the award for being the top salesman.
3. We *hurried* to the board meeting, but nobody *was* there.
4. The arbitration board *announced* that it *reached* agreement on the new contract.
5. The new assistant *knows* how to operate the word processor, but he *does not know* how to run the answering machine.
6. The carpenter *began* repairing the fence while the painter *painted* the walls.
7. The accountant *checked* the data, and then she *wrote* the profit and loss statement.
8. The nurse *checked* the patient, and then she *talked* to the doctor.
9. After we *ate* lunch yesterday, the boss *told* the employees about their new working hours.
10. When the weather gets better, I plan to *finish* the job.

Feedback 11-F

Possible answers are shown. If your responses differ, check with your instructor.

1. The doctor *visits* the patients early in the morning; at night he *makes* rounds again.
2. Finally, the architect *finished* the drawing, and she *won* an award for the design.
3. The reporter *hurried* to the scene of the accident, but no one *was* there.

4. The committee *notified* the board of trustees that it *reached* its decision at noon yesterday.
5. The receptionist *greeted* the callers while the assistant *started* the meeting.
6. Before the journalist *writes* a story, she carefully *checks* the facts.
7. After the nurse *took* the patient's blood pressure, the doctor *checked* his heart.
8. *Yesterday* afternoon, the computer *broke* down in the middle of a program.
9. I *wanted* to interview him tomorrow, but he *canceled* the appointment.
10. When summer *comes,* the farmers *look* forward to better weather.

Feedback 11-G

There may be more than one correct answer. If your responses differ, check with your instructor.

A field trip is a valuable experience for a student. For instance, a civil engineering student *benefits* from visiting various types of bridges. A nursing student *learns* a great deal from a trip to the hospital. In addition, an administrative assistant student *gets* helpful hints while he *visits* an office. On the whole, a relevant field trip enlightens a student.

Feedback 11-H

There may be more than one correct answer. If your responses differ, check with your instructor.

1. *Marty* would like to know where *he* could find a good mechanic.
2. *You* prepared the bids that *you* must submit to get the contract.
3. The *bookkeeper* balanced out the account, which *she* must total every day.
4. *They* reported for work early each morning to find a place to park *their* car.
5. *I* broke my microscope; *I* always hurry to finish the experiment on time.
6. If *one* is to finish the program for the computer on time, *he* probably will have to work overtime. (or) If *you* (or *we*) are to finish the program for the computer on time, *you* (or *we*) probably will have to work overtime.
7. *You* will receive your check from the comptroller after *you* complete the job. (Verb change)
8. *Anyone* can fill in the application if *he* (or *she*) concentrates. (Verb change) (or) *You* can fill in the application if *you* concentrate.
9. *Everybody* should develop a resumé, which *he* needs when applying for a job. (Verb change) (or) *You* should develop a resumé, which *you* need when applying for a job.
10. When *the contractors* finished with the shopping center project, *they* moved on to the next assignment—building a high-rise apartment.

Feedback 11-I

There may be more than one correct answer. If your responses differ, check with your instructor.

1. *I* asked the employment office where *I* could find an efficient assistant.
2. *Mr. Blevins* did the work *he* must do to qualify for the job promotion.
3. *We* checked the patients' charts, which *we* must look at every day.

4. *His* calculator was not working; therefore, *he* must check the warranty.
5. If *one* is to get paid for overtime, *he* first must work a 40-hour week. (or) If *you* are to get paid for overtime, *you* first must work a 40-hour week. (Verb change)
6. *You* will get a raise as soon as *you* pass the competency examination. (Verb change)
7. *Anyone* can do the job correctly if *he* (or *she*) reads the manual. (Verb change) (or) *You* can do the job correctly if *you* read the manual.
8. *Everybody* brought a stock portfolio, which *he* (or *she*) needs to sit on the Stock Exchange. (Verb change)
9. When *they* completed the job assignment, *they* went on to the next task. (or) When *you* completed the job assignment, *you* went on to the next task.
10. When a *person* goes for an interview, *he* (or *she*) should dress appropriately. (or) When *you* go for an interview, *you* should dress appropriately. (Verb change)

Feedback 11-J

There may be more than one correct answer. If your responses differ, check with your instructor.

A personnel manager may try in several ways to upset a job applicant to see how *he* handles an awkward situation. *He* may offer the interviewee coffee but no cream or sugar. Another trick is for the interviewer to have the applicant stand awkwardly without offering a seat. It would be wise for a prospective employee to be aware of possible attempts to frustrate *him.*

Feedback 11-K

There may be more than one correct answer. If your responses differ, check with your instructor.

1. (Colleges). . . They
2. (club). . . its
3. (Businessmen) . . . They
4. (Every one) . . . her
5. (All) . . . their
6. (group) . . . its
7. (company) . . . It
8. (We) . . . our
9. (accountant) . . . he (or she) *strives* (singular verb)
10. (team) . . . It was (singular verb)

Feedback 11-L

There may be more than one correct answer. If your responses differ, check with your instructor.

1. (agencies) . . . they
2. (board) . . . its
3. (Salespersons) . . . They

4. Every one . . . his or her
5. Both . . . their
6. group . . . its
7. company . . . its
8. We . . . our
9. server . . . He or she *knows* (singular verb)
10. staff . . . it

Feedback 11-M

Alternative possibilities appear in parentheses. To be correct, your paragraph must be consistent with either all of the italicized words or all of the words in parentheses. Other correct answers are possible. Check with your instructor if your responses differ.

Nurses (A nurse) *have* (has) many jobs to perform during a typical day. *They* (He or she) must check the patients' temperature and blood pressure at regular intervals. *They* (He or she) should also ask the patients if *they* (they) are having any complications. Furthermore, *nurses* (a nurse) must administer medication to *their* (his or her) patients and enter the dosage on *their* (their) charts. Truly, *nurses* (a nurse) *have* (has) a busy schedule.

Feedback 11-N

1. *The public relations officer planned the tour of the industry,* and the group of engineers arrived at 9:00 A.M. (Voice)
2. The tour guide was a petroleum engineer, and she *took* the group around the plant. (Tense)
3. The public relations officer planned the industrial tour, and *he* (or *she*) set up an itinerary for the group. (Number)
4. Anyone could participate in the tour if *he* (or *she*) wanted to. (Person)
5. The group took the tour; then there *was* a question-and-answer period. (Tense)
6. The engineers seemed to enjoy the tour; *they* got a complete view of the plant's operation. (Person and number)
7. The engineers enjoyed the tour; *they got* a complete view of the plant's operation. (Voice)
8. As the members of the group entered the processing room, *they saw* large vats. (Voice)
9. After the tour was completed, the guide *invited* the group to have lunch. (Tense)
10. Everyone should take advantage of such a tour if *he* (or *she*) would like to learn more about a company. (Number)

Feedback 11-O

There may be more than one correct answer. If your responses differ, check with your instructor.

1. VOICE: The salesman worked to meet his quota, and *he opened* 10 new accounts in one week.
2. TENSE: Bradford will repair the television, and Stillman *will* help him.
3. VOICE: We transported the tire to Indianapolis, and (*we*) *charged* it to the manufacturer.
4. VOICE: Sue totaled the daily receipts but (*she*) *made* several errors.

5. VOICE: Since Ross will retire at the conclusion of this project, *he offered* no suggestions.
6. VOICE: The supervisor installed and tested the new equipment. Next month, *he will* put it into operation.
7. TENSE: The hotel manager made arrangements for the convention, and his assistant *requested* the confirmations.
8. VOICE: *Murphy programmed* the computer, and he checked it for bugs yesterday.
9. NUMBER: A police officer holds a very important job in the community. Many people depend upon *him* (or *her*) for help.
10. PERSON: Because everyone works hard, *he* (or *she*) should take a midmorning break to relax.
11. VOICE: When the boss saw that an employee was sick, *he sent her* home to rest.
12. VOICE: Before I started to drive, I *fastened* my seat belt and *released* the emergency brake.
13. NUMBER: A tourist can stop frequently if *he* (or *she*) drives *his* (or *her*) own car.
14. VOICE: A person does well in an interview if *he* (or *she*) prepares ahead of time.
15. NUMBER: People should not trust rumors without checking for *themselves.*

Feedback 11-P

There may be more than one response. If your responses are different, check them with your instructor.

Travelers should welcome heightened security at airports (*voice*). Despite the inconvenience, many of the measures provide (*tense*) the assurance that flights will be as safe as humanly possible, and they (*number*) will take off on time if passengers follow a few commonsense guidelines. Travelers should pack sensibly (*voice*) and get to the airport well ahead of their (*person*) flight. Fellow passengers and airport personnel appreciate travelers who keep themselves informed (*voice*).

Feedback 11-Q

There may be more than one response. If your responses are different, check them with your instructor.

Even though many students today have extensive experience sending email, some students do not understand the importance of format and clarity when sending electronic communication. Email has several nuances that make it different than oral communication; for instance, it is impossible for readers to interpret tone or get any other clues about the communication from nonverbal clues, such as the speaker's inflection, body language, and gestures. Many electronic communicators try to replace the lack of body language with icons that indicate laughing, rolling the eyes, and angry expressions, but these icons are woefully inadequate since not all readers are familiar with these symbols, and they may misinterpret them. Furthermore, some students do not understand the importance of using a subject line and signing their email, which is especially important in professional and educational communication since some of these people receive hundreds of email messages on a daily basis. It is important for students to approach their email with instructors and professional contacts much as they would approach a formal report or memo, by organizing their information carefully, keeping the message concise yet thorough, and considering the readers and then writing specifically to meet the needs and expectations of their audience.

MODULE 12

Clarity

Objective: This module covers four areas that will help you prevent any misunderstanding in your writing.

Upon completion of this module, you will be able:

- To identify and to correct unclear pronoun reference.
- To identify and to correct unclear or misplaced modifiers.
- To define certain confusing pairs of words.
- To identify and to correct problems in five areas of parallel construction.

DIAGNOSTIC EXERCISE

Clarify pronoun, indefinite references, and misplaced modifiers.

1. We went to see the president and the vice president of the college because she wanted to hear our concerns.
2. The technician relayed my concerns to the supervisor, but he seemed unconcerned about the dilemma.
3. At DTCC, they have recently improved the facilities.
4. In the Rehoboth area, they have many outlet stores.
5. After collapsing from exhaustion, she took her daughter to the emergency room.

Underline the correct word.

1. If you visit the financial aid office, they will (advice/advise) you of the status of the funds.
2. Although the report has some limitations, (its/it's) well-written and thorough.
3. We hope that by discussing the issue (further/farther) at our next meeting, we will reach a consensus.
4. They have (fewer/less) members this year than they did last year.
5. She plans to (accept/except) the promotion next week.

PART I: PRONOUN REFERENCE

One way to make sure your writing is clear is to shift your point of view from that of the writer to that of the reader. When you sit down to write, put yourself in the place of the person who is going to read what you write. The importance of this technique is illustrated by the following incident, which occurred in a chemical laboratory.

On going off duty one evening, the senior laboratory technician left the following note for his night relief man, who was new on the job: "The flasks on the table probably have some sodium residue in them. Discard residues into a beaker, but check for water. Keep an eye on the B.B. Better use a metal one."

The new night man asked himself, "What does 'check' mean? To add water? To remove water? What does the note mean by 'a metal one'? A metal B.B.? A metal beaker?"

Fortunately, the assistant guessed right. He chose a metal beaker. He removed all moisture from it, poured in the sodium residue, and kept the beaker away from the Bunsen burner, which burned with a hot gas flame.

Had the assistant done otherwise, the action of sodium on water could have released pure hydrogen. If heated by the burner, this highly volatile gas could have exploded and seriously injured him.

In another case, a technician in a big planing mill wrote the following instructions to the night shipping clerk, who was to send out a load of door frames and a load of window frames. "The door frames go by rail this time and the windows by motor express. Have them stacked on loading platform B for 6 A.M. pickup Tuesday. Put the others on the flats." The clerk wondered: "Were the doors or the windows to be stacked for pickup?" He guessed wrong and shipped the windows to Miami and the doors to Alaska. Loss to the company in shipping charges and man-hours amounted to hundreds of dollars before the mess was straightened out.

Had the technician been thinking of the shipping clerk, he would have written something like this: "The door frames go by Seaboard Rail to Miami. The windows go by Ace Express to Anchorage and should be stacked on platform B for 6 A.M. pickup Tuesday."

The doors and windows were shipped to the wrong places because of two pronouns. One was **them,** which referred to the noun **windows.** The second was **others,** which referred to the noun **doors.** The technician had not made it clear what the antecedents were. (You will remember that an *antecedent* is the noun that the pronoun refers to.)

Make sure every pronoun has a clear antecedent. Do not use a pronoun if there is the slightest doubt about what it refers to. This practice does not always cause expensive errors, but it does confuse readers and makes them stop and reread the sentence. This is reason enough to correct the sentence.

POOR: Mellon bumped his SUV against the wall of his carport, **which** he hadn't yet paid for.

Does *which* refer to the SUV or to the carport?

BETTER: Mellon bumped his SUV, which he hadn't yet paid for, against the wall of his carport.

POOR: Norden picked up the wrench, removed the nut, and handed **it** to Robert.

What does **it** refer to? Again, the reader is obstructed in his or her reading. In this case, the word **wrench** must be repeated, or it must be replaced by a synonym for **wrench.**

BETTER: Norden picked up the wrench, removed the nut, and handed **the tool** to Robert.

NOTE Never let a pronoun "float" in space, unconnected to some noun. Make sure it has a specific antecedent.

POOR: Complaining angrily, Rudolph wrote it up and sent it to the newspaper. (*What is* **it**?)

BETTER: Angrily, Rudolph wrote up his **complaint** and sent it to the newspaper.

POOR: Not until Fred had heard his uncle talk about the pay scales in drafting did he want to become **one.**

BETTER: Not until Fred had heard his uncle talk about the pay scales in drafting did he want to become a **draftsman.**

ACTIVITY 12-A: Pronoun Reference

Rewrite these sentences to clarify the pronoun reference.

1. I went with Brad to Phil's place because *he* wanted company.
2. Tack an overlay on the drawing board to keep *it* clean.
3. Peter spoke to the timekeeper, and *he* was very rude.
4. The division manager always favored Swanson. *This* angered the other employees.
5. John showed the news reporter how to take good pictures, and *his* pictures turned out beautifully.
6. After the lab technician had trained an assistant, *she* enjoyed *her* work more.
7. Gail hired the waitress, *which* was a wise move on her part.
8. Plant three-foot azaleas in front of the seven-foot rhododendrons to make *them* stand out.
9. To get the students' grades to them as soon as possible, we feed *them* into a computer.
10. The policeman stopped the man who was speeding down the highway, and *he* was really mad.

Check your responses in Feedback 12-A at the end of this module. If your responses were correct, proceed to Other Indefinite References. If you missed any, do Activity 12-B.

ACTIVITY 12-B: Pronoun Reference

Rewrite these sentences to clarify the pronoun reference.

1. My problems in math were serious. Although my progress in English and reading was good, *this* brought down my overall record.
2. John likes his supervisor, and *he* is good to him.
3. As the ferry boat approaches the tugboat, *it* blows a warning.
4. After the electrician installed new switches in the motors, *some of them* did not work.
5. The car ran off the highway when the tire blew; *this* was a problem.
6. The beets were pickled, which made them last longer.

7. John is not only a very good lecturer but also a very good economist. I have always wanted to be *one.*
8. When the legislature convened, two members favored and three members opposed the bill; I agreed with *them.*
9. I almost signed a contract to buy a Mack, my favorite truck; then GM made me an attractive offer. *This* made me think a while longer.
10. A patient should work very closely with his doctor; then *he* would take an interest in *his* welfare.

Check your responses in Feedback 12-B at the end of this module. If your responses were correct, proceed to Other Indefinite References. If you missed any, review before continuing.

Other Indefinite References

- Try to avoid the use of the indefinite pronouns **it** and **they.**

POOR: In the college handbook, **it** lists the holidays we get in the spring semester.
BETTER: The college handbook lists the holidays we get in the spring semester.
POOR: At DuPont, **they** provide very reasonable health insurance.
BETTER: DuPont provides very reasonable health insurance.

- Also avoid explaining a term with ". . . is when" and ". . . is where."

POOR: A bear market **is when** stock prices fall.
BETTER: Stock prices fall in a bear market.
POOR: Early spring **is when** most new construction projects begin.
BETTER: Most new construction projects begin in early spring.
POOR: The fire station **is where** we vote for candidates for local offices.
BETTER: We vote for candidates for local offices at the fire station.

ACTIVITY 12-C: Indefinite References

Eliminate the vague **it, they, is when,** and **is where** in the following sentences.

1. At Aero International, **they** have an excellent in-service training program.
2. In the editorial in today's paper, **it** discusses the controversial busing issue.
3. In Oregon, **they** have passed a law which encourages the recycling of waste materials.
4. In the instruction manual, **it** explains how to operate an oscilloscope.
5. Inflation **is when** the dollar is worth less than previously.
6. Toxemia **is when** fluid builds up in the body.
7. At the Farmers' Auction Block **is where** they have many buyers of truck crops.

8. In the specifications, **it** clearly states the type of muffler to use on my car.
9. Talking on a telephone **is when** a secretary demonstrates finesse.
10. At the hardware center, **they** have all kinds of electrical equipment available.

Check your responses in Feedback 12-C at the end of this module. If your responses are correct, proceed to Part II. If you missed any, review the Indefinite References and then do Activity 12-D.

ACTIVITY 12-D: Indefinite References

Eliminate the vague **it, they, is when,** and **is where** in the following sentences.

1. On the drawing board **is where** this whole idea was conceived.
2. On Wall Street in New York, **they** have many brokerage companies.
3. In our Nursing Department's weight control booklet, **it** catalogs the approximate number of calories in all foods.
4. Surveying a plot of ground **is when** the boundaries are legally established.
5. For safety on all these switch boxes, **they** have a master lever.
6. In a computer, **it** stores information that may be used later.
7. The sign of a good switchboard operator **is when** he can make himself easily understood.
8. When tuning an engine, **it** requires time and patience.
9. Driving onto the freeway **is where** we must be alert.
10. On the editorial page in the evening paper, **they** printed many letters to the editor suggesting ways to resolve our tax problems.

Check your responses in Feedback 12-D at the end of this module. If your responses were correct, proceed to Part II. If you missed any, review before continuing.

PART II: MISPLACED AND UNCLEAR MODIFIERS

- Place a **modifier,** a word, phrase, or clause used to describe or enhance the meaning of another word in the sentence, *next* to the word it modifies. A modifier in the wrong place can cause confusion. Note the misplaced modifiers in the examples below and the various ways to unscramble the confusion and make the meaning clear.

MISPLACED
CLAUSE: Marjory waited to put her ring on in the bus, *which I had just bought her.* (*Bought the bus?*)
CLARIFIED: Marjory waited until we got on the bus to put on the ring, which I had just bought her.

MISPLACED PHRASE: *Earning time-and-a-half,* Joe was certain his secretary would remain on the job. (*Who was earning time-and-a-half? The secretary? Joe?*)

CLARIFIED: Joe was certain that his secretary, earning time-and-a-half, would remain on the job.
or
Earning time-and-a-half, the secretary assured Joe that she would remain on the job.

MISPLACED PHRASE: *To fly in to the airstrip,* the mountains must be crossed. (*Mountains flying?*)

CLARIFIED: To fly in to the airstrip, the pilot must cross the mountains.

NOTE Misplaced modifiers often occur with the passive voice, as in the last sentence above.

To avoid confusion, place the modifying clause or phrase immediately next to the word it modifies. If you begin a sentence with a verbal phrase, make sure the phrase modifies the subject of the sentence.

- Some nouns exist only in the careless writer's imagination. They are not actually expressed in the sentence. These nouns must be added to the sentence to keep the reader from stumbling.

POOR: *Excused at 3:30,* the office Christmas party began. (*Was the party excused?*)

BETTER: Excused at 3:30, the staff attended the office Christmas party.

NOTE Do not leave the reader guessing at what you are trying to say. Make sure that each pronoun has a clear antecedent and that each modifying phrase has a noun to link to.

POOR: *Despite typing all day,* no letters were finished. (*Did the letters type?*)

BETTER: Despite typing all day, the secretary did not finish any letters.

ACTIVITY 12-E: Misplaced Modifiers

Eliminate confusion by repositioning misplaced phrases or clauses next to the words they modify. Some rewording may also be necessary.

1. At the age of five, my father decided I would be an engineer.
2. Concerned about the grain market, a call was made to the broker.
3. While low on ink, James continued to operate the printer.

4. Worn thin from use, Bill replaced the shims on the wheels.
5. Although writing for several years, no articles have been published.
6. A photocopier was advertised in *The Reporter,* which was expensive.
7. Emily is writing a report on filmmaking in the college library.
8. The shoplifter admitted that she had stolen the dress while talking to the security officer.
9. Arriving at the police station, my license was returned.
10. I received instructions for operating the 10-ton crane by mail.

Check your responses in Feedback 12-E at the end of this module. If your responses were correct, proceed to Part III. If you missed any, review and do Activity 12-F.

ACTIVITY 12-F: **Misplaced Modifiers**

Eliminate confusion by repositioning misplaced phrases or clauses next to the words they modify. Some rewording may also be necessary.

1. Mrs. Allen complained about the lengthy report she had word processed while riding home in her car pool.
2. To reserve a room, the motel was called.
3. He repaired the computer for the boss's secretary, a run-down old model that needed replacing.
4. Feeling very sick at work, the company dispensary was where Jim saw the doctor.
5. Puzzled about the falloff in the current, the transformer was checked.
6. Smiling courteously, her offer was accepted.
7. Coming in on the bus, the factory is seen off to the left.
8. Not enough attention is devoted to quality-control instruction, giving seminars only once every three months.
9. He ordered a special lubricant for the 2-ton turbine shipped from New York.
10. The driver said he would never carry a firearm in a truck that was loaded.

Check your responses in Feedback 12-F at the end of this module. If your responses were correct, proceed to Part III. If you missed any, review before continuing.

PART III: WORD USAGE

Be careful about the words you use. Be sure that the word you choose means exactly what you want it to mean. Below is a list of pairs of words that are often confused. Study the definitions and examples carefully.

1. **Good** is usually an *adjective.*
   He is a **good** basketball player.

   Well is normally an *adverb.*
   He did **well** in chemistry.

   Well is an adjective only when it pertains to health.
   He doesn't feel **well.**

2. **Respectively,** an *adverb,* means *in the order given.*
   The board of directors appointed Harrison, Bonner, and Cook, **respectively,** as manager, comptroller, and secretary of the firm.

   Respectfully, an *adverb,* means *showing respect.*
   The salesman nodded **respectfully** to the manager and left the office.

3. **Precede,** a *verb,* means *to go before.*
   The sales meeting **preceded** the afternoon luncheon.

   Proceed, a *verb,* means *to advance or move forward.*
   They **proceeded** through the front door of the courthouse.

4. **Altogether** is most commonly used as an *adverb,* meaning *wholly, thoroughly.*
   He was **altogether** too emotional a person for that job.

   All together usually means *in a group, collectively.*
   They went **all together** to the graduation.

5. **Accept,** a *verb,* means *to take or receive something.*
   I will **accept** your job offer.

   Except, used most frequently as a *preposition,* means *with the exception of.*
   Everybody quit at five o'clock **except** me.

6. **Amount,** as a *noun* meaning *quantity,* is used with reference to things that *cannot be counted.*
   We have a tremendous **amount** of work to do.

   Number, as a *noun,* refers to *items that can be counted.*
   A large **number** of motorists were held up by the parade.

7. **About,** usually an *adverb,* means *approximately.*
   I made **about** $40 on the trade.

   Around, an *adverb* or a *preposition,* means *circling.*
   He went **around** the plant collecting union dues.

8. **Persecute,** a *verb,* means *to afflict or harass.*
   The Nazis **persecuted** the Jews in Germany.

Prosecute, a *verb,* means *to seek to accomplish by legal process.*
The district attorney will **prosecute** the defendant on a charge of fraud.

9. **Illegible,** an *adjective,* means *unreadable.*
Elaine's handwriting is **illegible.**

Ineligible, an *adjective,* means *not qualified.*
He was **ineligible** for a license because he had just moved to the state.

10. **Affect,** a *verb,* means *to influence.*
His action won't **affect** my decision.

Effect, most commonly used as a *noun,* means *result.*
The report had a bad **effect** on the morale of the office.

11. **Between,** a *preposition,* refers to the space or relationship between *two* persons or things.
The new accountant caused friction **between** the pay clerk and the timekeeper.

Among, also a *preposition,* refers to *three or more* persons or things.
The investigator caused trouble **among** all members of the staff.

12. **Uninterested,** an *adjective,* means *without interest or indifferent.*
He was **uninterested** in merchandising as a career.

Disinterested, also an *adjective,* means *having no desire for personal gain, impartial.*
The judge was wholly **disinterested** and evicted the dishonest attorney from the courtroom.

13. **Imply,** a *verb,* means *to suggest or hint to someone.* (The person speaking *implies.*)
Braden **implied** to me that he wanted a ride home.

Infer is just the opposite, a *verb* meaning *to perceive what is being suggested by someone else.* (The person listening *infers.*)
I **inferred** from what Braden said that he wanted a ride home.

Imply is an expression of *projecting;* **infer** is an expression of *receiving.*

14. **Complement,** a *noun* or *verb,* means *to fill up or complete.*
Mrs. Smith, a polite woman, provided a perfect **complement** to her successful husband.

Compliment, a *noun* or *verb,* means *praise.*
He showered **compliments** on her for her typing speed.

15. **Fewer,** an *adjective,* used with plural nouns, refers to the *number* of items or things that can be counted.
    The plant produced **fewer** cars in August than in July.

    Less, an *adjective,* refers to the *amount* of something that cannot be counted.
    There was **less** concrete in the mixer than he had estimated.

16. **Farther,** an *adverb,* usually refers to *physical distance.*
    He drove **farther** down the road.

    Further, an *adverb,* means *more distant in degree, time, or space.* It also means *to a greater extent* or *in addition.*
    The chairman will pursue the salary question **further.**

17. **To,** a *preposition,* means *in the direction of.*
    The electronics expert walked **to** the computer lab.

    Too, an *adverb,* means *also* or *extremely.*
    The new laser printer is **too** expensive.

18. **Its** is a *possessive pronoun.*
    The computer had **its** cover removed.

    It's is a *contraction* for *it is.*
    It's a well-written report.

19. **Advice,** a *noun,* means *counsel* or *information.*
    The employment counselor gave the graduate some good **advice.**

    Advise, a *verb,* means *to counsel.*
    The employment counselor will **advise** the new graduate.

20. **Got,** a *verb,* is past tense of **get** and means *obtained* or *acquired.*
    The technician **got** a raise.

    Have, a *verb,* means *to possess.*
    The technician will **have** a raise by next week

NOTE It is incorrect to use **got** as *became.* ("He **got** arrested" is wrong.) It is also incorrect to use **have got to** in place of *must.* ("I **have got to** go now" is wrong.)

ACTIVITY 12-G: Word Usage

Underline the correct word in the parentheses.

1. The first shift will (precede/proceed) the second shift at the pay window.
2. Jack, Joe, and Henry, (respectfully/respectively), covered the sales territories of Wilmington, Newark, and Philadelphia.

3. The TV advertisement brought (fewer/less) responses than expected.
4. Hearing the labor boss, members of the union (implied/inferred) that there will be a meeting tomorrow.
5. Left out in the rain, the pages of her report were almost (ineligible/illegible).
6. He performed very (good/well) as a master of ceremonies.
7. The treasurer distributed the money (among/between) the head of the board of directors and the representative of all the stockholders.
8. The price rise had a bad (affect/effect) on sales.
9. Please (except/accept) my apologies for disturbing you.
10. The company will pursue the matter (further/farther).
11. The bankruptcy referee was (disinterested/uninterested) and made no effort to show favoritism to the creditors.
12. (It's/Its) (to/too/two) soon to make a decision.
13. The professional counselor's (advise/advice) was good.
14. The state will (persecute/prosecute) him in the superior court.

Check your responses in Feedback 12-G at the end of this module. If your responses were correct, proceed to Part IV. If you missed any, review Part III and then do Activity 12-H.

ACTIVITY 12-H: Word Usage

Underline the correct word in the parentheses.

1. His letter of recommendation was very (complimentary/complementary).
2. The members of the jury could not agree (between/among) themselves.
3. The (further/farther) he drove, the worse the storm became.
4. Inflation increased the cost of steel (around/about) 10 percent.
5. The police officers will (precede/proceed) to their squad cars.
6. The students were (disinterested/uninterested) in seeking a B.A. degree.
7. (Less/Fewer) motorists are putting up with freeway traffic than before.
8. She did very (good/well) in writing the memo.
9. The president (has/has got) to make a decision.
10. The table had (it's/its) leg broken.
11. The used Chevrolet is priced (all together/altogether) too high.
12. The nonunion members of the company were (prosecuted/persecuted) by the union leaders.
13. He ordered all the options (accept/except) power windows.
14. The senior employees can (advise/advice) you.
15. Without an associate degree, he was considered (ineligible/illegible) for the position.

Check your responses in Feedback 12-H at the end of this module. If your responses were correct, proceed to Part IV. If you missed any, review before continuing.

PART IV: PARALLEL CONSTRUCTION

A good sentence functions like a well-lubricated car, carrying the reader from one thought to the next without any squeaks or rattles. A sentence that draws attention to its wording—no matter how beautifully written—is a BAD SENTENCE. The reader should be wholly unaware of the passage of words. Sometimes the jolts in a sentence that interrupt the reader's flow of thought are errors in spelling or grammar. Often, however, they are structural blunders, such as violations of parallel construction. These occur most often in sentences using words joined by **and** or **or.** We will look at three types.

1. *Parallel construction with the word **and.*** Words or word groups preceding and following the word **and** should be similar in form. They should both be gerunds, for example, or infinitives or clauses or the same part of speech.

   POOR: I like **engineering** and **to fish.** (Here a gerund, *engineering,* is mistakenly paired with an infinitive phrase, *to fish.*)

   BETTER: I like **engineering** and **fishing.** (Two gerunds)

   POOR: The workers began to feel as **if they had confidence** and **happy.** (A clause, *as if they had confidence,* is mistakenly paired with an adjective, *happy.*)

   BETTER: The workers began to feel **confident** and **happy.** (Two adjectives)

   POOR: Jefferson plans **to study engineering** and then **going to work** at NCR. (Here an infinitive, *to study,* is paired with the verbal *going.*)

   BETTER: Jefferson plans **to study engineering** and then **to go to work** at NCR. (Two infinitive phrases)

2. *Parallel construction in lists.* Technical people often have to draw up lists. The items on a list should be parallel. Notice the two items in the following list which do not match the others:

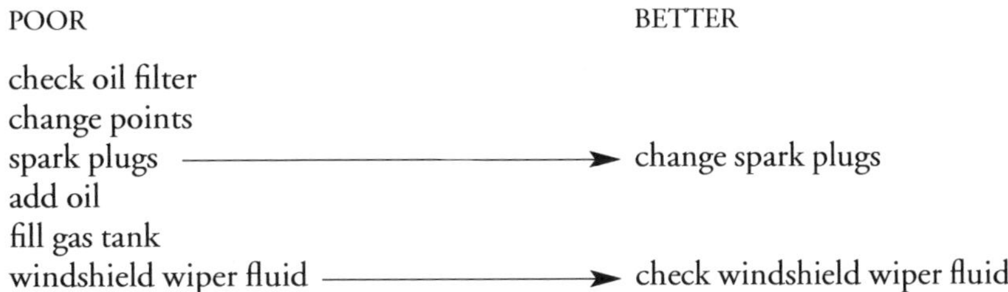

POOR
BETTER
check oil filter
change points
spark plugs
change spark plugs
add oil
fill gas tank
windshield wiper fluid
check windshield wiper fluid

3. *Parallel construction in a series.* A series of words or word groups in a sentence should maintain the same form.

PARALLELISM BY NOUN

POOR: Desmond had ability, knowledge, honesty, and **was courageous.** (Here an adjective, *courageous,* has been mixed in with a series of nouns. As a result, the sentence has a bad "rattle.")

BETTER: Desmond had **ability, knowledge, honesty,** and **courage.** (All nouns)

PARALLELISM BY ADJECTIVE

POOR: Desmond was **intelligent, able, honest,** and **had courage.** (Here a verb phrase, *had courage,* has been mixed in with a series of adjectives.)

BETTER: Desmond was **intelligent, able, honest,** and **courageous.** (All adjectives)

PARALLELISM BY PHRASE

POOR: Desmond spoke **on the same subject, to the same people, when the time was identical.** (Here a clause, *when the time was identical,* has been mixed in with phrases.)

BETTER: Desmond spoke **on the same subject, to the same people,** and **at the same time.** (All prepositional phrases)

PARALLELISM BY CLAUSE

POOR: Desmond, **who was intelligent** and **had honesty,** was hired for the position.

BETTER: Desmond, **who was intelligent and who was also honest,** was hired for the position. (Similar clause structures)

PARALLELISM BY SENTENCE

POOR: To operate the projector, first **plug the cord** into the electrical outlet. Then the **slide tray should be positioned** on zero. Next, **you turn** the fan on. After that the **lamp should be** switched on. Finally, **advance** to the first slide. (Note the mixture of second person, second person commands, and passive voice.)

BETTER: To operate the slide projector, first **plug the cord** into the electrical outlet. Then **position the tray** on zero. Next, **turn on the fan.** After that, **switch on the lamp.** Finally, **advance** to the first slide. (All second person commands in the active voice.)

ACTIVITY 12-I: Parallel Construction

Draw a line through the words or word groups that are not parallel. Write the correct form above the line.

1. He has been taking instruction in drafting, surveying, and how to operate a die-casting machine.
2. The transportation chief supervises the service crew, and he is giving directions to the drivers.
3. The counselor advises the students on preparing schedules, getting financial aid, and to carry reasonable course loads.
4. We saw that Borden's Porsche is beautiful, that it is a lot of excitement to drive, and brand new.
5. During our class in layout and design, we learned how to lay out ads, to develop a Web page; and proofreading.
6. To become a successful business administrator, a person must have ability, patience, and be enthusiastic.
7. Our classes were held on Wednesday afternoon, Thursday evening, and we also attended every other Friday morning.
8. On weekends, the employees usually tend to their gardens, fix up their houses, go shopping, exchanging visits with their relatives.
9. The students' grades were entered in the computer, recorded in Banner, and the students received them as an e-mail.
10. In the emergency room at the hospital, a nurse looked at my eyes, checked my throat, a thermometer was put in my mouth, and she took my blood pressure.

Check your responses in Feedback 12-I at the end of this module. If your responses were correct, proceed to the section on Parallel Construction in Outlines. If you missed any, review and then do Activity 12-J.

ACTIVITY 12-J: Parallel Construction

Draw a line through the word or word groups that are not parallel. Write the correct form above the line.

1. Answering the phone, typing letters, e-mails that must be answered, and filing documents are only parts of my assistant's job.
2. We learned how to gauge points, how to adjust a carburetor, checking the spark plugs, and how to grease a car.
3. To make a good impression during an interview, act like a lady or a gentleman, speak as well as you can, and dressing is very important.

4. We saw the bulldozer when it pushed down the trees, when it cleared the lot, and it leveled a ridge toward the center.
5. An advertisement should be written to be easily understood, to attract attention, a little color would help, and to be sensational.
6. Helen particularly enjoys sterilizing equipment, preparing mediums, growing cultures, and the analysis of results.
7. When we arrived at the Student Center, we were cordially welcomed, questioned, and someone gave us counsel.
8. To listen, to think, and speaking clearly are the three primary responsibilities of a good speaker.
9. During a political campaign, everyone should think about political views, talk to the candidates, and then he votes for his choice.
10. Regardless of your technology, you will constantly be involved with communications—reading, writing, an occasional speech.

Check your responses in Feedback 12-J at the end of this module. If your responses were correct, proceed to the section on Parallel Construction in Outlines. If you missed any, review before continuing.

Parallel Construction in Outlines

One area where parallel construction is of great importance is in outlines. When you make an outline, check to see that the items are equal in grammatical structure; that is, make sure its elements are all nouns or noun phrases, all verbs or verb phrases, etc.

ACTIVITY 12-K: Parallel Construction in Outlines

In the following outline, draw a line through the items that are not parallel. Write the correct form above the line.

Proper Telephone Techniques for Businesses

1. Answer on first or second ring
2. Identify company
3. Be sure to identify yourself
4. Politeness and friendliness
5. Respond helpfully
6. Product and service information given
7. Close call courteously

Check your responses in Feedback 12-K. If your responses were correct, proceed to the section on Parallel Construction in Correlatives. If you missed any, do Activity 12-L.

ACTIVITY 12-L: Parallel Construction in Outlines

In the following outline, draw a line through the items that are not parallel. Write the correct form above the line.

Proper Telephone Techniques in Business

1. Answering on first or second ring
2. Identify company
3. Identifying yourself
4. Being polite and friendly
5. Helpfulness
6. Giving product and service information
7. Close call courteously

Check your responses in Feedback 12-L. If your responses were correct, proceed to the section on Parallel Construction in Correlatives. If you missed any, review before continuing.

Parallel Construction in Correlatives

Correlatives are conjunctions that are usually used in pairs. Here are the most common ones:

CORRELATIVES

not only . . . but also
either . . . or
neither . . . nor
both . . . and
whether . . . or

Parallel construction is also important when correlatives are used. The wording that follows the first correlative must be in the same form as that which follows the second correlative.

NOT PARALLEL: He was **not only** courteous to supervisors **but also** he went out of his way to be pleasant to fellow employees.

Since an adjective *courteous* follows **not only,** an adjective must, therefore, also follow **but also.**

PARALLEL: He was **not only** courteous to supervisors **but also** pleasant to fellow employees.

NOT PARALLEL: Eddie was **either** dodging the sheriff **or** he would buy everybody in town a drink.

PARALLEL: Eddie was **either** dodging the sheriff **or** buying everybody in town a drink.

NOT PARALLEL: He was **neither** somebody who was getting ahead **nor** putting anything by.

PARALLEL: He was **neither** getting ahead **nor** putting anything by.

NOT PARALLEL: She **either** was angry **or** upset.

PARALLEL: She was **either** angry **or** upset.

ACTIVITY 12-M: Correlatives

Correct the sentence by using parallel word groups with the correlatives.

1. She was both worried at the employee's absence and became furious at John.
2. Whether I go to the business conference or if you should be going makes no difference to me.
3. She was not only efficient but also had a great deal of attractiveness.
4. I am neither interested in the job nor is Baltimore a town I would be eager to live in.
5. We have good luck growing not only Fordhook lima beans but also Burpee limas produce a good crop.
6. She was concerned whether to accept the offer at the hospital or it may be better to continue in school toward a degree.
7. Before the contractor lays the foundation, we will either increase the size of the two bedrooms or another plan will be chosen.
8. The mechanic checked both the oil dipstick and gave special attention to the right front tire.
9. After the jury foreman pronounced the verdict, the judge was neither lenient about the defendant's sentence nor did he become severe.
10. A swimming pool at a motel either supplies desired recreation or advertising and promotion is improved.

Check your responses in Feedback 12-M at the end of this module. If your responses were correct, proceed to Activity 12-O. If you missed any, review and then do Activity 12-N.

ACTIVITY 12-N: Correlatives

Correct the sentences by using parallel word groups.

1. The excavated area not only filled in nearly full from the heavy rains but a lot from the sidewalls trickled in.
2. Figuring income taxes has become so complicated that the average wage earner will either hire an accountant or he can buy a computer program.

3. This applicant is very good at both answering the phone and her ability to create spreadsheets is very good too.
4. The decrease in electrical power lies neither in the fuse box nor does there seem to be anything wrong with the wires.
5. We are concerned whether to employ a nurse to live at home or my grandfather may do better in a long-term care facility.
6. These men either operate the precision machines or they are good at assembling the equipment.
7. On most farms, a soil sample not only gives the farmer an idea about the condition of his field but also he can plan his crop rotation better.
8. A police officer is both a regulator of law and order and he performs many other services for people.
9. A computer cannot produce an accurate result if either the facts are entered inaccurately or if the figures are entered incorrectly too.
10. The engineers debated whether the old aqueduct would be used for an increase in service or should they build a new one.

Check your responses in Feedback 12-N at the end of this module.

ACTIVITY 12-O: **Editing Practice**

Edit the following paragraph to eliminate problems in pronoun reference, agreement, word usage, and parallel structure.

Clarity is critical for comprehension in business and technical writing because it can create expensive problems for a company. Clear, correct writing has a major affect both on instructions and it can cause a financial burden among a company and its vendors. When it is not written clearly, it delays production and delivery of services. Companies trying to reduce the amount of problems resulting from poor written communication frequently forbid employees to use pronouns in their documents and to require them to attend business writing workshops.

Check your responses in Feedback 12-O at the end of this module.

ACTIVITY 12-P: **Editing Practice**

Edit the following paragraph to eliminate problems in pronoun reference, agreement, word usage, and parallel structure.

Technology can be an asset in the academic arena, but it also has its critics. For example, some feel that the emergence of e-learning represents degradation of the educational institution. Others disagree, and they point out that distance learning aided by technology not only significantly increases access to education for many students, but also it provides flexible scheduling, which is increasingly necessary as the amount of students who are returning to school after many years in the workforce increases.

Both proponents of e-learning and it's critics except that technology will continue to be implemented in educational institutions at a rapidly growing rate, and they insist that it is important for educators too use the tools available and allowing technology to compliment existing courses, but not rely on them so heavily that the learning environment becomes sterile and one-dimensional.

Check your responses in Feedback 12-P at the end of this module.

DIAGNOSTIC FEEDBACK

Clarify pronoun, indefinite references, and misplaced modifiers.

1. Because the president wanted to hear our concerns, we went to see her and the vice president of the college.
2. Although the technician seemed unconcerned about the dilemma, he relayed my concerns to the supervisor.
3. DTCC has recently improved the facilities.
4. The Rehoboth area has many outlet stores.
5. After her daughter collapsed from exhaustion, she took her to the emergency room.

Underline the correct word.

1. If you visit the financial aid office, they will (advice/advise) you of the status of the funds.
2. Although the report has some limitations, (its/it's) well-written and thorough.
3. We hope that by discussing the issue (further/farther) at our next meeting, we will reach a consensus.
4. They have (fewer/less) members this year than they did last year.
5. She plans to (accept/except) the promotion next week.

FEEDBACK FOR MODULE 12

Feedback 12-A

There may be more than one correct answer. If your responses differ, check with your instructor.

1. Because Brad wanted company, I went with him to Phil's place.
2. To keep the drawing board clean, tack an overlay on the board.
3. Peter spoke very rudely to the timekeeper.
4. Because the division manager always favored Swanson, the other employees were angry. (or) The division . . . Swanson. This action angered . . .

5. . . . the reporter's pictures turned out beautifully.
6. . . . the assistant enjoyed her work more. (or) . . . the technician enjoyed her work more.
7. Gail's hiring of the waitress was a wise move on her part. (or) Gail hired the waitress. This move was wise on her part.
8. . . . to make the rhododendrons (or the azaleas) stand out.
9. . . . we feed the grades into a computer.
10. . . . the policeman (or the man) was really mad.

Feedback 12-B

There may be more than one correct answer. If your responses differ, check with your instructor.

1. My problems in math were serious. Although my progress in English and reading was good, my math performance brought down my overall record.
2. John likes his supervisor, who is good to him.
3. The ferry boat blows a warning as it approaches the tugboat.
4. . . . some of the switches did not work.
5. . . . the tire was a problem.
6. Pickling the beets caused them to last longer. (or) The beets lasted longer because they were pickled.
7. . . . I have always wanted to be an economist (or a lecturer).
8. . . . I agreed with those who favored (or those who opposed).
9. . . . This offer made me think a while longer.
10. . . . the doctor would take an interest in the patient's welfare.

Feedback 12-C

There may be more than one correct answer. If your responses differ, check with your instructor.

1. Aero International has an excellent in-service training program.
2. The editorial in today's paper discusses the controversial busing problem.
3. Oregon has passed a law which encourages the recycling of waste materials.
4. The instruction manual explains how to operate an oscilloscope.
5. Inflation occurs when the dollar is worth less than previously.
6. Toxemia occurs when fluid builds up in the body.
7. Many buyers of truck crops are at the Farmers' Auction Block.
8. The specifications clearly state the type of muffler to use on my car.
9. A secretary demonstrates finesse when talking on the telephone.
10. The hardware center has all kinds of electrical equipment available. (or) All kinds of electrical equipment are available at the hardware center.

Feedback 12-D

There may be more than one correct answer. If your responses differ, check with your instructor.

1. This whole idea was conceived on the drawing board.
2. Wall Street in New York has many brokerage companies.
3. Our Nursing Department's weight control booklet catalogs the approximate number of calories in all foods.
4. The boundaries of a plot of ground are legally established by surveying.
5. All of these switch boxes have a master lever for safety.
6. A computer stores information that may be used later.
7. A good switchboard operator can make himself easily understood.
8. Tuning an engine requires time and patience.
9. We must be alert when driving onto the freeway.
10. The editorial page in the evening paper printed many letters to the editor suggesting ways to resolve our tax problems.

Feedback 12-E

There are other possible answers. If yours differ, check with your instructor.

1. *When I was five,* my father decided I would be an engineer.
2. Concerned about the grain market, *the investor* called his broker.
3. James continued to operate the printer while *it was low* on ink.
4. Bill replaced the wheel shims, *which were worn thin from use.*
5. Although writing for several years, *she* has never published any articles.
6. A photocopier, *which was expensive,* was advertised in *The Reporter.* (or) *An expensive photocopier.*
7. Emily is *in the college library* writing a report on filmmaking.
8. *While talking to the security officer,* the shoplifter admitted that she had stolen the dress.
9. Arriving at the police station, *I* had my license returned.
10. I received by mail instructions for operating the 10-ton crane.

Feedback 12-F

There may be more than one correct answer. If your responses differ, check with your instructor.

1. *While riding home in her car pool,* Mrs. Allen complained about the lengthy report she had word processed.
2. To reserve a room, *we* called the motel.
3. He repaired the computer, *a run-down old model that needed replacing,* which belonged to the boss's secretary.
4. *Feeling very sick at work,* Jim saw the doctor at the company dispensary.
5. *Puzzled about the falloff in current,* the operator checked the transformer.
6. *Smiling courteously,* Mary accepted her offer.
7. *Coming in on the bus,* tourists can see the factory off to the left.
8. Not enough attention is devoted to quality-control instruction since *the company holds seminars* only once every three months.
9. He ordered a special lubricant *shipped from New York* for the 2-ton turbine.
10. The driver said he would never carry in a truck *a firearm that was loaded.*

Feedback 12-G

1. precede
2. respectively
3. fewer
4. inferred
5. illegible
6. well
7. between
8. effect
9. accept
10. further
11. disinterested
12. It's, too
13. advice
14. prosecute

Feedback 12-H

1. complimentary
2. among
3. farther
4. about
5. proceed
6. uninterested
7. Fewer
8. well
9. has
10. its
11. altogether
12. persecuted
13. except
14. advise
15. ineligible

Feedback 12-I

1. . . . drafting, surveying, and *operating* a die-casting machine.
2. . . . supervises the service crew and *gives* directions ...
3. . . . preparing schedules, getting financial aid, and *carrying* reasonable course loads.
4. . . . that Borden's Porsche is beautiful, *that it is exciting to drive,* and *that it is* brand new.
5. . . . how to lay out ads, to develop a Web page, and to *proofread.*
6. . . . must have ability, patience, and *enthusiasm.*
7. . . . held on Wednesday afternoon, Thursday evening, and *every other* Friday morning.
8. . . . tend to their gardens, fix up their houses, go shopping, and *visit* with their relatives.
9. . . . entered in the computer, recorded in Banner, and *mailed to the students.*
10. . . . looked at my eyes, checked my throat, *put* a thermometer in my mouth, and *took* my blood pressure.

Feedback 12-J

1. Answering the phone, *typing* letters, *responding* to e-mails, and filing documents are only . . .
2. . . . how to gauge points, how to adjust a carburetor, *how to check the spark plugs,* and how to grease a car. (or) . . . how to gauge points, adjust a carburetor, check the spark plugs, and grease a car.
3. . . . act like a lady or a gentleman, speak as well as you can, and *dress well.*
4. . . . when it pushed down the trees, when it cleared the lot, and *when it leveled a ridge toward the center.*
5. . . . to be easily understood, to attract attention, *to be colorful,* and to be sensational.
6. . . . sterilizing equipment, preparing mediums, growing cultures, and *analyzing results.*
7. . . . we were cordially welcomed, questioned, and *counseled.*
8. To listen, to think, and *to speak clearly* are . . .
9. . . . think about political views, talk to the candidates, and then *vote for his choice.*
10. . . . reading, writing, and occasionally *speaking.*

Feedback 12-K

1. Answer on first or second ring
2. Identify company
3. *Identify yourself*
4. *Be polite and friendly*
5. Respond helpfully
6. *Give product and service information*
7. Close call courteously

Feedback 12-L

1. Answering on first or second ring
2. *Identifying company*
3. Identifying yourself
4. Being polite and friendly
5. *Being helpful*
6. Giving product and service information
7. *Closing call courteously*

Feedback 12-M

There may be more than one correct answer. If your responses differ, check with your instructor.

1. She was **both** *worried* at the employee's absence **and** *furious* at John.
2. **Whether** *I go* to the business conference **or** *you go* makes no difference to me.
3. She was **not only** *efficient* **but also** *attractive.*
4. I am **neither** *interested* in the job **nor** *eager* to live in Baltimore.
5. We have good luck growing **not only** *Fordhook lima beans* **but also** *Burpee limas.*
6. She was concerned **whether** *to accept* the offer at the hospital **or** *to continue* in school toward a degree.
7. Before the contractor lays the foundation, we will **either** *increase* the size of two bedrooms **or** *choose* another plan.
8. The mechanic checked **both** *the oil dipstick* **and** *the right front tire.*
9. After the jury foreman pronounced the verdict, the judge was **neither** *lenient* **nor** *severe* about the defendant's sentence.
10. A swimming pool at a motel **either** s*upplies some desired recreation* **or** *improves advertising and promotion.*

Feedback 12-N

There may be more than one correct answer. If your responses differ, check with your instructor.

1. The excavated area filled in **not only** *from the heavy rains* **but also** *from the trickle from the sidewalls.*

2. Figuring income taxes has become so complicated that the average wage earner will **either** *hire* an accountant **or** *purchase* a computer program.
3. This applicant is very good at **both** *typing* **and** *shorthand.*
4. The decrease in electrical power lies **neither** *in the circuit breaker* **nor** *in the wires.*
5. We are concerned **whether** *to employ* a nurse to live at home **or** *to put* my grandfather in a long-term care facility.
6. These men can **either** *operate* the precision machines **or** *assemble* the equipment.
7. On most farms, a soil sample gives the farmer an idea about **not only** *the condition* of his field **but also** *crop rotation.* (or) **not only** *gives* . . . **but also** *allows* him to plan . . .
8. A police officer is **both** *a regulator of law and order* **and** *a performer of many other services for people.*
9. A computer cannot produce an accurate result if **either** *the facts are entered inaccurately* **or** *the figures are entered incorrectly.*
10. The engineers debated **whether** *to use the old aqueduct* for an increase in service **or** *to build a new one.*

Feedback 12-O

Corrections regarding clarity, usage, and parallelism have been bolded. If your responses differ, check them with your instructor.

Clarity is critical for comprehension in business and technical writing because **unclear writing** can create expensive problems for a company. Unclear, incorrect writing has a major **effect** on instructions and can cause a financial burden **between** a company and its vendors. When **instructions** are not written clearly, they delay both the production and the delivery of services. Companies trying to reduce the **number** of problems resulting from poor written communication **often either** forbid employees to use pronouns in **business** documents **or require** them to attend business writing workshops.

Feedback 12-P

Corrections are shown in bold.

Technology can be an asset in the academic arena, but it also has its critics. For example, some feel that the emergence of e-learning represents degradation of the educational institution. Others disagree, and they point out that distance learning aided by technology not only significantly increases access to education for many students, but **also provides** flexible scheduling, which is increasingly necessary as the **number** of students who are returning to school after many years in the workforce increases. Both proponents of e-learning and **its** critics **accept** that technology will continue to be implemented in educational institutions at a rapidly growing rate, and they **both** insist that it is important for educators **to** use the tools available and **allow** technology to **complement** existing courses, but not **rely on technological advances** so heavily that the learning environment becomes sterile and one-dimensional.

MODULE 13

Accelerating Techniques

Objective: This module will help you make your writing more concise.

Upon completion of this module, you will be able:

- To eliminate unnecessary words in a sentence.
- To eliminate clichés and slang in writing samples.
- To combine like subjects and verbs for the purpose of brevity.
- To subordinate ideas.
- To reduce dependent clauses to single words.

DIAGNOSTIC EXERCISE

Without changing the meaning, reduce the italicized expressions to one or two words.

1. We like to spend time reading *in the evening hours.*
2. Electronic communication *has proved itself to be* fast and efficient.
3. We have *different variations* to choose from.
4. The conference is to be held *in the city of Chicago.*
5. *Due to the fact that* enrollment is down, we have cancelled three classes.

Use word reduction techniques to combine like subjects or verbs or reduce clauses to phrases.

1. Technicians must have excellent communication skills. They often communicate with varied audiences.
2. The computer lab is outdated. It is in need of renovations. The updates can't be made until we receive the grant money.
3. She did not do an outline so that she could save time writing the report.
4. The books required for the nursing program are very expensive. Books for just one semester can cost more than $1000. Buying used books is a way to cut the cost of books.
5. Randall did not like the corporate environment, and so he changed careers and became a teacher.

PART I: ELIMINATING UNNECESSARY WORDS

There is an old saying in industry: *The professional writer writes in sand; the amateur writer writes in concrete.* This means that the professional works his sentences over and over, knowing that the first version is seldom the best. You must train yourself to take a second look at your own writing so that you can catch and correct any errors.

One of the most common errors is using unnecessary words. This practice draws attention to itself and slows down the reader. You should cut out any dead wood that is making your sentences too long. Notice how unnecessary words are eliminated in the following examples.

LENGTHY: Each and every employee will report in writing and complete and turn in form number 402 by August 31 and not later.

BETTER: Each employee will complete and turn in form 402 by August 31. (10 words saved)

LENGTHY: The employers cooperated together and endorsed a confirmation of the important essentials of the concurring agreement.

BETTER: The employers cooperated and endorsed the essentials of the agreement. (6 words saved)

Redundant expressions are those which say the same thing more than once. They cause extra wordage in your writing and should be eliminated. Look at the redundant phrases below and their correct versions. Learn to avoid redundancy in your own sentences.

obviously apparent (apparently)
consensus of opinion (consensus)
mix together (mix)
combine together (combine)
connect together (connect)
for the purpose of (for *or* to)
a speech about the subject of (a speech on)
noticeable to the eye (noticeable)
visible to the eye (visible)
audible to the ear (audible)
alone all by himself (alone)
during the winter months (during winter)
a minor who has not yet reached the age of 18 (a minor)
endorse the check on the back (endorse the check)
in the month of May (in May)
in the city of Detroit (in Detroit)
as to whether (whether)
past experience (experience)
past history (history)
in the final analysis (finally)
honest truth (truth)
final conclusion (conclusion)
bought and paid for (bought)
around in circles (around)
half in two (in half)
whole entire (entire)
winning another victory (another victory)
center around (center on)
might possibly (might)
here in this place (here)
different variations (variations)
square corner (corner)
two twins (twins)

resulting consequences (consequences)
fluid liquid (liquid)
written literature (literature)
in this day and age (today)
blue in color (blue)
round in shape (round)
at 8:30 A.M this morning (at 8:30 A.M)
retrieve back (retrieve)
small in size (small)
bitter in taste (bitter)
due to the fact that (due to)
has proved itself to be (is)
prior to the time that (before)
during the years between (between)
foreseeable future (future)

ACTIVITY 13-A: Unnecessary Words

Without changing the meaning, reduce the italicized expressions to one or two words.

1. The clerk reviewed the statement *for the purpose of checking for* errors.
2. We visited Assateague Island *on a single occasion.*
3. He works in Ocean City *during the summer months.*
4. He works in the research lab *all alone by himself.*
5. All the students must know the *absolutely basic fundamentals* of grammar.
6. The politician tried to *make his influence felt among* the citizens.
7. *Mix together* all the dry ingredients before adding the eggs.
8. The bank teller asked the customer to *endorse the check on the back.*
9. The governor's assistant gave *a speech on the subject of* the resources of Texas.
10. The patient was to take his medicine *at regular intervals of time.*

Check your responses in Feedback 13-A at the end of this module. If your responses were correct, proceed to Part II. If you missed any, review Part I and then do Activity 13-B.

ACTIVITY 13-B: Unnecessary Words

Without changing the meaning, reduce the italicized expressions to one or two words.

1. The military family often *changed living quarters.*
2. *A minor who has not yet reached the age of 18* is not permitted to vote.

3. He has *a great amount of* time to prepare for his trip.
4. Greg was standing on the corner *at the time that* the accident occurred.
5. *He is of the opinion* that women make good lawyers.
6. On Friday we should know *as to whether* she passed the oral exams.
7. The room was constructed to accommodate *a large number of* people.
8. He is to *make a recommendation* that the employee receive a raise.
9. The war was *finally brought to an end.*
10. There was a *consensus of opinon* that the class be cancelled.

Check your responses in Feedback 13-B at the end of this module. If your responses were correct, proceed to Part II. If you missed any, review before continuing.

PART II: AVOIDING CLICHÉS, SLANG, AND "IMGLISH"

A cliché is an overused, worn-out expression, such as "it's a cake walk." Slang is a word or words that are used outside of their dictionary meaning, such as "getting played." "IMglish" is an abbreviated series of letters and numbers. All these types of expressions indicate that the writer is too lazy to find an appropriate, concise, or fresh way to convey the meaning. They also can confuse the reader, and complicate the intended message. In order to eliminate these words and expressions from your writing, become familiar with and avoid clichés, slang, and "IMglish."

Clichés

Excessive use of certain phrases has caused them to lose their impact, especially in the world of business. They are no longer striking or effective, and readers may view them as weak and/or wordy. Use the following list of common business clichés and learn to rephrase them to make your writing more effective.

at the end of the day (concluding)
on the same page (everyone understands)
on the radar (keep in mind)
take it offline (talk about privately)
sniff test/scratch test (test)
back burner (items of lesser importance; keep in mind)
20-20 hindsight (knowledge that is too late)

cover all the bases (check)
kick the tires (check it out, test it)
touch base (contact)
push the envelope (test the boundaries)
reinvent the wheel (revolutionize)
visibility (see)
deliverable (work)

at the 11th hour (last minute)
bring to the table (offered at a meeting)
dog and pony show (financial presentation)
fence-mending (apologies)
draw the line in the sand (make final)
jump through hoops (work hard)
keep a low profile (lay low)
learning curve (speed at which one learns)
level the playing field (equal treatment)
number crunching (accounting)
savvy (smart, aware, knowledgeable)
slam dunk (complete success)
the bottom line (result; basic meaning)
tongue in cheek (jokingly)
tweaking (slight adjustment)
what makes her tick (what motivates)
value-add (makes better)
knock it out of the park (succeed)
core competencies (things you should know how to do)
ball is in your court (your turn)
800-pound gorilla (person or company that dominates an area)
take a bath (to lose money)
making money hand over fist (making excessive money)
think outside the box (creative)
paradigm shift (change in the way things are done)
wipe the slate clean (start over)
synergistic (mutually beneficial)
win-win situation (mutually beneficial)
24/7 (all the time)
action items (to-do list)

Slang

Slang, like the Internet, cell phones, and large-screen televisions, is fleeting. What is popular one year, the next year can be as outdated as "golly" or "groovy." Some words and expressions hold up through the ages, such as "chill" and "dude," both of which originated in the 1970s. Slang is used predominantly in speech, and in technical writing it is out of place and confusing. You can accelerate your writing by avoiding such words and phrases.

props (respect, recognition)
off the hinges, off the hook (outstanding)
clueless (unaware)
drop (arrive)
burnt out (extremely tired)
pimp (alluring, seductive)
no-brainer (easy)
school (as verb) (to teach)
peeps (friends)
shorty (girl)
straight (OK, fine)
hook up (liaison, meeting)
kick it (relax, have fun)
jock (imitate)
spent (tired)
play (to cheat or fool)
crib (house, residence)
my bad (my fault)
represent (make a good impression)
all that (superior)

"IMglish"

Instant messaging is meant to be just as it says—instant. In the rush to get the words out, many become abbreviated, a series of letters, or a combination of letters and numbers, such as "How R U? C U L8R." This sort of abbreviation should never be used in professional writing, under any circumstances. Too often, employees use the same methods—such as email—to talk to both their professional and personal contacts, and casual writing styles can carry over into their business communication. It is best to use proper English whenever using email, regardless of the recipient. Below are some examples of common IM/email abbreviations that should never be used in professional writing.

LOL (laugh out loud)
L8R (later)
CYA (see you)
OMG (oh my god)
OIC (oh, I see)
IMHO (in my humble opinion)
TTYL (talk to you later)
SO (significant other)
LTNS (long time, no see)
thru (through)
BRB (be right back)
BFF (best friends forever)
WT? (what the)
KIT (keep in touch)
TCOY (take care of yourself)
PLZ (please)

ACTIVITY 13-C: Clichés, Slang, and "IMglish"

Select a more appropriate way of wording the italicized clichés, slang expressions, and "IMglish"

1. Jill has a *never say die* attitude about life.
2. Our problems are growing *by leaps and bounds.*
3. *IMHO* the instructor demands too much time.
4. I hope the retailers will not automatically *jack up* the price.
5. If you are going to learn to ski, good equipment is *a must.*
6. The politics in the city government was *rotten to the core.*
7. *In this world today,* there are no easy solutions to our problems.
8. *At this point in time,* we do not anticipate any cuts in the budget.
9. *PLZ* respond to this request.
10. Finding a good solution is usually *easier said than done.*

Check your responses in Feedback 13-C at the end of this module. If your responses were correct, proceed to Activity 13-D. If you missed any, review before continuing.

ACTIVITY 13-D: Clichés, Slang, and "IMglish"

Select a more appropriate way of wording the italicized clichés and slang expressions.

1. There was *method to his madness.*
2. Good jobs are *few and far between.*
3. The choices were *six of one, half a dozen of another.*
4. She is *as pretty as a picture.*
5. *Last but not least,* the company will publish its annual report in June.
6. The project's failure was *my bad.*
7. The hotel accommodations were *fit for a king.*
8. *Little by little,* we learned the facts of the case.
9. *OIC* what is expected of the new technician.

Check your responses in Feedback 13-D at the end of this module. If your responses were correct, proceed to Part III. If you missed any, review before continuing.

PART III: COMBINING LIKE SUBJECTS AND VERBS

A sentence is sometimes slowed down by a needless interruption of thought. Compare the following sentences.

> She lives in a new development. Usually, she has no trouble getting a bus.
>
> She lives in a new development and usually has no trouble getting a bus.

Both examples are grammatically correct. However, the second sentence, in which the two subjects are combined, is much smoother. Look in your own writing for instances where sentences that have the same subject can be combined and the verb made compound.

SLOW: Digital television took time catching on, but soon digital TV had swept the country.

SMOOTHER: Digital television took time catching on but soon swept the country.

SLOW: Mr. Redford has a leadership quality, and he uses it at the office.

SMOOTHER: Mr. Redford has a leadership quality and uses it at the office.

Similarly, when you have two sentences (or two parts of a compound sentence) with the same verb, you can combine the verbs and make the subject compound.

SLOW: Bob drove to Chicago, and Allison also took her car.
SMOOTHER: Bob and Allison both drove to Chicago.
SLOW: The union voted for Smith, and the administration did the same thing.
SMOOTHER: Both the union and the administration voted for Smith.

ACTIVITY 13-E: Combining Subjects or Verbs

Speed up these sentences by combining like subjects or like verbs.

1. Douglas got a job in design at Universal Drafting, and Harry was also hired in the very same department.
2. William preregistered, and thus he avoided the long lines on registration day.
3. ABC Company offers free health insurance and a pension plan, and the same is true at Acme Bolt, Inc.
4. She operates the Docutech, and she operates the copier.
5. Morrison established a very good sales record. Then he went right to the top with the company.

Check your responses in Feedback 13-E at the end of this module. If your responses were correct, proceed to Part IV. If you missed any, review Part III and do Activity 13-F.

ACTIVITY 13-F: Combining Subjects or Verbs

Speed up these sentences by combining like subjects or like verbs.

1. The supervisor for Shift A makes out the assignment schedule every morning, and so does the supervisor for Shift B.
2. The nurse took the patient's temperature today, and the doctor took it, too.
3. The assistant types letters for her boss, and she also keeps the books.
4. The school board approved of the new policy, and the administrative staff also favored it.
5. The doctor performed duties in the emergency room, and she also worked with patients in ICU.

Check your responses in Feedback 13-F at the end of this module. If your responses were correct, proceed to Part IV. If you missed any, review before continuing.

PART IV: SUBORDINATING IDEAS

Short, choppy sentences are easy to read when they are interspersed at reasonably long intervals; however, when they are used frequently, they give an unpleasant, "bumpy" impression. You can usually smooth bumpy sentences by using clause signals and subordinating secondary thoughts into dependent clauses. This process can be accomplished in three steps. Let's consider the following three choppy sentences.

(1) It stopped raining.
(2) We drove to New York in Fred's car.
(3) It had just been washed.

First Step: Which is the dominant thought? Obviously, number 2. Therefore, we will make this the main (independent) clause and try to subordinate numbers 1 and 3.

Second Step: What kind of clause signals should be used? Number 1 tells *when* we went to New York; therefore, we should try an *adverb* clause signal. Number 3 *describes* Fred's car; therefore, we should look among the *adjective* signals.

Here are some of the clause signals divided into two types: those that introduce clauses that function as adverbs within a sentence and those that introduce adjective clauses. (A more complete list of clause signals appears in Module 7.)

ADVERB CLAUSE SIGNALS		ADJECTIVE CLAUSE SIGNALS	
(To be used when the clause does the job of an adverb)		(To be used when the clause does the job of an adjective)	
after	since	MOST COMMON:	that
although	unless		which
as	until		who
because	when	OTHERS:	what
before	where		whatever
if	while		whom
			whomever

Third Step: We select the signal **when** from among the adverbs to subordinate the adverb clause and **which** from among the adjectives to subordinate the adjective clause. This gives us the following smooth sentence.

When it stopped raining, we drove to New York in Fred's car, **which** had just been washed.

Here are more examples of choppy sentences linked to make the writing flow more speedily.

(1) First the basement is excavated.
(2) The foundation is dug by using a backhoe.
(3) This is operated by one man.

Which is the most important thought? Number 2. Again, number 1 serves as an adverb telling *when* the action occurs. Number 3 again acts as an *adjective* describing the noun *backhoe.* Here is the smooth, combined sentence.

> **After** the basement is excavated, the foundation is dug by using a backhoe, **which** is operated by one man.

Again, here are three choppy sentences:

(1) The new employee relieved George.
(2) The new man had been hired for quality-control work.
(3) Then George returned to work and took over.

Which is the dominant thought? In this case, number 1. Number 2 tells something about the new man and, therefore, acts as an adjective. So we select an adjective clause signal. Number 3 tells how long the new man relieved George and, therefore, acts as an adverb; thus, we select an adverb clause signal.

> The new employee, who had been hired for quality-control work, relieved George until he returned and took over.

If a series of choppy sentences contains two thoughts of equal importance, do not subordinate one to the other; combine them with a coordinating conjunction.

(1) John went to work for First National Bank.
(2) He graduated from Western Community College in 2007.
(3) Warner went on to San Francisco University.

Numbers 1 and 3 are of equal importance and can be combined with the conjunction **and**. Number 2 describes John and, therefore, should be subordinated as an adjective clause.

> John, **who** graduated from Western Community College in 2007, went to work for First National Bank, **and** Warner went on to San Francisco University.

Remember that when coordinated clauses have a similar subject or verb, these can be combined (see Part III of this module).

(1) The Mackenzies bought the old Rob house.
(2) It was located in a wooded area.
(3) They restored it in 2000.

Numbers 1 and 3 are of equal importance, can be joined by **and,** and have a similar subject. Number 2 should be subordinated.

> The Mackenzies bought the old Rob house, **which** was located in a wooded area, **and** restored it in 2000.

It is important to determine correctly when coordination is called for and when one clause should be subordinated to another. Look at the following sentence.

> Mary was telephoning me, and lightning struck the courthouse steeple.

Grammatically, this sentence is correct. It has two independent clauses joined by the conjunction **and,** which is properly preceded by a comma. However, it is obvious that something is wrong. The writer has placed a second-class thought in a first-class position, thus pulling the sentence out of balance. The information about Mary merely sets the stage for the lightning account and should be subordinated. This is easily done by adding the clause signal **while** and putting Mary in a dependent adverb clause.

> **While** Mary was telephoning me, lightning struck the courthouse steeple.

Here are two examples in which the clause signal **who** was inserted as a relative pronoun, subordinating one of the thoughts to a dependent adjective clause.

UNBALANCED: The workers liked to deal with their supervisor, and he spoke their own language.

BALANCED: The workers liked to deal with their supervisor, **who** spoke their own language.

UNBALANCED: Ms. Birch spoke fluent Spanish, and the President summoned her.

BALANCED: The President summoned Ms. Birch, **who** spoke fluent Spanish.

ACTIVITY 13-G: Subordinating Ideas

Following the three steps described in the text, eliminate choppiness in the following groups of sentences by subordinating secondary thoughts into dependent adverb or adjective clauses. If two thoughts are of equal importance, join them with a coordinating conjunction. If necessary, rewrite the entire sentence. Remember to punctuate properly.

1. I was typing. Mr. Wellington talked to a woman. She had known him in real estate.
2. Mark off the center of the room. The room is about 15 feet long. Do this when the paint dries.
3. A heavy wrench is harder to handle. It completes the job in less time, however. It cuts labor costs.
4. The proposition sounded attractive to me. It appealed to my partner. We turned it down.
5. The union organizers approached the company executives yesterday. I spoke to the workers before that. The workers agreed to listen.
6. George didn't follow up on his application at JBK Co., and then he received a notice to report.
7. The personnel manager had a splendid speaking voice, and he represented the company on TV.
8. We paid Frank our dues; prior to that we had elected him treasurer.
9. I complained to the timekeeper, and then he found out he had misplaced my card.
10. Joanna had worked for Everett Norton, but she claimed she had never been employed.

Check your responses in Feedback 13-G at the end of this module. If your responses were correct, proceed to Part V. If you missed any, do Activity 13-H.

ACTIVITY 13-H: Subordinating Ideas

Combine these sentences into one sentence as in Activity 13-G.

1. The old die-cutting machine was in continuous use. It was operated by McNiel. Then the replacement unit arrived.
2. The employees formally demanded a wage hike. The management agreed to negotiate. The Board of Directors was violently opposed to a wage increase.
3. The plant closed. However, before that Jack drove into town with the president. He was due to speak at five.
4. Inflation could be corrected. It robs all of us. Oh, that the government would act intelligently and promptly!
5. The nurse was checking the patient's chart. The doctor was talking to another patient. He had gone to college with her.
6. The sales manager turned down the appointment, and so the position went to Jones.
7. Alicia had no privacy in the main office, and so she moved into a cubicle of her own.

8. Newlson was a good welder, but on the other hand he was very slow.
9. Jack lived just down the block, and so he joined our car pool.
10. Dobbles was fired, following which action the company hired Barnard.

Check your responses in Feedback 13-H at the end of this module. If your responses were correct, proceed to Part V. If you missed any, review before continuing.

PART V: REDUCING DEPENDENT CLAUSES

Just as you can often make a sentence flow better by reducing an independent clause to a dependent clause, you can save words by reducing a dependent clause to a phrase or a word.

1. *Reducing Dependent Clauses to Prepositional Phrases.* Look for clauses that can be turned into prepositional phrases.

CLAUSE: **When you come to the loading platform,** sound your horn.
PHRASE: **At the loading platform,** sound your horn. (3 words saved)
The man **who is wearing the white coat** is the lab chief.
The man **in the white coat** is the lab chief. (2 words saved)
While we were going through Los Angeles, we saw the GM executive.
In Los Angeles we saw the GM executive. (4 words saved)
When the executives had finished the meeting, they went to dinner.
After the meeting, the executives went to dinner. (4 words saved)

2. *Reducing Clauses to Infinitive Phrases.* An infinitive phrase is composed of the word **to** with the present tense of a verb: **to write**, **to know**, **to drive**. Infinitive phrases are particularly useful in eliminating an awkward dependent clause beginning with **so that**.

I skipped lunch **so that I could reduce** my calorie consumption.
I skipped lunch **to reduce** my calorie consumption. (2 words saved)
He took Technical Writing **so that he would be prepared** for future work assignments.
He took Technical Writing **to prepare** for future work assignments. (4 words saved)

3. *Reducing Clauses to Participles or Participial Phrases.* The present participle is the **-ing** form of the verb. The past participle of a regular verb is formed by adding **-ed** to the verb after deleting any final **e**. The most common irregular past participles are listed in Module 1. Participles can be very useful in reducing dependent clauses.

While he read all of the morning mail, he planned the next meeting.

Reading the mail, he planned the next meeting. (5 words saved)

Although George was hired on Wednesday, he did not report until Friday.

Hired on Wednesday, George did not report until Friday. (3 words saved)

Because Mary had worked as a programmer, she advanced rapidly at B & D.

Having worked as a programmer, Mary advanced rapidly at B & D. (2 words saved)

4. *Reducing Clauses to Adverbs.* Sometimes an adverbial clause can be reduced to one word that does the same job in the sentence.

The boss argued **in a manner that was very angry** with the workers.

The boss argued **angrily** with the workers. (6 words saved)

All morning she awaited his return at the airport, **in the course of which she became nervous.**

All morning she **nervously** awaited his return at the airport. (7 words saved)

5. *Reducing Clauses to Adjectives.* An adjective dependent clause often can be reduced to a single adjective.

He wore a tie **that had a lot of stripes on it.**

He wore a **striped** tie. (7 words saved)

In Miami he picked up a Chevy **that somebody had either turned in or sold outright to a dealer.**

In Miami he picked up a **used** Chevy. (11 words saved)

Candace, **who worked at a full-time job at Hercules,** did typing for the Humane Society.

Candace, **a full-time Hercules worker,** did typing for the Humane Society. (4 words saved)

6. *Reducing Clauses to Nouns.* Often you can reduce adjective clauses by simply eliminating the clause signal (*who* or *which*) and the verb. In the sentences below, the adjective clauses (underlined) become appositives renaming the subjects and coming immediately after the words they describe.

Our instructor, (**who was**) <u>an intelligent person</u>, disagreed with the newspaper editorial. (2 words saved)

The soy bean crop, (**which is**) <u>an important factor in our local economy</u>, is late this year. (2 words saved)

Our car payments, (**which impose**) <u>a real burden on the budget</u>, will continue for two years. (2 words saved)

7. *The Four-Step Reduction Technique.* If you have trouble reducing clauses to single words, try this simple technique. A clause modifying a noun or pronoun can be converted into an adjective by using the following procedure.

He designed a house that a family could live in.

Step 1: Find the dependent adjective clause. ("that a family could live in")
Step 2: Which is the most important word in this clause? (**live**)
Step 3: Convert the key word live into an adjective, using one of the following adjective endings:

-ful	**-d** or **-ed**
-less	**-y**
-able	**-ing**

Step 4: Shorten the sentence.
He designed a **livable** house. (5 words saved)

Until the general election, he was the candidate who led all of the rest of the people running.

Step 1: Dependent clause? ("who led all the rest of the people running")
Step 2: Key word? (**led**)
Step 3: Which adjectival ending is applicable? (**-ing**)
Step 4: Shortened sentence:
Until the general election, he was the **leading** candidate. (8 words saved)

Sometimes a rambling dependent clause can be reduced to an adverb. Follow the same general procedure as with adjectives.

He addressed the workers as a dictator would address his troops.

Step 1: Dependent clause? ("as a dictator would address his troops")
Step 2: Key word? (**dictator**)
Step 3: Turn this into an adverb? (**dictatorially** [**-ly** is the most common adverb ending])
Step 4: Shortened sentence:
He addressed the workers **dictatorially.** (6 words saved)

If a sprawling dependent clause cannot be reduced to an adjective or adverb, try converting the key word into a noun. You can probably use one of the following noun endings.

-ness
-tion, -sion
-ence, -ance
-ment
-ing

A clause that functions as a noun can often be reduced to a single noun.

One of the basic rules of the laboratory is that employees must keep things very clean.

Step 1: Dependent clause? ("that employees must keep things very clean")
Step 2: Key word? (**clean**)
Step 3: Turn into a noun? (**cleanliness**)
Step 4: Shortened sentence:
One of the basic rules of the laboratory is **cleanliness.** (6 words saved)

In reducing dependent clauses to prepositional phrases, identify the key word, change it into a noun if it is not in that form already, place a preposition before the noun, and position the phrase appropriately. Add minor words as needed.

He was a very pleasant man who maintained an appearance of being gruff and rude.

Step 1: Dependent clause? ("who maintained an appearance of being gruff and rude")
Step 2: Key word? **(appearance)**
Step 3: Add preposition **behind** and add **his.**
Step 4: Shortened sentence:
Behind his gruff and rude appearance, he was a very pleasant man. (3 words saved)

Because he was very angry, he shouted at the assistant.

Step 1: Dependent clause: ("Because he was very angry")
Step 2: Key word? **(angry)**
Step 3: Add preposition **in.**
Step 4: Shortened sentence:
In anger, he shouted at the assistant. (3 words saved)

ACTIVITY 13-I: **Reducting Clauses**

Employing the four-step reduction technique, reduce the dependent clauses in the following sentences to a *single word.* Strike out the clause and insert the word in the appropriate place.

1. They began excavating on a day that the sun was shining.
2. You are fortunate in having an employee who is obviously a person that you can depend upon.
3. One of the reasons for our poor profits this year is that inflationary influences are operating against us.
4. He was a worker who did outstanding work on his job.
5. She spoke to him in a manner that revealed her impatience.

Check your responses in Feedback 13-I at the end of this module. If your responses were correct, proceed to Activity 13-K. If you missed any, review Part V and then do Activity 13-J.

ACTIVITY 13-J: Reducting Clauses

Reduce the dependent clause to a single word. Strike out the clause and insert the word in the appropriate place.

1. A decision that operates impartially for all is sometimes difficult to make.
2. Anne Johnson, who earned her degree in biology, visits here every summer.
3. The farmer, who became very furious in the course of the incident, ordered the hunters off his property.
4. He bought a computer with microsoft programs that had been installed at the factory.
5. A worker who comes part-time every day was injured in the assembly department.

Check your responses in Feedback 13-J at the end of this module. If your responses were correct, proceed to Activity 13-K. If you missed any, review before continuing.

ACTIVITY 13-K: Reducting Clauses

Without changing the meaning, convert the dependent clauses into prepositional phrases. Cross out the clause and insert the phrase where appropriate.

1. When the noon hour finally arrived, he would retreat and read.
2. While summer warmed the land, the surveyors set the boundaries of our property.
3. As soon as everybody quit work, he would start moonlighting in his cab.
4. When the hunting season came around once more, he sold licenses.
5. When you come to the corner of Third Street and Folsome Avenue, turn right.

Check your responses in Feedback 13-K at the end of this module. If your responses were correct, proceed to Activity 13-K. If you missed any, do Activity 13-L.

ACTIVITY 13-L: Reducting Clauses

Without changing the meaning, convert the dependent clauses into prepositional phrases. Cross out the clause and insert the phrase where appropriate.

1. The woman who is now wearing the white suit works at General Foods.
2. While we were going down Michigan Avenue, we saw the builders repairing the hotel.

3. When the convention guests had finally finished the last of their dinner, they went into the conference room.
4. Our supervisor, who is an extremely diplomatic person in working with people, handles all of the personnel problems.
5. The request which asked for an interview came in Friday's mail.

Check your responses in Feedback 13-L at the end of this module. If your responses were correct, proceed to Activity 13-M. If you missed any, review before continuing.

ACTIVITY 13-M: Reducing Clauses

Rewrite the following sentences, using any of the word-reducing methods in this module.

1. Ellen took the Pontiac so that she could go to work.
2. After he called Mr. Newton, he completed the memo.
3. Although Horace was fired on Monday, he did not leave his job until Wednesday.
4. After Mrs. Bremmer had completed her in-service training, she reported to the makeup section.
5. The supervisor gave orders to the crew, and he did this in an angry way.
6. She walked alone down the dark corridor, in the course of which she became very nervous.
7. The salesman arrived in Samoa during the season when it rains much of the time.
8. My partner sent me a pipe that had been carefully carved by hand.
9. Helguard is a draftsman who is very talented.
10. He turned in a production record that was a surprise to everybody.
11. Just as dawn was breaking in the east, we entered the factory, which was old.
12. He lowered his eyelid in a wink that was meant to warn us about the high-pressure salesman.
13. The job that Henrietta did on the reports simply impressed everybody.
14. The orders from the boss, which amazed all of us, upset the program in a way that was complete to say the least.
15. The boss seemed to delight in making us feel confused.
16. Some office worker without the slightest sense of responsibility left the safe unlocked.
17. They had set up temporary headquarters in the section of the warehouse in which various materials of different kinds were no longer stored.
18. The supervisor showered upon us compliments that were wholly unexpected on our part.

19. For his business trip he picked up a Buick that had been bought new the year before and recently traded in.
20. Mr. Stern, the man who is my employer at the office, reports to work at eight o'clock.

Check your responses in Feedback 13-M at the end of this module.

ACTIVITY 13-N: **Editing Practice**

Edit the following paragraph using any word reduction techniques presented in this module.

In service training to update constantly all people who are employed both full-time and part-time by the company is necessary without a doubt. Each and every day new advances are being made and are implemented by the powers on high. The men and women in the trenches are unable to utilize without the proper in-service training all of this technology at their fingertips, and all of this costly equipment is a total waste of the shareholders' piece of the pie. In addition and more importantly is the need to consult with these worker ants what is and what is not working for them.

Check your responses in Feedback 13-N at the end of this module.

ACTIVITY 13-O: **Editing Practice**

Edit the following paragraph using word reduction techniques (combine like subjects and verbs and eliminate slang, clichés, and wordy phrases).

When writing a report or essay, it is important to spend a significant amount of time planning the structure of the report. It is also important to spend time organizing the information. In fact, there is a consensus of opinion among writing instructors that most of the time that is put into writing a report should be spent before the first version of it is drafted. Instructors insist that spending this time on preparation will actually save time on the overall project. They say this is due to the fact that when the information has been carefully organized and the structure is clear, it makes it a no-brainer for the students to begin to weave their own ideas in with the information that they have gathered. Students who are clueless as to the benefits of spending time carefully planning and organizing their work before writing often put themselves at a disadvantage. If they would wake up and smell the coffee, they just may write reports that knock it out of the park.

Check your responses in Feedback 13-N at the end of this module.

DIAGNOSTIC FEEDBACK

Changes are shown in italics.

1. We like to spend time reading *in the evening.*
2. Electronic communication *is* fast and efficient.
3. We have *variations* to choose from.
4. The conference is to be held *in Chicago.*
5. *Because* enrollment is down, we have cancelled three classes.

Use word reduction techniques to combine like subjects or verbs or reduce clause to phrases

1. Technicians must have excellent communication skills and must often communicate with varied audiences.
2. The computer lab is outdated and in need of renovations, but the updates can't be made until we receive the grant money.
3. To save time writing the report, she did not do an outline.
4. The books required for the nursing program are very expensive, sometimes up to $1000 for one semester, so one way to cut costs is to buy used books.
5. Because Randall did not like the corporate environment, he changed careers and became a teacher.

FEEDBACK FOR MODULE 13

Feedback 13-A

These are suggested answers. Yours may differ and still be acceptable. Check with your instructor.

1. for
2. once
3. during summer
4. alone
5. fundamentals
6. influence
7. Mix
8. endorse the check
9. a speech on
10. regularly

Feedback 13-B

These are suggested answers. Yours may differ and still be acceptable. Check with your instructor.

1. moved
2. A minor
3. much
4. when
5. He thinks
6. whether
7. many
8. recommend
9. finally ended
10. consensus

Feedback 13-C

These are suggested answers. Yours may differ and still be acceptable. Check with your instructor.

1. positive
2. rapidly
3. I think, I believe
4. raise the price
5. very important, crucial, essential
6. corrupt
7. Today
8. Today, Nowadays
9. Please
10. difficult

Feedback 13-D

These are suggested answers. Yours may differ and still be acceptable. Check with your instructor.

1. purpose to his actions
2. hard to find, rare
3. Today, Nowadays
4. equal
5. pretty, lovely, beautiful
6. Finally
7. my mistake, my error
8. superior, excellent, luxurious
9. Gradually
10. I understand, I see

Feedback 13-E

1. Douglas and Harry got jobs in design at Universal Drafting.
2. William preregistered and thus avoided the long lines on registration day.
3. Both ABC Company and Acme Bolt, Inc., offer free health insurance and pension plans.
4. She operates the Docutech and the copier.
5. Morrison established a very good sales record and went right to the top with the company.

Feedback 13-F

1. The supervisors for Shifts A and B make out the assignment schedule every morning.
2. Both the nurse and the doctor took the patient's temperature today.
3. The assistant types the letters for her boss and also keeps the books.
4. The school board and the administrative staff approved of the new policy.
5. The doctor performed duties in the emergency room and worked with patients in ICU.

Feedback 13-G

These are suggested answers. Your answers may differ and still be acceptable. Check with your instructor.

1. While I was typing, Mr. Wellington talked to a woman who had known him in real estate.
2. After the paint dries, mark off the center of the room, which is about 15 feet long.
3. Although a heavy wrench is harder to handle, it completes the job in less time and cuts labor costs.
4. Although the proposition sounded attractive to me and my partner, we turned it down.
5. Before the union organizers approached the company executives yesterday, I spoke to the workers, who agreed to listen.

6. Although George didn't follow up on his application at JBK Co., he received a notice to report.
7. The personnel manager, who had a splended speaking voice, represented the company on TV.
8. After we had elected Frank treasurer, we paid him our dues.
9. After I complained to the timekeeper, he found out he had misplaced my card.
10. Although Joanna had worked for Everett Norton, she claimed she had never been employed. (or) Joanna, who had worked for Everett Norton, claimed she had never been employed.

Feedback 13-H

These are suggested answers. Your answers may differ and still be acceptable. Check with your instructor.

1. The old die-cutting machine, which was operated by McNiel, was in continuous use until the replacement arrived.
2. Although the Board of Directors was violently opposed to a wage increase, the management agreed to negotiate when the employees formally demanded a wage hike.
3. Before the plant closed, Jack drove into town with the president, who was due to speak at five.
4. Inflation, which robs all of us, could be corrected if the government would act intelligently and promptly.
5. While the nurse was checking the patient's chart, the doctor talked to another patient with whom he had gone to college.
6. Because the sales manager turned down the appointment, the position went to Jones.
7. Since Alicia had no privacy in the main office, she moved into a cubicle of her own.
8. Although Newlson was a good welder, he was very slow.
9. Jack, who lived just down the block, joined our car pool.
10. After firing Dobbles, the company hired Barnard.

Feedback 13-I

These are suggested answers. Your answers may differ and still be acceptable. Check with your instructor.

1. They began excavating on a *sunny* day.
2. You are fortunate in having a *dependable* employee.
3. One of the reasons for our poor profits this year is *inflation.*
4. He was an *outstanding* worker.
5. She spoke to him *impatiently.*

Feedback 13-J

These are suggested answers. Your answers may differ and still be acceptable. Check with your instructor.

1. An *impartial* decision is sometimes difficult to take.
2. *Biologist* Anne Johnson visits here every summer.

3. The farmer *furiously* ordered the hunters off his property.
4. He bought a computer with *factory* installed Microsoft programs.
5. *A part-time* worker was injured in the assembly department.

Feedback 13-K

Your answers may differ. Check with your instructor.

1. *At noon,* he would retreat and read.
2. *In summer,* the surveyors set the boundaries of our property.
3. *After work,* he would start moonlighting in his cab.
4. *During hunting season,* he sold licenses.
5. *At the corner of Third and Folsome,* turn right.

Feedback 13-L

Your answers may differ. Check with your instructor.

1. The woman *in the white suit* works at General Foods.
2. *On Michigan Avenue,* we saw the builders repairing the hotel.
3. *After dinner,* the convention guests went into the conference room.
4. Our supervisor handles all the personnel problems *with diplomacy.*
5. The request *for an interview* came in Friday's mail.

Feedback 13-M

If your responses differ, check them with your instructor. There are many possible correct answers.

1. Ellen took the Pontiac *to work.*
2. *After calling Mr. Newton,* he completed the memo.
3. *Fired on Monday,* Horace did not leave his job until Wednesday.
4. *Her in-service training completed,* Mrs. Bremmer reported to the makeup section. (or) *After in-service training,* Mrs. Bremmer . . .
5. *Angrily,* the supervisor gave orders to the crew.
6. *Nervously,* she walked alone down the dark corridor.
7. The salesman arrived in Samoa *during the rainy season.*
8. My partner sent me a *hand-carved* pipe.
9. Helguard is a very *talented* draftsman.
10. He turned in a *surprising* production record.
11. *At dawn* we entered the *old* factory.
12. *He warned us with a wink* about the high-pressure salesman. (or) He winked to warn us . . .
13. Henrietta did an *impressive* job on the reports.
14. The *amazing* orders from the boss *completely* upset the program.
15. The boss seemed to delight in *confusing us.*
16. Some *irresponsible* office worker left the safe unlocked.
17. They set up temporary headquarters in an *unused* section of the warehouse.

18. The supervisor showered *unexpected* compliments on us.
19. For his business trip he picked up a *year-old* Buick.
20. Mr. Stern, *my employer,* reports to work at eight o'clock.

Feedback 13-N

Your responses may differ. Check with your instructor.

Regularly scheduled in-service training for all employees is necessary. The new advances being implemented daily by company management are costly to shareholders because the workers cannot use the technology without instruction. The employees should be consulted before the company considers future changes.

Feedback 13-O

Your responses may differ. Check with your instructor.

When writing a report or essay, it is important to spend a significant amount of time planning the structure and organizing the information. In fact, there is consensus among writing instructors that most of the time that is put into writing a report should be spent before the first version of it is drafted. Instructors insist that spending this time on preparation will actually save time on the overall project because when the information has been carefully organized and the structure is clear, it is easier for the students to begin to weave their own ideas in with the information that they have gathered. Students who are unaware of the benefits of spending time carefully planning and organizing their work before writing often put themselves at a disadvantage. If they change their approach to the assignments, they just may write reports that are successful.

MODULE 14

Report Writing

Objective: Structurally, the report is an expanded version of the paragraph. This module takes you into report writing and lets you work with five common types of reports.

Upon completion of this module, you will be able:

- To define the function of an outline in multiparagraph writing.
- To prepare a multiparagraph report outline given three principles of organization.
- To identify and to use appropriately two report formats.
- To write five reports using appropriate report format for each.

PART I: REVIEW OF PARAGRAPH WRITING

Reviewing the essential points of constructing a unified paragraph will aid in understanding how a report is constructed. First, the topic sentence must have a subject (what you are talking about) and a controlling idea (what you are saying about the subject).

SAMPLE PARAGRAPH

Topic Sentence	S: Opening a fast food franchise / CI: several steps
	Opening a fast food franchise involves several steps.

Next, there should be several supporting sentences that help to prove the controlling idea.

Supporting Sentences	First, arrange to finance the operation. Then find a suitable building site. Next, recruit and hire personnel, and finally, advertise topromote the business.

Last of all, there should be a concluding sentence that summarizes the main point of the paragraph.

Concluding Sentence	If you follow these steps, you will soon have a successful restaurant.

If you have mastered the parts of the unified paragraph, you possess the basic tools for report writing. This is so because each sentence of the paragraph can be enlarged into a paragraph itself. Here is how you do it.

Topic Sentence	becomes →	Introductory Paragraph
Supporting Sentences	become →	Supporting Paragraphs
Concluding Sentence	becomes →	Concluding Paragraph
Paragraphs	become →	Report

You can now apply this process to the sample paragraph above and turn it into a report.

SAMPLE REPORT

Introductory Paragraph	If you have investigated many careers and have decided you would like to be your own boss, then perhaps you would like to open your own business. Although opening a fast food franchise (S) can be difficult for some, if approached in a businesslike way and broken down into several steps (CI), it could prove to be a highly profitable commercial undertaking.

Compare this introductory paragraph with the topic sentence in the sample paragraph.

Supporting Paragraphs 1	First, you must arrange to finance the business. Discuss the possibility of a loan with bankers and other businesspeople, making an itemized list of capital needs. Plan to borrow money from a bank or find financial backers to go into business with you.
2	Then find a suitable building lot in an appropriate spot in a retail area after comparing several different locations. Keep in mind, in selecting a site, such features as accessibility from major arteries, customer parking, drive-in window, and an area of stable population.
3	Next, after making a list of qualifications for all employees, recruit and hire personnel. You will need a manager with experience and good references. Also, you will need to hire short-order cooks and counter help, plus part-time employees.
4	Finally, advertise to promote the franchise. Consider billboards along main highways and discount coupons in local newspapers. Radio and television are excellent media to appeal to hungry patrons. Another good advertising device is a catchy slogan or jingle.

Compare these four supporting paragraphs with the supporting sentences.

Notice that these supporting paragraphs do not have concluding sentences. A paragraph does not need a concluding sentence if it leads into the next paragraph. Only paragraphs that stand alone must have a concluding sentence.

Concluding Paragraph	If you follow these steps, you could soon be the owner of a thriving fast food franchise. As you master all of the techniques involved in your business venture, you will make a place for yourself in a world that offers a variety of opportunities.

Compare the concluding paragraph with the concluding sentence in the sample paragraph.

The formats for the paragraph and for the report are almost identical. The most important principle is that of logical organization, and you can be assured of having logical organization if you lay out the framework or skeleton before writing the report. You develop the framework by outlining. An outline is a way to categorize neatly all the various points to be included in the report and to get all your ideas down in the proper order. In Module 10, you learned to jot your ideas down in list fashion. In order to write a report, you will need a more detailed outline.

PART II: OUTLINING

When you set out to write a report, your task will go smoothly if you approach it in a systematic manner. A disorganized, inefficient student might simply sit down with a pencil and paper or at a computer and hope the jumble of thoughts will jump from his or her mind to the paper. As you learn to be an organized writer, you will begin the task more logically.

First, you must select a broad topic; then you narrow it to a specific topic geared to an appropriate length for your report. As an example, you might consider a report on the general topic of careers and narrow it to the specific topic of "Starting a Business." The next step is to formulate a topic sentence which states what focus you will develop regarding your specific topic. In this example, a possible topic sentence would be *Starting a business is relatively easy if you follow a definite plan.*

Once these three steps (selecting a broad topic, narrowing it to a specific topic, and constructing a topic sentence) are complete, you are ready to proceed with the outline for the report.

Outlining is not as difficult as many writers think it is. First, you must understand the function of an outline. The outline, when done with care, will help you present the purpose of your report and set forth your procedure for developing your ideas. It can also be an effective way of testing your idea for a paper because it will let you know *before* you write whether you have enough information and detail to develop your ideas.

The outline should present the subject of your report and a procedure for discussing the subject. Your topic is what you are talking about and what you have to say about it. The procedure, on the other hand, is the actual organization of details. This organization of details is important, for you must choose details that will support your main topic, and you must present them in the most effective order to gain support.

If given the topic "Starting a Business" for a report, you must first determine what to say about it and how to say it best. The easiest way to do this is to make a scratch outline. A scratch outline is merely a list of ideas that come to mind when you think of your topic. Brief phrases are better than complete sentences. Do not be concerned at this point with organization or spelling or appropriateness. Concentrate on getting down as many solid ideas as possible. A scratch outline for "Starting a Business" might look like this:

SCRATCH OUTLINE

Recruiting and hiring personnel	Customer parking
Billboards along main highways	Locating site in retail area
Leisure time on weekends	Area of stable population
Advertising merchandise	Students as part-time employees
Find financial backers	Borrow from bank
Drive-in window	Cooks and counter help
Family problems at home	List of capital needs
Catchy slogan or jingle	Discussion of possibility of loan with bankers and businesspeople
Financing the business	Compare several locations
Experienced manager	Accessibility from major arteries
Radio and TV	Discount coupons in local newspaper
Political survey	

Now you should study your list carefully and start grouping ideas together. Look for general ideas first rather than details. These broad ideas will later be the main topics or headings in the body of your paper. In the scratch outline, for example, the first item, "Recruiting and hiring personnel," is a general idea that will be one of the major topics of your paper. The second item, "Billboards along main highways," is not general and can serve only to support one of the broad major topics. After studying this particular list, you should see four major ideas that would be helpful in "Starting a Business." Pull these out of the list as your main divisions; don't worry yet about details to develop them. Put them in the proper order, in this case the order you would follow if you were a businessperson. Sometimes the order you choose will be decided by chronology, as in this case of what must be done first, then next, and so on. In other cases, you may organize the main points in order of importance, usually from greatest to least. Your outline at this time would look like this:

SKELETON OUTLINE

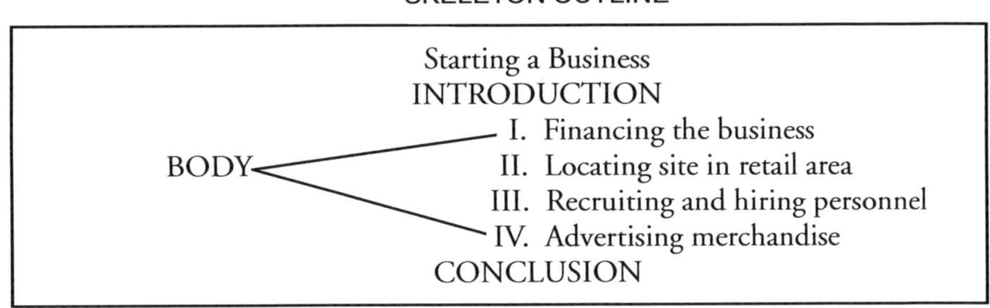

Starting a Business
INTRODUCTION
BODY
I. Financing the business
II. Locating site in retail area
III. Recruiting and hiring personnel
IV. Advertising merchandise
CONCLUSION

Once you have the major topics for the body of your paper, you should go back to your list to look for details that will develop these ideas. Group all related ideas together under one general heading. If your scratch outline does not have any details for a certain topic, add some at this time from your own experience and knowledge or from research in books or magazine articles. If you cannot come up with any details to develop a topic, you will know that your main divisions should be changed to topics that will lend themselves to development. At this point, you should also eliminate items in your list that have nothing to do with the general topics. In this scratch outline, the following items are irrelevant: leisure time on weekends, family problems at home, political survey. Cross them out. Remember that a scratch outline is rough, and you do not have to use every item you put down. The detailed outline resulting from the sample scratch outline might look as follows.

DETAILED OUTLINE

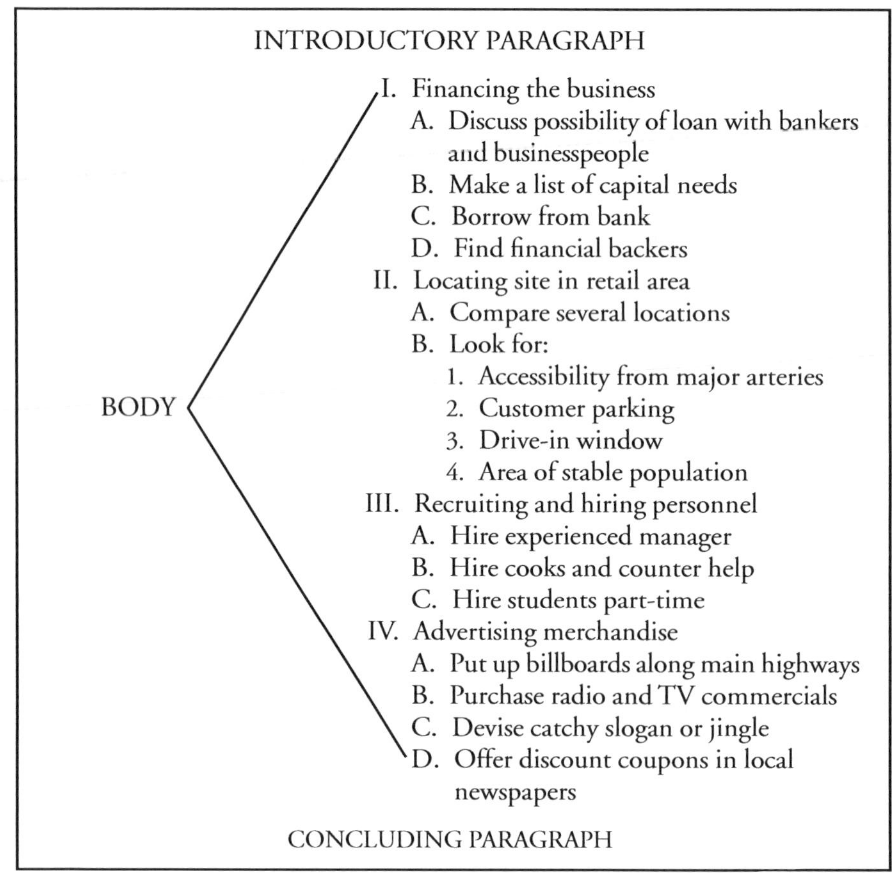

INTRODUCTORY PARAGRAPH
BODY
I. Financing the business
A. Discuss possibility of loan with bankers and businesspeople
B. Make a list of capital needs
C. Borrow from bank
D. Find financial backers
II. Locating site in retail area
A. Compare several locations
B. Look for:
1. Accessibility from major arteries
2. Customer parking
3. Drive-in window
4. Area of stable population
III. Recruiting and hiring personnel
A. Hire experienced manager
B. Hire cooks and counter help
C. Hire students part-time
IV. Advertising merchandise
A. Put up billboards along main highways
B. Purchase radio and TV commercials
C. Devise catchy slogan or jingle
D. Offer discount coupons in local newspapers
CONCLUDING PARAGRAPH

Note these important factors in translating a scratch outline into a completed topic outline:

1. You do not need to use every item on the scratch outline.
2. The introduction and conclusion are not found on a scratch outline.
3. You should choose a minimum number of main divisions and try to develop these well on the completed topic outline.
4. The final topic outline is written in parallel form for clarity. All headings should be parallel (that is, all noun phrases, all verbs, all clauses, etc.) and all items under each heading should be parallel. (Refer to Module 12 for more on parallel construction.)
5. The purpose of outlining is to divide ideas into parts, so there is no need to break down an idea if it has only one part. In other words, if you have a I, you must have a II. If you have an A, you must have a B.

ACTIVITY 14-A: Organizing a Scratch Outline

Change the scratch outline below into a working topic outline. Use these principles of organization to prepare to write your own reports: (1) Eliminate the unrelated items. (2) Arrange the remaining items into an outline with five major ideas or divisions and two or more subdivisions supporting each major part. (3) Write "Introduction" and "Conclusion" in the proper place on the outline.

TOPIC: COPING SKILLS FOR STRESS MANAGEMENT

No caffeine
Appearance
No sugar
Perfectionism
Have a contingency plan
Delegation of authority
Use deep breathing exercises for relaxation
Accumulate several chores to do at once
Smile
Ulcers
Have children do certain household chores
Organization
Make a daily plan
No drugs
Eliminate duties that frustrate you
Overcommitment
Exercise
Share jobs with others at work
Include fun things in your schedule
Hire someone to do certain jobs
Lack of honesty

No alcohol
Nutrition
Wear clothes you feel good in
Run, walk, bicycle, swim, or play tennis or racketball regularly
Pay attention to neatness and cleanliness
Work out aerobically at least three 20-minute sessions per week

After completing the scratch outline assignment, check your outline in Feedback 14-A at the end of this module.

PART III: REPORT INTRODUCTIONS

Once you understand the principles of the outline, you are ready to set up your report. Because a report involves development of details, there are other considerations that will impact its effectiveness. Organizationally, you may want to consider one of two reliable introductions that will be discussed. Aesthetically, there are a number of visual enhancing aids that will affect the overall appearance of the report for your reader. These techniques will enable your reader to follow your discussion more easily and quickly.

The Introduction

Introductions serve various purposes, but the most important are to clearly set up the purpose of the report in a topic sentence, to raise audience interest, and sometimes to give a succinct overview of what content a report contains. The following two introductions—the inverted pyramid and the report plan types—allow you to achieve these goals, but each is different in purpose and approach.

The Inverted Pyramid

The *inverted pyramid* introduction, also known as the *funnel* or *inverted triangle*, is aptly named because of its visual representation, an upside-down triangle. This type of introduction works for virtually any piece of writing. It is especially effective with lengthy pieces.

This technique begins with a general discussion to introduce the topic and to raise audience interest. Additional sentences, based on the scope of the piece, narrow to a precise controlling idea presented in the introduction's last sentence, the topic sentence. There is no indication of discussion to follow in this type of introduction.

The Report Plan

The *report plan* introduction isn't quite as versatile as the inverted pyramid; however, it is extremely concise because it gives a quick overview of what content a report covers. This approach works best when there are only a few main supporting ideas because these ideas are listed in parallel form in a report plan sentence, usually at the end of the introduction. These ideas are actually the headings derived from the accompanying outline or plan for the report. Longer reports should use a pyramid approach since it becomes unwieldy to list all main ideas.

Visual Representation of Introductions

Compare the visual representation of these two kinds of introductions. Then read the comparison of how each report is composed. Notice that composing techniques for the body and the conclusion of the report are identical. Even the topic sentence can be the same, except for its location. Only the introductions differ in approach according to the amount of support the writer intends to include—pyramid for a longer, more involved paper and report plan with an overview of topics to follow.

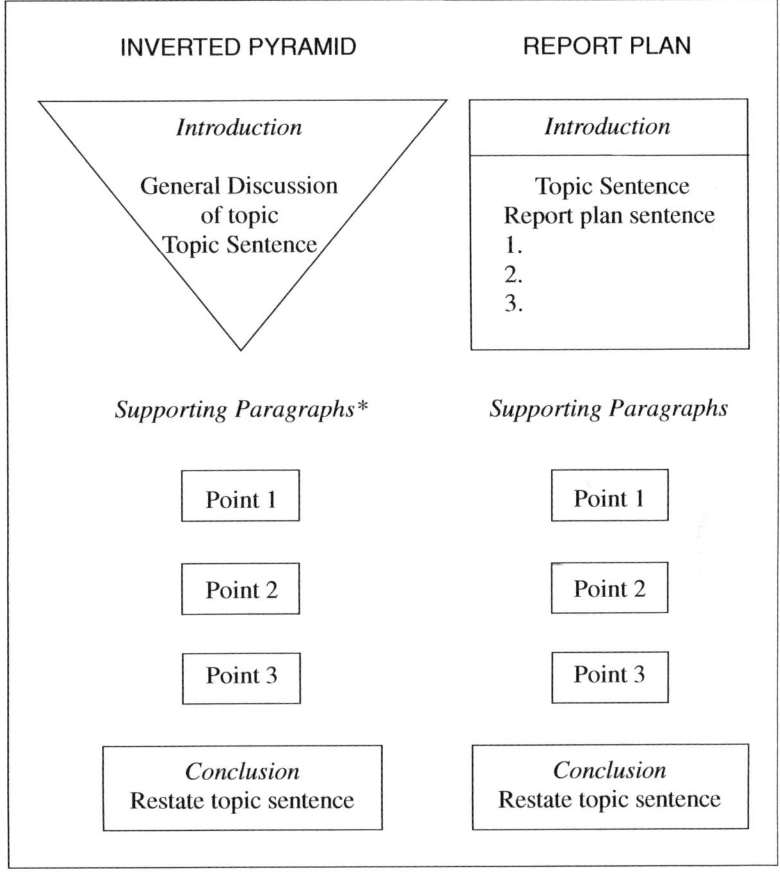

*Obviously, there can be more than three supporting paragraphs, but there should be at least two to form a multiparagraph piece.

TECHNIQUES FOR INVERTED PYRAMID AND REPORT PLAN FORMATS

INVERTED PYRAMID FORMAT	REPORT PLAN FORMAT
Introduction	*Introduction*
Open with a general statement to set the context for the subject area. Then gradually narrow to the main point containing the subject and controlling idea—usually called the thesis statement or topic sentence—preferably in the last sentence of the opening paragraph.	Open with the thesis statement or topic sentence (the subject and controlling idea of the report). Following that, state the report plan, which lists the main points to be presented in the order in which they will occur and in parallel form. These points are the headings from the outline.
Supporting Paragraphs	*Supporting Paragraphs*
Each supporting paragraph should have its own topic sentence and at least two others containing detail. Use a separate paragraph for each major point and development. Use transitional expressions to link paragraphs smoothly. Statements within the paragraph can consist of reasons, examples, details, statistics, comparison and contrast, negation, classification, definition, cause, and process.	Each supporting paragraph should have its own topic sentence and at least two others containing detail. Use a separate paragraph for each major point and development. Use transitional expressions to link paragraphs smoothly. Statements within the paragraph can consist of reasons, examples, details, statistics, comparison and contrast, negation, classification, definition, cause, and process.
Conclusion	*Conclusion*
Rephrase the thesis or topic sentence.	Rephrase the thesis or topic sentence.

PART IV: FORMAT TIPS

Writers can facilitate the understanding of their ideas immensely through the use of visual enhancing aids or formatting techniques. These include the use of white space, headings, paragraphing, and listing techniques. A reader will be attracted to a visually appealing document. It also requires less effort for the reader to follow. Finally, formatting techniques allow writers to guide the reader through discussions.

Unless otherwise indicated, you might want to use the following guidelines to present your writing:

1. Use 1-inch margins.

2. Use full-block (no indenting) style when single spacing the document. Insert blank lines between paragraphs. If you prefer to double space your document, indent each paragraph. Do not insert extra blank lines between paragraphs when double spacing; there should be one blank line between paragraphs.

3. Keep your paragraphs between 9 and 12 typed lines. Paragraph by separating ideas with topic sentences or subheadings.
4. Likewise, follow the guidelines of keeping sentences between 15 and 25 words. Longer sentences can be unwieldy.
5. Create headings and subheadings to guide the reader through content. Make sure, however, that headings look different from subheadings. You can achieve this through font size or by use of all capitals. Make sure to keep your headings on the same page as the accompanying text.
6. Insert blank lines before and after headings.
7. Set font size at the standard 12 point, not 10, for regular text. Use a slightly larger size for headings.
8. Choose clean, legible fonts such as Times Roman, Arial, or Courier for standard text.
9. Use bullets and listing techniques when possible. See Part VI, Listing Technique.
10. Limit your use of enhancing aids; less is best. In other words, don't underline, bold, and italicize the same text.

PART V: THE PERSUASIVE REPORT

The **persuasive report** presents an argument to readers and then asks them to react. It presents only one side of the picture and tries to persuade readers that the point of view given is the logical one. Keep in mind that this report is designed to convince readers of your point of view and to get them to take some action. The topic should be a controversial issue or at least one that has more than one side to it.

The following persuasive report will illustrate the two introductions. Notice that the supporting paragraphs and conclusion remain the same in both formats. The same report has been used to illustrate both formats so that you can see how both would work. An outline is included so you can see how headings become elements of the report plan, which matches in sequence.

OUTLINE

Block Scheduling

Introduction

I. Effect on transportation
   A. Time spent commuting
   B. Cost of commuting

II. Impact on finances
   A. Five free days for work
   B. Two days of childcare expenses
III. Elimination of wasted instructional time
   A. Classroom chores
      1. Check attendance
      2. Return tests and papers
      3. Make announcements
      4. Review of previous discussion
   B. Presentation of material
   C. Break time

COMPARISON OF INTRODUCTIONS

INVERTED PYRAMID INTRODUCTION

Recruiting new students is a major goal of most community colleges. One deciding factor for prospective students is a schedule convenient to family and employment commitments. *Block classes are a perfect alternative for mature, employed community college students.*

Transportation

Transportation is a concern of many community college students. Many students discover that the number of hours spent in commuting to school exceeds 90 minutes per day. If students schedule classes for five days per week, this equates to students expending more than seven

REPORT PLAN INTRODUCTION

Block classes are a perfect alternative for mature, employed community college students. Block scheduled classes are scheduled to meet one day per week for the prescribed instructional time. With block classes, for a full-time schedule of 12 credits, students enroll in two classes on two days; if students wish an additional class, it could be scheduled for an evening one of the days the students are already scheduled to be on campus. Students should request these classes because they require less transportation, they provide a potential for financial benefits, and they maximize instructional time.

Transportation

Transportation is a concern of many community college students. Many students discover that the number of hours spent in commuting to school exceeds 90 minutes per day. If students schedule classes for five days per week, this equates to students expending more than seven hours a week commuting. Frequently, students ascertain they are driving to campus once or twice a week for only one class with the traditional scheduling arrangement of classes. In addition, students must also consider the financial ramifications of driving to campus five times per week instead of two. Students must consider not only the cost of gas required but also the less obvious costs associated with wear on the engine and tires and the need for more frequent servicing of the vehicle.

Financial Benefits

In addition to the time and cost associated with commuting to the community college, students must also evaluate other financial factors they may be facing as a result of commuting five times per week to school. If they had five days totally free for scheduling work hours instead of weekends and a few hours each day of the week, even part-time employment would be easier to arrange. Perhaps students could work eight hours for three of the five free days instead of four hours six times a week. Moreover, students may be paying for childcare to attend classes. Many students discover they are paying for three hours of childcare to attend a one-hour class. Obviously, this could be a cost saving area for those students requiring day care services.

Time Management

Students attending one class per week instead of the traditional three classes should notice a different

hours a week commuting. Frequently, students ascertain they are driving to campus once or twice a week for only one class with the traditional scheduling arrangement of classes. In addition, students must also consider the financial ramifications of driving to campus five times per week instead of two. Students must consider not only the cost of gas required but also the less obvious costs associated with wear on the engine and tires and the need for more frequent servicing of the vehicle.

Financial Benefits

In addition to the time and cost associated with commuting to the community college, students must also evaluate other financial factors they may be facing as a result of commuting five times per week to school. If they had five days totally free for scheduling work hours instead of weekends and a few hours each day of the week, even part-time employment would be easier to arrange. Perhaps students could work eight hours for three of the five free days instead of four hours six times a week. Moreover, students may be paying for childcare to attend classes. Many students discover they are paying for three hours of childcare to attend a one-hour class. Obviously, this could be a cost saving area for those students requiring day care services.

Time Management

Students attending one class per week instead of the traditional three classes should notice a different utilization of instructional time. The classroom management style is altered as a result of block scheduling. At the beginning of class, typically the instructor checks attendance, returns tests and assignments, makes announcements, and reviews material covered the previous class. The amount of time necessary to accomplish these tasks is greatly reduced with block scheduling since each task is done only once rather than three times. A complicated theory can be discussed, and its applications can be practiced during a block class, whereas just the theory might require more than one of the typical one-hour class sessions. Typically, the next class session, the students would be presented with an opportunity to practice the application of the material. The concentrated learning environment of the block class is a more efficient usage of the students' educational time. Finally, instead of rushing to the next class, both the instructor and the students may resolve problems during the break period.

Conclusion

Because family and employment limit the time available for education, because finances are always a concern, and because effective utilization of instructional time is important, community colleges need to consider alternatives to traditional scheduling. An alternative that addresses the various demands challenging the mature, employed adult is the block class format.

utilization of instructional time. The classroom management style is altered as a result of block scheduling. At the beginning of class, typically the instructor checks attendance, returns tests and assignments, makes announcements, and reviews material covered the previous class. The amount of time necessary to accomplish these tasks is greatly reduced with block scheduling since each task is done only once rather than three times. A complicated theory can be discussed, and its applications can be practiced during a block class, whereas just the theory might require more than one of the typical one-hour class sessions. Typically, the next class session, the students would be presented with an opportunity to practice the application of the material. The concentrated learning environment of the block class is a more efficient usage of the students' educational time. Finally, instead of rushing to the next class, both the instructor and the students may resolve problems during the break period.

Conclusion

Because family and employment limit the time available for education, because finances are always a concern, and because effective utilization of instructional time is important, community colleges need to consider alternatives to traditional scheduling. An alternative that addresses the various demands challenging the mature, employed adult is the block class format.

ACTIVITY 14-B: Persuasive Report

Write a persuasive report following the procedures below:

1. Choose a general topic for the report.
2. Narrow it to a specific topic.
3. Write a thesis statement.
4. Outline the report.
5. Proofread carefully using the following checklist.
   _____ Spelling
   _____ Verb forms and endings
   _____ Punctuation
   _____ Pronoun agreement
   _____ Subject–verb agreement
   _____ Fragments
   _____ Shifts
   _____ Voice (consistency with active or passive)
   _____ Tense (consistency with past, present, future)
   _____ Person (consistency with 1st, 2nd, 3rd)
   _____ Number (consistency with singular or plural)
   _____ Parallel structure
   _____ Possessives (correct use of apostrophe, no contractions)
   _____ Misplaced modifiers
   _____ Correct word usage
   _____ Wordiness
   _____ Clichés
   _____ Slang
6. Hand in to your instructor your outline, rough draft, and final copy.

PART VI: TECHNICAL PROCEDURE REPORT

A **technical procedure report** explains how to do something. Although it is quite similar to the process paragraph that you wrote in Module 10, it is more detailed. The process paragraph deals with a rather simple, uncomplicated process that can be related in a few fairly short steps. The technical procedure report is lengthier because it describes a more complex process, and it contains much more detail.

There are various ways to approach the procedure report depending upon the purpose. Sometimes, the purpose is to be able to perform the procedure, so you will set it up showing the various steps using direct commands as in the process paragraph. Then there are procedures where the emphasis is on understanding what happens, not necessarily how to make it happen. These resemble standard expository pieces based on information. More than likely if a procedure is required, the emphasis will be on how to do something; therefore, the following sample will show an effective way to set up a procedure requiring discussion and detail as opposed to simple, straightforward steps.

Sample Procedure

Since good writing is a direct result of good planning, the following procedure report will show how to create a working outline. In some situations, a sentence outline will suffice for a procedure if it is clear and concise. Here is how a standard outline on "Creating a Working Outline" can be turned into a procedure report.

HOW TO CREATE A WORKING OUTLINE

Introduction

- I. Brainstorm ideas
  - A. Work from a topic
  - B. Consider anything that comes to mind
  - C. Don't worry about organization or repetition at this point
- II. Organize ideas
  - A. Find major headings
  - B. Group ideas
  - C. Eliminate repetition
  - D. Throw out stray ideas
- III. Rank ideas
  - A. Chronological order
  - B. Order of importance
  - C. Spatial order
- IV. Copy into correct format
  - A. Roman numerals
  - B. Capitals
  - C. Periods
  - D. Alignment

Conclusion

The Procedure Report

On its own, the preceding outline might be useful for someone familiar with the procedure of making an outline. However, the outline would be absolutely meaningless for anyone who hasn't performed the procedure often.

Therefore, a procedure report would be helpful to fill in some of the necessary, missing details about outlining.

Parts of the procedure report. Like other pieces of writing, a procedure report will begin with an introduction (you can use either approach according to the amount of discussion) that clearly sets up the idea of process and what specifically you will be telling the reader how to do. Then there should be a section called "Preparation" where you would discuss what needs to occur before the procedure begins. This, too, varies in length according to topic. At this point, you are ready to present your procedure itself, the steps along with accompanying discussion as needed. Finally, like all pieces of writing, there is a conclusion, which, in this case, would probably discuss the importance of the procedure. Essentially, the concluding section lets the reader know that the procedure is complete. Note, however, that the conclusion is never the last step of the procedure. This is a frequent error in this type of report.

Format. Commands and the use of second person point of view are appropriate for procedure. Establish the "you" in your introduction, and use commands to set up the steps. Because of the utilitarian nature of the procedure report, you will want to utilize headings (see Part IV, Format Tips). In addition, a procedure usually has many details which need to be presented in sequential order; therefore, a checklist is the perfect format. You provide easy access to information with a separation of details in a limited space.

Listing technique. Using the listing technique is a simple process. First, you need to write a lead-in sentence that works as a topic sentence for the list. The lead-in sentence ends with a colon. A bullet or number is used to separate each item in the list. These items should be written in parallel structure. Concluding remarks must follow the list to indicate closure; in other words, you never end a document with a bulleted or numbered item. Do not forget to use white space to separate the lead-in sentence from items in the list and the conclusion. Below is an example of listing technique.

If you use a list, please be sure to do the following:

- Have a lead-in sentence.
- Use numbers or bullets.
- Make sure items are parallel.
- Have a separate conclusion.
- Use plenty of white space.

Following these guidelines will ensure that your list is effective and reader friendly.

Sample Procedure Report

The following procedure report uses the inverted pyramid introduction and shows how the featured outline can be turned into a procedure report with headings and a listing technique.

HOW TO CREATE A WORKING OUTLINE

TO: Mrs. Young
FROM: Lucas Lynch
SUBJECT: Technical Procedure Report
DATE: April 14, 2007

In writing, the use of an effective outline can reduce your time and effort. More than likely, you will also get a better product. Writers who outline can usually save at least one-third of their worktime. *Here's how you, too, can create a working outline to save you time and energy.*

Preparation

Before you start, you will need to prepare carefully. Make sure you understand clearly your assignment. Complete your reading and notetaking, if necessary. Then gather your paper and pencil or ready your computer. If your computer has an outliner, familiarize yourself with it before you start.

Procedure

A working outline results from these relatively quick steps:

1. *Brainstorm your topic.* During the act of brainstorming, write down quickly anything that comes to mind about your designated topic. Use short phrases. Don't worry about organization, repetition, spelling, or anything else at this time. Instead, concentrate on getting the idea down before you forget it.
2. *Organize your ideas.* Now you can start to look for major headings and details. On scrap paper, make a list of headings and fill in the columns with supporting details from your original list. Eliminate duplicate wording and throw out any stray ideas that don't work with your headings. Better yet, try to use these ideas in your introductory or concluding remarks if they work there. Now you have a scratch outline.
3. *Rank your ideas.* It is now time to make judgments about presentation of your ideas. Should they be presented chronologically, spatially, or by order of importance? Rank your main ideas with roman numerals and then do the same with your details using ABCs.
4. *Format your outline.* Once your ideas are ordered, you are ready to turn the scratch outline into an outline using correct form. If you are using your computer's outliner, you can turn that feature on and type up your list. If you are writing your outline, get a fresh sheet of paper and neatly copy your outline in ink using roman numerals, capital letters, periods, and alignment as needed.

Conclusion

If you take the time to think and organize your ideas by preparing a working outline before you write, you will save valuable time and energy in the writing process. If you have never used outlines before, try this method. You may be pleasantly surprised at the extent to which outlining eases the process of writing.

Do not forget to use transitional expressions. Below is a list for particular use in a process report.

SUGGESTED TRANSITIONAL EXPRESSIONS FOR PROCEDURE REPORT

first, second (etc.)	to
next	also
then	in addition
afterwards	furthermore
finally	moreover
lastly	besides

ACTIVITY 14-C: **Technical Procedure Report**

Write a technical procedure report following the procedures below.

1. Choose a procedure to explain for the report.
2. Write a thesis statement.
3. Outline the report, including Preparation and Procedures.
4. Write the final draft from the outline.
5. Proofread carefully using the following checklist.

_____ Spelling
_____ Verb forms and endings
_____ Punctuation
_____ Pronoun agreement
_____ Subject–verb agreement
_____ Fragments
_____ Shifts
    _____ Voice (consistency with active or passive)
    _____ Tense (consistency with past, present, future)
    _____ Person (consistency with 1st, 2nd, 3rd)
    _____ Number (consistency with singular or plural)
_____ Parallel structure
_____ Possessives (correct use of apostrophe, no contractions)

_____ Misplaced modifiers
_____ Correct word usage
_____ Wordiness
_____ Clichés
_____ Slang

6. Hand in to your instructor your outline, rough draft, and final copy.

PART VII: INTERVIEW REPORT

The techniques of interviewing should be very valuable to you on the job in order to collect the information you need on a particular subject. To conduct an interview, you will need to rely upon several skills you have already learned.

For this **interview report,** you will be asked to interview someone currently employed in your technology to prepare for writing an interview report. Since the interview is intended to give you another point of view from someone actually working in your field, *do not interview one of your technology instructors or a member of your family.* Furthermore, this assignment is designed to give you practice both in interviewing and in writing, helpful tools to use on the job. By utilizing the skills of planning ahead and organizing facts, as indicated below, you will improve your ability to communicate.

Selecting the Interviewee

Your technology may be a very broad area, giving you many choices of people to interview. If you are enrolled in business administration, for instance, you will have to narrow the field to a specific area, such as accounting, sales, or management. Thus, the first thing for you to decide is the particular facet of your technology you wish to make your career. (If you are not certain, choose your favorite among the possibilities.) Then find a person employed in this area. For a list of people, consult your technology instructors, the telephone directory, or a local firm.

Preparing for the Interview

When you have selected the individual you want to interview, telephone to ask for an appointment convenient to both of you. Be sure to tell the interviewee who you are, why you would like the interview, what the specific subject of the interview is, and the amount of time you would like. Discuss a time limit for the interview so you will both know how to plan. It would be courteous also to tell the interviewee that you will send a copy of the report to read before it goes to your instructor. Find out as much as possible about the interviewee beforehand.

The second part of the preparation before the actual interview is drawing up a list of questions. Make these as specific as possible so that you can control the direction of the interview. Ask about things you personally want to know about. Since this interviewee is working in your chosen career, this person can give you many ideas as to what to expect on the job. Here are some specific areas you may have questions about:

Type of person required for job
Educational requirements for job
Internship
Opportunities for graduates in field
Possibilities for advancement
Salary
Benefits
Duties
Advantages and disadvantages
Recommendations to persons entering field
New developments and proposed changes in field
Communication requirements for job

As soon as you have compiled a list of questions which you would like to ask in the interview, review them with your instructor (see Activity 14-D). Include the name and address of the person you are interviewing so that your instructor can send a letter of appreciation for this person's time and interest. You should also send the person a thank you letter (see business letters in Module 15).

ACTIVITY 14-D: Interview Questions

After securing an appointment for an interview, review the following information with your instructor.

1. Name of person to be interviewed
2. Position held
3. Place of employment
4. Address
5. Date and time set for interview
6. Questions you intend to ask

Conducting the Interview

Arrive early for the interview. Be sure that you are neatly and appropriately dressed. As soon as the interview begins, be prepared to direct the discussion. Your purpose is to collect information about the job, so do not be timid in asking questions. It is preferable to begin with such subjects as job opportunities and responsibilities. Save the topic of money for last. Be pleasant and courteous, yet assert yourself. Indicate your interest by remaining alert, sitting up straight, and looking the interviewee in the eye.

Let your interviewee do most of the talking, but do not allow the person to lose focus and discuss irrelevant subjects. Remain objective; keep your convictions to yourself. Don't take sides. Ask questions in the order in which they come up in the discussion; new questions are certain to arise that you did not include on your original list. Concentrate on the person's remarks. Take notes only briefly so as not to disturb the interviewee's train of thought. Do not use a large notebook, but have a small note pad and pencil available. You may use a tape recorder if the interviewee agrees when you make the appointment.

Remember to thank the interviewce for the time and information as you leave. Do not stay any longer than it takes you to ask your questions. The interviewee is a busy person and will appreciate your being as brief as possible.

SAMPLE OUTLINE: INTERVIEW REPORT

Introduction

Person interviewed: Sally Short
Position: Medical Assistant
Company: All State Pediatrics
Education: Diploma in Licensed Practical Nursing from DTCC

I. JOB DUTIES
   A. Prepares patients for exams and physicals
      1. Height, weight, temperature, BP
      2. Symptoms
   B. Gives necessary immunizations
   C. Gives eye examinations
   D. Performs hearing screenings

II. ADVANTAGES
   A. Working with people from diversified backgrounds and cultures
   B. Working with children/personal fulfillment
   C. Earning good wages
   D. Acquiring excellent benefits/health coverage

III. DISADVANTAGES
   A. Repetitiveness
   B. Lack of advancement
   C. Very busy times during winter cold/flu season
   D. Bimonthly Saturday hours (small children)

IV. PERSONAL CHARACTERISTICS
- A. Compassion
- B. Caring
- C. Patience
- D. Honesty
- E. Integrity
- F. Outgoing, pleasant personality
- G. Organizational skills

V. Communication
- A. Written
  - 1. Time-consuming/75 percent
  - 2. Charts
    - a. Height, weight, BP
    - b. Symptoms
  - 3. Forms
    - a. School/sports physicals
    - b. Prescription requests
    - c. Insurance and specialist referral
    - d. Urine and blood laboratory requests
- B. Oral
  - 1. About 25 percent
  - 2. Patients
    - a. Medical history
    - b. Follow up appointments
  - 3. Doctor
    - a. Patients' charts
    - b. Appointments

Conclusion

Enlightening and informative
Confirmation of career choice

Writing the Report

As soon after the interview as possible, while your impressions are still fresh, sit down and make detailed notes. If you wait too long, you may forget some of the important points.

Once your note-taking is completed, you are ready to organize all the facts by constructing an outline. You have already gained some skill in this procedure.

First, pick out the headings. Then, organize them in a logical sequence. Finally, group all of the facts obtained in the interview under appropriate headings. With this outline completed, you have done the hardest part of the task. The actual writing of the report is easy once you have organized the material.

The standard report format is similar to the one you learned for the process report and the persuasive report. It is made up of three sections:

1. *Introduction.* This should contain pertinent background information about the person interviewed, as well as the date, time, and place of the interview. It should also include a report plan sentence for the body of the report.
2. *Supporting Paragraphs.* These should discuss a minimum of five areas, including communication as a part of the job. You will probably want to devote a paragraph to each heading. Remember to tie the paragraphs together with transitional expressions.
3. *Conclusion.* Here you should restate the essential facts learned in the interview. You may also include any conclusions you have drawn as a result of the interview; you can express your own opinion here.

Here is a sample interview report. Note the use of headings to make it easier for the reader to follow. First person pronouns are acceptable in the introduction and conclusion of the interview report.

SAMPLE INTERVIEW REPORT

TO: Ms. Instructor
FROM: Brent Presnell
SUBJECT: Interview with Sally Short
DATE: April 8, 2007

On March 20, 2007, I interviewed Sally Short, a licensed practical nurse employed as a medical assistant by All State Pediatrics in Georgetown, Delaware, in her home. Ms. Short received a diploma in Licensed Practical Nursing from Delaware Technical and Community College in 1987 and has been in the medical profession for almost 20 years; she worked 15 of these years in a hospital setting, but she prefers the more intimate one-on-one patient relationship that occurs in a physician's office. Many areas of the profession were discussed; however, the most important, detailed aspects of the position were job duties, the advantages and the disadvantages of this position, personal characteristics of prospective employees, and communication.

Job Duties

Daily, Ms. Short's responsibilities remain constant. She spends most of her workday preparing patients for exams and physicals. This requires that she obtain and record the patient's height, weight, temperature, blood pressure, and symptoms on the patient's chart. Also, Sally gives the children necessary immunizations, eye exams, and hearing screenings when needed.

Advantages

During the interview, Ms. Short shared a variety of advantages of the medical assistant's position. The most important advantage is the enjoyment of working with many people from diversified backgrounds and cultures. She delights in working with children, and she receives personal fulfillment from her job. Ms. Short states, "My love for the job makes the day a little easier for my sick patients." Also, the post offers very good wages. The starting salary depends upon individual experience and knowledge and includes an annual raise. Furthermore, the position offers excellent fringe benefits, including health coverage.

Disadvantages

There are several disadvantages in working as a medical assistant in a private office. The main inconvenience is the repetitiveness of the work day. Every day contains the same activities with no variety in job duties. Another important hindrance is no possibility of advancement in this position; however, if the employee works in a hospital setting, job openings and advancements do become available at times. Also, the office is extremely busy during the winter cold-and-flu season. This can be an obstacle if personal time is needed during office hours. Finally, the bimonthly Saturday hours can be very difficult if the employee has small children at home.

Personal Characteristics

Many personal characteristics are needed to perform this job. First, the children are sick and in need of attention; therefore, the most important traits required are compassion, caring, and patience. Honesty and integrity are necessities when dealing with the sensitive, personal medical records of patients. Also, an outgoing, pleasant personality helps to establish a rapport with the children and their parents. In addition, organizational skills are extremely important when handling the medical chart of a patient.

Communication

Ms. Short spends approximately 75 percent of her workday writing and 25 percent talking with patients and the doctor filling out patient charts. For example, she records the physical statistics of the patient and the symptoms of the illness as well as completing physical forms for schools and sports. In addition, she completes medicine requests, insurance and referral forms, and urine and blood laboratory requests. Her oral communication skills are important when she takes a patient's medical history or schedules follow up appointments. Ms. Short also discusses patient's charts and appointments with Dr. Smith.

Conclusion

Overall, the interview was very enlightening and extremely informative. As stated earlier, there were many areas of the vocation that were discussed, and the most consequential aspects of the post are detailed above. Meeting Ms. Short has confirmed and increased my desire to obtain employment in a doctor's office.

ACTIVITY 14-E: Interview Report

Conduct your interview, create an outline from your notes, and write your report and thank you letter.

PART VIII: RECOMMENDATION REPORT

When you are on the job, it is likely that you will be asked to make a decision or recommendation on whether to purchase a particular piece of equipment or to adopt a particular program. You would have to examine several alternatives, compare the results, and recommend one for adoption, presenting the results of your comparative study in the form of a **recommendation report.**

Memorandum Format

One approach to a recommendation report is a memorandum accompanied by tabulated data. The advantage of the tabulated form is that the reader can see everything at a glance and need not wade through a sea of words. This format is preferable when the report contains a great deal of hard data.

In a recommendation report, the introduction should set the purpose of the report, mentioning the items under consideration, and also stating your choice at the outset. It should also indicate why you are making the recommendation. The supporting paragraphs should analyze the main features of the best choices available for consideration. The conclusion should recommend which item to adopt and tell *why.*

Note that the first paragraph of the memorandum contains the background information that would be in the introduction of a standard recommendation report. The conclusion states the recommendation and summarizes the data that support that decision. In all recommendation reports, be sure to compare a sufficient number of alternatives. Be sure to draw conclusions in a final paragraph stating why you made the choice that you did. It is helpful if you not only give reasons for your choice but also give reasons for rejecting the other items.

SAMPLE OUTLINE: RECOMMENDATION REPORT

Recommendation for an Allied Health Journal

INTRODUCTION

Journals: *Health Care* and *Journal of the Allied Health Professional (JAHP)*

I. Scope
  A. *Health Care*
    1. 10–15 articles
    2. Broad range of current issues
  B. *JAHP*
    1. 5–6 articles
    2. Narrow in scope
    3. Studies

II. Readability
  A. *Health Care*
    1. Reader friendly
    2. Easy to comprehend
    3. Terms defined
  B. *JAHP*
    1. Difficult to read
    2. Technical terms

III. Audience
  A. *Health Care*
    1. Allied health providers
    2. Allied health students
  B. *JAHP*
    1. Geared toward researchers, health instructors, and practitioners
    2. Data oriented

IV. Format
  A. *Health Care*
    1. Headings/Subheadings
    2. Graphics

- B. *JAHP*
  1. Headings/Subheadings
  2. Charts, graphs
  3. Emphasis on statistics

V. Documentation
- A. *Health Care*
  1. Researched articles
  2. References lists not always included
  3. Statistics
- B. *JAHP*
  1. Abstracts
  2. References listed

VI. Professional Resources
- A. *Health Care*
  1. CEUs
  2. Information on insurance, conferences, jobs, products
- B. *JAHP*
  1. Same as *Health Care*
  2. Higher caliber of job opportunities

CONCLUSION

SAMPLE RECOMMENDATION REPORT: MEMO FORMAT

TO: Dr. Thomas Sampson
FROM: Joseph Hill
SUBJECT: Recommendation of Allied Health Journals
DATE: September 25, 2007

There are many different allied health journals for an allied health worker to choose from, but it is essential to have one that discusses relevant topics and is easy to understand. *Health Care* and the *Journal of the Allied Health Professional* are two of the many journals that examine topics involving patient care and different procedures used in health care. Though both of these journals have the same goal, to provide allied health care workers with useful information about the field of medicine, *Health Care* is clearly the better choice for students.

	Health Care	**Journal of the Allied Health Professional**
Scope	10–15 articles on broad range of current topics like treatment, therapy, and ethical issues	5–6 articles based on medical research and its impact on health care
Readability	Easy to understand; technical terms defined	Difficult; very technical terminology
Audience	Health care providers and anyone interested in health care issues	Researchers, health instructors, and practitioners
Format	Reader friendly; headings; graphics	Headings; many charts; graphics; statistically oriented
Documentation	Yes, but not all articles have a reference list	Yes, abstracts and comprehensive reference lists included
Resources	CEUs; announcements concerning insurance, publications, conferences, classified ads, products, and discounts	CEUs; announcements concerning insurance, publications, conferences, classified ads, products, and discounts

Recommendation

Although both journals are very interesting and pertinent to future health care personnel, *Health Care* is the better of the two for practicing health care professionals and students interested in the field. This is because the journal is easier to understand, and it addresses a broad range of relevant topics. This journal's section on resources for health care providers is more appropriate for the allied health student.

Here is the same recommendation report set up without using a table.

SAMPLE RECOMMENDATION REPORT: PARAGRAPH FORMAT

TO: Dr. Thomas Sampson
FROM: Joseph Hill
SUBJECT: Recommendation of Allied Health Journals
DATE: September 25, 2007

There are many different allied health journals for an allied health worker to choose from, but it is essential to have one that discusses relevant topics and is easy to understand. *Health Care* and *Journal of the Allied Health Professional* are two of the many journals that examine topics involving patient care and different procedures used in health care. Though both of these journals have the same goal, to provide allied health care workers with useful information about the field of medicine, *Health Care* is clearly the better choice for students.

Scope

One of the crucial points for making this decision is the scope of the articles. *Health Care* is a journal that addresses many interesting allied health topics. It includes about 10 to 15 articles that discuss a broad range of current issues in the field of health today. These articles include information about innovative treatments, therapy, and ethical issues affecting the health care system. *Journal of the Allied Health Professional* contains only five to six articles discussing topics of a much more narrow scope than the previous journal. The articles are reports of actual studies based on medical research and how those results can impact healthcare. "Clinical Trials of Penicillin in the Treatment of Streptococcal Pneumonia" is the title of one of the studies, indicating that the article discusses one specific approach to the treatment of one specific condition.

Readability

Students choosing a journal need to be mindful of the language used. *Health Care's* articles are very reader friendly and easily understood. Technical terms are defined. *Journal of the Allied Health Professional's* articles are more difficult to read because of their technical level of terminology.

Audience

Both magazines have different target audiences. It is obvious that *Health Care's* articles are directed to allied health providers and students pursing a career in that field. Written mainly for researchers, health instructors, and practitioners, *Journal of the Allied Health Professional* has articles that are researched and data oriented.

Format

Reader-friendly formats should also be considered in the recommendation. In *Health Care,* the articles are set up with headings and subheadings. There are some graphics. Although headings, subheadings, charts, and graphs are used throughout *Journal of the Allied Health Professional,* its articles are harder to follow because of their technical level of terminology and emphasis on statistics.

Documentation

Health care providers in training need to be reassured of accurate information indicated by documented sources. Research is apparent throughout *Health Care's* articles. Although there is not a reference list at the end of each article, the use of statistics and references to similar works assure the reader that the author has fully investigated the topic. The research in *Journal of the Allied Health Professional* begins with an abstract and ends with a reference list with up to 50 entries.

Professional Resources

Availability of professional resources is a major asset to health care providers. Opportunities to acquire continuing education units (CEUs) through subscription and completion of enclosed tests are highly desirable because of licensure restrictions. In addition, information about insurance, conferences, classified ads, uniforms, products, discounts, etc., provides subscribers with current resources that affect their careers. Both of the journals provide readers with plenty of these resources with the only notable difference being the caliber of job opportunities. The *Journal of the Allied Health Professional* lists positions requiring advanced degrees.

Recommendation

Although both journals are very interesting and pertinent to future health care personnel, *Health Care* is the better of the two for practicing health care professionals and students interested in the field. This is because the journal is easier to understand, and it addresses a broad range of relevant topics. This journal's section on resources for health care providers is more appropriate for the allied health student.

ACTIVITY 14-F: **Recommendation Report**

Obtain information on any two topics you wish to compare. You may want to consider equipment, programs, ideas, or policies. Prepare your outline and then write a recommendation report using either the paragraph or the table format.

PART IX: SUMMARY REPORT

Another type of writing you may be asked to do on the job is to summarize a magazine article, progress on a project, or research on a subject. You will do this in a **summary report.** This type of report should be as brief as you can make it yet as clear and complete as possible. You have to condense the essential points and eliminate all of the extra material.

Let's suppose you have been asked to summarize a magazine article. First, read the article thoroughly so that you understand it completely. You may even want to reread parts and highlight major ideas to make sure you do not miss any important points.

Your summary report should include an introduction, which states the name of the magazine, italicized; the date of the magazine; the name of the article, in quotes; its general subject; supporting paragraphs, which describe the main points of the article; and a conclusion, which emphasizes the heart of the article. Do not inject your own opinion, even if you disagree, since your purpose is merely to summarize.

The summary should be 15 to 20 percent of the length of the original article. Condensing material to the essentials will give you practice in distinguishing between primary facts and minute details.

Be very careful to avoid plagiarism. If you use the author's exact words anywhere in your report, be sure to give the author credit by enclosing those words in quotation marks and inserting a citation about the source. If you express the author's thoughts in your own words, no quotation marks are needed.

Read the following magazine article; then study the sample planning form, outline, and summary of the article. The article is approximately 2,400 words, and the summary is 236 words, about 10 percent of the original length.

Speaking of Writing—Interviews with People on the Job

Madeline Hamermesh
Normandale Community College

With considerable frequency, articles appear in *The Wall Street Journal* and other business-related periodicals lamenting the state of written communication in business. The authors of these articles point out the avoidable costs in employee time, poor product quality, and customer dissatisfaction that are entirely due to miscommunication of the written word. Examples range from nonuse or misuse of commas, wrong word choices, cloudy syntax, and jumbled organization to factual errors and misinformation.

For years I have been collecting such articles in order to motivate students in the business writing course I teach. I don't know just how seriously the students take these articles. (After all, I have my priorities and they have theirs.) But I can say that the articles give me much to think about. And my thoughts are these: How can I teach so as to send these young people out to their first jobs able to compose, at least, a clear two-sentence or one-paragraph memo, and, if I'm lucky, a soothing letter to an irate customer? Is drill in the mechanics the answer? Just how much time should be spent on the basic principles of written communication and how much on specific types of letters, memos, reports? Should I follow the textbook faithfully? And do I really know what these students will need in order to write effectively on their future jobs?

Like most academics, my experience in the real world of business is limited to being a consumer rather than a producer or a service person. Thus I tend to follow the precepts and patterns of business communication textbooks as guides. They advocate the several C's (conciseness, clarity, completeness, courtesy, correctness, coherence, etc.); the triangle of sender-message-receiver; the psychological patterns of good news, bad news, and persuasion; empathy and the "you"-attitude (or the "you-view," as I term it); good diction and tone; and avoidance of jargon and redundancy. But my doubts about the content of my course in business writing have grown each time I read an article decrying the lack of writing skills young people bring to their jobs. A sabbatical year has given me the chance to test what the textbooks say.

Through contacts with friends, colleagues, and students, I compiled a list of several dozen people in business whom I might be able to interview. The names given to me ranged from vice-presidents of international corporations through middle managers (usually in human resource training) to individual small entrepreneurs. I wrote to these people asking if they would be willing to talk with me for an hour or so in order to answer this question: What should I teach my business writing students in order to prepare them as well as possible for the writing they will do on the job? As you might expect, more responses came from those near the top of the corporate structure than from those nearer the bottom.

Over four months, January to April, 2002, I interviewed a dozen people in business. I must keep them anonymous since I do not have their permission to specify them by name or company. They include a vice-president of a multinational high-tech corporation; a communications manager for the same corporation who is a former college English instructor; the vice-president of a large manufacturing firm; the training manager of a firm that makes products for factories and defense contractors; the manager for public affairs communications for a food processing conglomerate; a specialist underwriter and a personnel director of an insurance broker serving businesses and industries; a "director of corporate materials" for a manufacturer of insulated shipping containers: a vice-president for communications for a financial services corporation; an account executive, one of ten serving this area for a national training and development corporation; a "personnel and training coordinator" for a small company that serves all the stores in the state of a national fast food chain; the manager of education in the human resources department of another multinational high-tech manufacturer; and a program manager of supervisory development in the corporate headquarters of the same company. I believe I was fortunate in talking with people who are especially aware of problems in communication: those in training and development and those directly involved in communication themselves.

The interviews lasted about one hour each and were conducted informally. I took notes, but the conversations were not structured. I did go with some basic questions:

What do you see as the qualities of good writing?

Do you feel that miscommunication due to poor writing is a problem in your company?

What are your personal writing practices?

What are your expectations in the writing skills of entry-level employees?

What are your suggestions about how such people should be prepared in a business writing course?

Overall, their answers more than support the precepts to be found in typical business communication textbooks. Although they lack the terminology with which to name these qualities, they were unanimous in citing conciseness, even brevity, as a top priority in business writing. Apparently, the lack of time and the effort needed to plough through excess verbiage and irrelevant material is the reason they said things like, "Get to the point" and—"Put it on one page, or don't bother writing me." While not all cited conciseness as a number one quality of effective writing, everyone mentioned it.

Similarly, there was consensus in valuing correctness in the mechanics. One person said, "There's no such thing as a typo," and another proofreads outgoing memos and letters several times, even asking a third person to check for errors. The financial services company vice-president for communication pointed out the obvious result of faulty mechanics: the waste of time and money when work has to be redone several times. And another specified "poor grammar, misspellings, and homonym confusion" on her list of writing sins. For some, mechanical correctness is not a problem. Typically, they stated, "That's the secretary's responsibility," and, in one company, a special perk is a secretary who can compose an effective, error-free letter.

A quality often mentioned by the textbooks is conversational tone, naturalness, avoidance of "corpspeak." Whatever it is called, it was named by each person I talked with as a desirable quality. Some call it sincerity; others, less concise, said that a letter should sound as if "we were talking face to face." One said he does not like "lofty, third-person stodginess," and his own letter reflected this attitude. Another, with some academic experience, did mention a "friendly, conversational tone." And one said he likes an "upbeat, affirmative tone." Only one failed to note the quality of ease and friendliness as desirable in writing, perhaps because he himself was stiff and unforthcoming in the interview.

Surprisingly, almost all noted the awareness of audience as a necessary prerequisite to effective written communication. One, who was a former college English instructor, hence sophisticated in his terminology, mentioned the necessity of "writer's sensitivity to the audience, which implies not only avoiding jargon but also using tact, indirection, and subtlety." Another saw the problem of lack of audience awareness when writers use "unnecessarily complicated constructions, buzz words, pomposity." Some spoke of considering the probable attitude of the reader and of the amount of time, precious to the reader, needed to cover a long document. Another mentioned the need for the writer's empathy that takes into account the reader's needs, whether she or he has the background for understanding the communication and its purpose, as well as the attitude and receptivity of the reader. And all but one mentioned this sensitivity to the audience—in short, what we teach as the "you-view." This would subsume several related ideas: conciseness, conversational tone because the reader will be put off by pretentious diction and complicated syntax;

avoidance of jargon because the reader might not understand, particularly if it is used in order to impress. One executive was quite vehement in his dislike of long letters and memos and said that he throws away, unread, anything over one page!

Surprising, too, was the mention of logical organization. Almost everyone noted the need for a structure within a piece of writing. The former English teacher even expressed the need for writers to follow the classical rhetorical structures of arrangement, as, for example, according to importance of details or by comparison and contrast. Most were not as sophisticated in naming the devices of organization, but all were aware of its importance. A person who prepares training manuals mentioned her use of numbered paragraphs and underlining for emphasis as tools to help readers.

Finally, the vice-president in charge of communication for the investment services company mentioned, quite understandably, the need for writers not only to be aware of the corporate culture but also to express that culture, whenever communication occurs, both within and outside of the company.

When those interviewed were asked about their personal writing practices, they sounded like classic textbooks. It was clear that all took their written expression quite seriously, especially at the higher levels of corporate structure. One vice-president uses handwritten, short notes to colleagues and dictates longer messages. He works hard at sounding conversational, he said, but what he dictates is always improved on the typed drafts. Interestingly, when he is faced with a ticklish writing situation, one that demands thought and care, he reverts to longhand. A training director follows the orthodox procedure of producing first a sentence outline, then a first draft in longhand, then a dictation or a re-write in longhand for the final typescript, and finally a careful proofreading.

Another person, a training and development supervisor, does all her own writing and proofs all outgoing correspondence from her department. The industrial insurance specialist must collect statistical data before submitting his proposals (which is what most of his writing consists of), but the writing follows a pattern that is circumscribed and "pre-formed" because of the legal implications of his work. Whatever the method, it was clear that my informants took effective written expression very seriously and took the time and effort necessary to achieve their best result.

Whether or not they were saying what they thought an English teacher might want to hear, they were unanimous in citing good writing skills as a prerequisite for advancement in the job. One executive quoted his chief engineer, who said that competent engineers could be hired by the dozen, but there's a shortage of those who can put their ideas on paper clearly. This executive feels that a career can be advanced significantly by good writing skills. One of the representatives of a small training and development business said that while he and his colleagues had few opportunities for writing, he often heard clients' complaints about the poor skills of entry-level employees and told an anecdote of a memo at a large, multi-national organization which was "read" and initialed through seven levels without anyone detecting a major error in it.

The training director of a manufacturing company said several times that poor writing detracts from the effectiveness of the message and gives a poor image of the company and the writer because both come across as ignorant. The training director of another company in charge of the after-hours educational program for some 17,000 employees said that the several writing-improvement courses offered each quarter are always filled to capacity, even though they carry no credit and guarantee no job advancement or salary increase. What this does indicate, she said, is a desire to improve a very important job skill. A manufacturing company executive feels that not only recent graduates, but people generally are deficient in writing skills. All agreed with the major comment in articles critical of the current state of clear and effective writing: This is a skill crucial to achievement in the corporate world.

If no new or startling research findings are themselves significant results, then what business people told me is valid since it confirms the tenets of the textbooks and consequently the content of business writing courses. Bolstered by the comments of those I spoke with, I'll return to the classroom with more confidence in what I'm teaching. I'll also be able to speak of the importance of writing skills as perceived by people of substance in the business community. Some of them have volunteered to speak to my classes or to be interviewed on videotape. Maybe what they have to say will be more convincing than the articles about why the junior executive can't write.

OUTLINE: SUMMARY REPORT

Background Information (to be included in Introduction)

Title of article: "Speaking of Writing—Interviews with People on the Job"
Author: Madeline Hamermesh, Normandale Community College
Publication: *The American Business Communication Association Bulletin*
Date: March 2003

I. Six qualities of good writing
   A. Conciseness a top priority
      1. Brevity
      2. No excess verbiage and irrelevant material
   B. Correctness in mechanics
      1. Eliminating all typos
      2. Proofreading
      3. Saving of time and money
   C. Conversational tone
      1. Naturalness
      2. No "corpspeak"
      3. No stodginess
      4. Friendliness

- D. Awareness of audience
  1. Avoid jargon
  2. Consider attitudes and receptivity of reader
  3. Incorporate "You-view"
- E. Logical organization
  1. Select
     - a. Order of importance
     - b. Comparison and contrast
  2. Number paragraphs
  3. Underline for emphasis
- F. Awareness of corporate culture

II. Interviewees' personal writing practices
- A. Awareness of importance of written expression
- B. Procedure of outline, rough draft, and final draft
- C. Taking time and effort for best results

Conclusion

These business professionals firmly believe that good writing skills are a prerequisite to career advancements. Moreover, "Poor writing detracts from the effectiveness of the message and gives a poor image of the company and the writer. . . ." The author's research interviews confirmed that the content of business writing courses is relevant to the business world.

SAMPLE SUMMARY REPORT

TO: Ms. Morley
FROM: Jonathan Layton
SUBJECT: Summary Report
DATE: May 1, 2007

The March 2003 issue of *The American Business Communication Association Bulletin* published an article by Madeline Hamermesh entitled "Speaking of Writing—Interviews with People on the Job." The article reports the results of interviews with business people concerning written business communication.

Six qualities were consistently mentioned as requisites for good business writing. Foremost, conciseness and brevity were stressed because professionals have no time for "excess verbiage and irrelevant material." Another area of value was mechanical correctness. Typos were just not acceptable; thus, proofreading, saving time and money, was a critical part of writing. Each person also mentioned conversational tone, naturalness, and friendliness in the correspondence language rather than "corpspeak" or stodginess. Furthermore, logical organization, a planned approach, "according to importance of details or by comparison and contrast," along with enumerated paragraphs and underlining, was strongly recommended. A final feature mentioned was awareness of corporate culture.

The experts were quite serious about their personal written expression. They emphasized an outline, rough draft, and final draft, with careful proofreading. Taking the time and making the effort produced the best results.

In conclusion, interviewees unanimously cited "good writing skills as a prerequisite for advancement on the job." Hamermesh concluded, ". . . what business people told me is valid since it confirms the tenets of the textbooks and, consequently, the content of business writing courses."

ACTIVITY 14-G: Summary Report

In the library find a magazine article or report that is related to your technology and is at least two pages long. Make a copy of the article to hand in with your report. Outline the article; then write the summary report.

FEEDBACK FOR MODULE 14

Feedback 14-A

This is a suggested plan; you might have a different order.

Topic: Coping Skills for Stress Management

I. Organization
   A. Make a daily plan
   B. Have a contingency plan
   C. Accumulate several chores to do at once
   D. Eliminate duties that frustrate you
   E. Include fun things in your schedule
II. Delegation of authority
   A. Have children do certain household chores
   B. Share jobs with others at work
   C. Hire someone to do certain jobs
III. Appearance
   A. Smile
   B. Wear clothes you feel good in
   C. Pay attention to neatness and cleanliness

IV. Exercise
    A. Use deep breathing techniques for relaxation
    B. Work out aerobically at least three 20-minute sessions per week
    C. Run, walk, bicycle, swim, or play tennis or racketball regularly
V. Nutrition
    A. No caffeine
    B. No sugar
    C. No drugs
    D. No alcohol

MODULE 15

Business Letter Writing

Objective: This module will teach you how to write the main types of business letters and communications.

Upon completion of this module, you will be able:

- To define the purpose and focus of business letter writing.
- To write five types of business letters using appropriate form and focus.
- To compare the business letter and the office memo.
- To write two types of interoffice memos.

PART I: PSYCHOLOGY OF BUSINESS WRITING

When you graduate and move into the job market, in order to get a good position, you will need to master two important areas of knowledge: (1) the technical skills necessary to perform your job well, and (2) the communication skills required to convey information effectively. While your technology courses are designed to give you proficiency in the technical aspects of your job, your English courses are set up to prepare you for the kinds of writing and speaking you will do as part of your duties. In particular, this course will enable you to communicate in writing with forceful letters that will not only enhance the company you work for but also give you personal credibility in your field. Letter writing techniques should not be minimized; your letters may become important company records.

Purpose

First, take a look at the purpose of business writing. When you write a letter, it is critical that the reader understand the message. In addition, the letter should build and maintain the company's goodwill through an attitude of making and keeping friends. Ultimately, the letter should motivate readers to accomplish the writer's purpose.

Focus

To fulfill this purpose, your letter should focus on the reader. Put yourself in the place of the reader; remember that he or she will be looking at the letter to determine how to benefit from it. Apply the principles of psychology about what motivates people: the need for financial gain, personal comfort, status, and physical well-being. Living in the computer age makes it even more important to give readers a sense of personal recognition. Use the person's name once in the body of the letter. Follow the "you approach" by avoiding too many **I**'s or **We**'s in the message. The use of these psychological principles will let the reader know that his or her interest is your concern.

Wording

The wording of your business correspondence can help you achieve your purpose and focus on the reader. Using the following list of 15 C's will allow you to maintain the overall positive tone that you want to achieve.

courteous—pleasant, polite
cordial—friendly, congenial
clear—understandable
concise—brief
complete—comprehensive

coherent—unified, flowing
concrete—exact, specific
common—familiar, jargon-free
candid—forthright, open
concerned—interested, helpful
considerate—tactful
convincing—persuasive
credible—believable
conversational—not stiff and formal
correct—error-free

No matter what your message, whether positive or negative, use this checklist to avoid wording that is abrasive, stiff, unfriendly, or unclear. Use active rather than passive voice. A positive manner and conversational tone can help you influence the reader and accomplish your purpose.

Tone

You cannot compose anything without being aware of tone. The tone of your correspondence will depend on the writer's position in relation to the person to whom it is addressed. When writing, you should try to strike a balance in the level of your language. You should avoid:

wordiness—*in this day and age, prior to the time that*
clichés—*selling like hotcakes, stick to your guns*
slang—*awesome, bad*
technical jargon—*prioritize, impacted*
outdated language—*as per our conversation, pursuant to*

Your letters should reflect the tone you use in conversation rather than the formal business phrases traditionally associated with business letters and legal documents. Since correspondence is often retained as company records, keep your language objective and factual.

One good way to evaluate your tone is to read your letters as if you were receiving them. Would you respond favorably to their tone?

Guidelines

To conclude the discussion on psychology of business writing, consider a few remaining general guidelines. As a superior writer, you must know your subjects thoroughly. In addition, it is worthwhile to offer to be helpful to the reader whenever you can. Even if it is not required of you, you can volunteer useful information for the reader's benefit. You can facilitate action by making it easy for the reader to respond with a tearsheet, a self-addressed card, or even a phone number. Take care to be prompt in responding to business correspondence, and let the reader know you are dealing with the situation immediately. You can achieve success in your on-the-job writing by paying careful attention to (1) your purpose of clear communication, (2) your emphasis on the reader's self-interest, and (3) your positive wording.

PART II: PLANNING

Parts

A good business letter does not just happen; it comes from thoughtful preparation and planning. If you compare a letter to a conversation with a friend, you can break it into three distinct parts:

1. Greeting and purpose
2. Details
3. Closing

A typical social conversation on your part might go something like this:

> Hello. How are you?
> I was hoping that you could go to the theater with me. (*Greeting and purpose*)
> The show will be on Saturday at the college auditorium starting at 2 P.M.
> Tickets are $10 each. I will meet you in the lobby at 1:30. (*Details*)
> I'll look forward to seeing you Saturday.
> Bye. (*Closing*)

Breaking a task into its parts always makes it simpler to accomplish. If you are careful to include all three parts in your letters, you will have a well-balanced communication.

Outline

Using the three parts of a letter as a skeleton, you can outline your message so that it communicates effectively.

First, decide on an appropriate opening sentence. Do not jump right into the body of the letter; have at least one sentence that is introductory. For example, **Thank you for your** (**order, letter, reply,** etc.); or, **We appreciate your business.**

Next, determine the purpose of the letter. State it briefly in the sentence following your introductory sentence. If you are responding to a letter, you should mention its subject. For instance, **I appreciate being asked to speak to your group.**

Then gather all the information (details) you need to achieve your purpose. Ask yourself: who? what? when? where? why? how? as they apply to the situation. Then organize this information in an orderly flow in your next paragraph or paragraphs. If you have a great deal of information, you may want to use additional paragraphs.

To close, construct an appropriate paragraph of leave-taking, one that will ensure goodwill. For example, **We are happy to do business with you** or **We look forward to hearing from you,** etc. If you desire certain action (follow-up), you should suggest it before closing.

Following this plan will enable you to construct a proper business letter. Be sure to include all three sections.

Emphasis

A significant consideration in the overall plan of your letter is emphasis. How do you give prominence to your most important ideas? You can do this by managing (1) space, (2) location, and (3) mechanics. The amount of space you devote to an idea indicates its importance. Obviously, the greater the development, the greater the emphasis. Also, emphasis can be achieved by location in a prominent position; for example, state your strongest reason first. The use of mechanics is another way to highlight ideas. Such techniques as enumeration (lists), indentation, capitalization, underlining, italicizing, and bold print can call the reader's attention to points of importance.

In summary, planning can be a productive effort when it (1) utilizes the three parts of a letter (*greeting and purpose, details,* and *closing*), (2) establishes an outline using those parts, and (3) gives proper emphasis to the ideas of greatest importance.

PART III: FORMAT

Letter Style

When writing a business letter, you have certain options in the area of style. Once you are on the job, you will discover what style your company prefers for its letters. It is wise to follow that preference. Two basic styles emerge as the common ones found in most businesses:

1. The block style
2. The modified block style

In the block letter, every line begins at the left margin—unless, of course, the printed letterhead is centered at the top of the page. See the following sample entitled "Sample Block Format."

SAMPLE BLOCK FORMAT

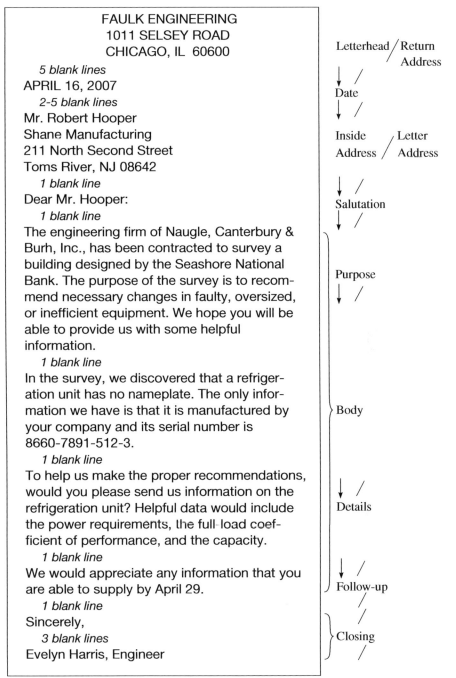

FAULK ENGINEERING
1011 SELSEY ROAD
CHICAGO, IL 60600

5 blank lines

APRIL 16, 2007

2-5 blank lines

Mr. Robert Hooper
Shane Manufacturing
211 North Second Street
Toms River, NJ 08642

1 blank line

Dear Mr. Hooper:

1 blank line

The engineering firm of Naugle, Canterbury & Burh, Inc., has been contracted to survey a building designed by the Seashore National Bank. The purpose of the survey is to recommend necessary changes in faulty, oversized, or inefficient equipment. We hope you will be able to provide us with some helpful information.

1 blank line

In the survey, we discovered that a refrigeration unit has no nameplate. The only information we have is that it is manufactured by your company and its serial number is 8660-7891-512-3.

1 blank line

To help us make the proper recommendations, would you please send us information on the refrigeration unit? Helpful data would include the power requirements, the full-load coefficient of performance, and the capacity.

1 blank line

We would appreciate any information that you are able to supply by April 29.

1 blank line

Sincerely,

3 blank lines

Evelyn Harris, Engineer

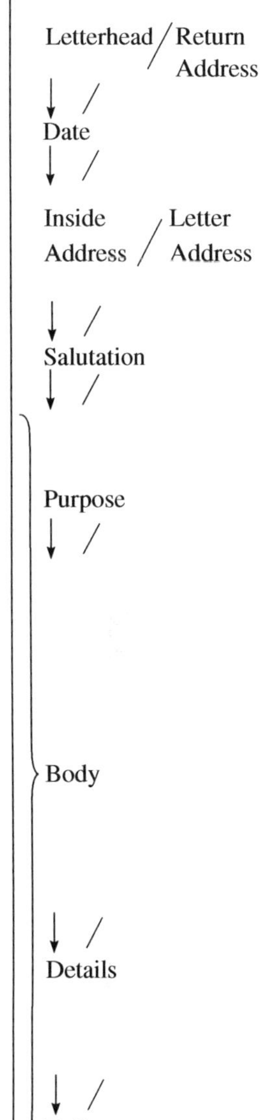

In the modified block letter, the date and complimentary closing begin at the center point. Often it has indented paragraphs, as in the following sample. However, another acceptable version of the modified block letter does not have indented paragraphs.

SAMPLE MODIFIED BLOCK FORMAT
(WITH INDENTED PARAGRAPHS)

Faulk Engineering
1011 Selsey Road
Chicago, IL 60600

April 15, 2007

Mr. Robert Hooper
Shane Manufacturing
211 North Second Street
Toms River, NJ 08642

Dear Mr. Hooper:

The engineering firm of Naugle, Canterbury & Buhr. Inc., has been contracted to survey a building designed by the Seashore National Bank. The purpose of the survey is to recommend necessary changes in faulty, oversized, or inefficient equipment. We hope you will be able to provide us with some helpful information.

In the survey, we discovered that a refrigeration unit has no nameplate. The only information we have is that it is manufactured by your company and its serial number is 8660-7891-512-3.

To help us make the proper recommendations, would you please send us information on the refrigeration unit? Helpful data would include the power requirements, the full-load coefficient of performance, and the capacity.

We would appreciate any information that you are able to supply by April 29.

Sincerely,

Evelyn Harris, Engineer

Sections of a Letter

As you can see from the sample block letter, there are six sections of a standard business letter:

1. Letterhead or return address
2. Date
3. Inside address or envelope address
4. Salutation
5. Body
6. Closing

The **letterhead** or **return address** gives the writer's complete address. Many businesses provide stationery with preprinted letterheads. Usually, if you use printed letterhead, the address is centered. Do not create letterheads for your assignments in this book. Use the return address format.

NOTE Currently, it is common to place the return address of a personal business letter (no letterhead) below the sender's typed name in the closing. In this case, you would begin your letter with the current date. Use the two-letter, all-capitals abbreviations for states (see list at the end of this module). See the example below.

> Sincerely,
>
> Nancy Atkins
> 875 Dogwood Lane
> Rehoboth Beach, DE 19971

Place the **date** below the company letterhead. Be sure to write out the month; do not abbreviate. Remember to place a comma between the day of the month and the year. The correct style is this: June 25, 2007.

The **inside** or **letter address** is approximately five spaces below the date, depending on the length of the letter, and begins at the left margin. You should include the name and title of the person to whom you are writing, as well as the company name and address. Write out such words as *Street, Route, Road, Drive,* etc.

The salutation begins two spaces below the inside address starting at the left margin. *Be sure to note that it is followed by a colon in a business letter.* (You can use a comma in a social business letter.) Use the person's name and courtesy title (Mr., Mrs., Captain) when you can. The salutation should agree with the first line of the inside address. If you do not know the person's name, call the receptionist of the company to find out before writing. *Ms.* is always correct for women unless you know that they would prefer to be referred to as *Miss* or *Mrs.* Do not use the person's first name in the salutation.

Dear Professor Bartlett:
Dear Senator White:
Dear Ms. Abbott:
Dear Mrs. Canfield:

When you do not have a specific person to write to, it is customary to use some of the following salutations for a company:

Dear Sir or Madam: (Used for a person whose gender you do not know)
Ladies and Gentlemen: (Used for companies and organizations)
Dear Order Department Staff: (Used for a specific department)

NOTE Do not use "To Whom It May Concern."

The letter should follow your plan as you have outlined it. It should contain a minimum of three paragraphs, with a paragraph for the greeting and purpose, at least one paragraph for the details, and a paragraph for the closing and follow up. These paragraphs are single spaced with double spacing between each. In the block style, the paragraphs begin at the left margin. In the modified block style, you have the option of beginning them at the left margin or indenting them five spaces.

The **closing** consists of the complimentary close, such as *Sincerely* or *Cordially yours,* the writer's signature, the typed name, and the person's job title. Note that the second word in a closing, such as *Cordially yours,* is not capitalized. In the block style, the closing is found at the left margin. In the modified block style, it is at the midpoint of the page. The complimentary close is typed two spaces after the last paragraph. The typed name is four spaces below the complimentary close, leaving room for the handwritten signature. If a job title is included, it follows immediately after the typed name.

Examine the final copy of your letters to see that you have included all sections so that you can be sure of having a polished, professional letter that reflects the business image you wish to convey.

Mechanics

If you pay careful attention to mechanical details, your business correspondence will project the image of a professional organization. The proper use of elements such as abbreviations, numbers, and capitalization is crucial in making your writing effective. Here are a few pointers concerning these mechanical elements as they occur in business letters. For a more detailed discussion, consult a handbook, grammar text, or dictionary.

Abbreviations

- Use abbreviations rarely in your business letters. Basically, in the return address and the inside address, use the two-letter, all-capitals abbreviations for states (see p. 340 for a complete list).

  DE for Delaware
  CA for California
  TX for Texas

- When using the name of a state in the text of a letter (not in the form of an address), spell out the state name.

  The new business is located in Flint, Michigan.

- Write out words such as *Street, Route, Road, Lane,* etc., in an address. Also write out *East, West, North,* and *South.*

  Mr. William Freeman
  Route 1, Box 218
  Lewes, DE 19958

  Ms. Carmen Ortega
  301 East Peach Lane
  Salisbury, MD 21801

- Write out the months of the year in a date.

  February 27, 2008

- Write out titles following names.

  Mr. Lamden Carey
  Director of Personnel

- You may abbreviate the name of an organization if you spell it out at the first use.

  Registration for students at Delaware Technical and Community College will be on March 9, 2008. Students participating in DTCC orientation should report at 9 A.M.

Numbers

- Check carefully to see if you should use words or figures. The basic rule is to use words for **one** through **ten** and figures for **11** and up.
- In a date, do not use the ordinal ending (**th** or **nd**) unless it precedes the month.

  15th of February (not **February 15th**)

- Use the proper sequence of month, day, and year for dates.

  February 15, 2007 (not **15 February 2007**)

Capitalization.

- Capitalize all first words and all important words in a subject line or title. It is not necessary to capitalize the articles (**a, an, the**) or the prepositions under four letters (**of, in, to,** etc.) unless they come at the beginning of the letter.

- Underline or italicize the titles of books and the names of newspapers and magazines. Enclose the titles of chapters, articles, short stories, and poems in quotation marks and place periods and commas inside closing quotation marks.

  In your textbook, *Writing Skills for Technical Students,* your assignment is to read Module 15, "Business Letter Writing."

- Use lowercase abbreviations for **a.m.** and **p.m.**

  9 p.m.
  10:30 a.m.

Length

The question of length of a letter has no firm rules as far as number of sentences or number of paragraphs. You will have to pull some items from the list of C's to determine proper length. Ask yourself: "Is the letter clear, concise, and complete?" If you can say "Yes" to all three, your length is appropriate.

More definite guidelines can be given regarding sentence and paragraph length. A sentence should average 20 words; however, it is wise to keep in mind that variety in length makes for more pleasant reading. Basic paragraph length is about 100 words for the body (details) and 40 or 50 words each for the introduction (greeting and purpose) and conclusion (closing). Generally speaking, a paragraph should be no longer than 8–10 typewritten lines.

Appearance

The appearance of your letter is not to be overlooked because it reflects the kind of person you are and the type of company you represent. Neatness is a critical factor. Use a letter-quality printer. The quality of paper is also a consideration. Professional-looking letterhead makes a good impression. Finally, the way the letter is balanced on the page can enhance the image. In other words, use spacing to balance the white space on your sheet of paper.

Summary

You will become increasingly proficient at developing the kind of business communications that enhance your company's public relations and build your own reputation as an employee of merit if you remember to do the following:

1. Apply the psychological principles of effective business writing.
2. Focus on the reader.
3. Use positive tone and proper wording.
4. Plan well by outlining the three parts of a letter while giving proper emphasis to your key points.
5. Follow the guidelines on style, format, and appearance.
6. Proofread carefully for correct mechanics.
7. When in doubt, consult a reference manual.

PART IV: REQUEST LETTER

The most common type of letter that you will write is a letter of request. It is used to request information, services, or products. As the writer making the request, you must make it as easy as possible for the receiver to answer your request. This can be accomplished through proper planning and consideration for the reader.

To make it easier for the reader to comply, be sure to include the following specific information:

What is wanted
Who wants it
Why it is wanted
How it will be used
List of a few clear, direct questions (if appropriate)
Deadline for necessary action
Expression of appreciation

In the request letter, the "you approach" is very helpful because it allows you to indicate how the reader can benefit by sharing his or her knowledge and services. Whenever possible, show the reader the advantages of responding positively and promptly to your request.

Your choice of words will have a direct effect on the response you get. For example, if you are asking someone to be a guest speaker, **Would you consider addressing our group** is preferred to **I would like you to speak.** The second example is really not a request; it is a polite command. Likewise, **Would you send me information about** is more appropriate than **I need information on.**

The main parts of a request letter consist of an opening, a body, and a conclusion—at least three paragraphs. The purpose of the opening is to involve the reader by gaining his or her attention and to establish the purpose of the letter. The body contains all the necessary details the recipient will need to make a response. In your closing, be sure to include a due date or a specific time by which you need to have the response. Most of the time, the reader will respond to a reasonable request. Remember that the reader cannot know what you want if you do not give specific instructions.

For a sample of the content of a request letter, see the Sample Block Format. Then proceed to Activity 15-A.

ACTIVITY 15-A: Writing a Request Letter

Write a request letter using one of the following situations. Supply the necessary details of who, what, when, where, how, and why to make the letter complete.

1. Write a letter asking a person to speak at a meeting of a professional organization of which you are a member.
2. Write a letter asking an expert in your field to judge a professional contest related to your technology.
3. Write a letter asking a person working in your technical field to grant you an interview for your class assignment in the Report Module.
4. You have been offered a job with a particular company. Write a letter asking a person working for that firm to give you some information about the company and the particular job you have been offered.

PART V: LETTER THAT SAYS "NO"

A refusal letter is, of course, the opposite of a request letter. However, each is based on the same psychology: Both the writer and the receiver want something. The writer who views the request from both sides will write a better refusal letter—and keep the goodwill of the customer.

An objective of the "No" letter is to appeal to the requester's reason and, in so doing, avoid hurt feelings.

One of the most effective techniques for preparing the reader for a refusal is to begin with a brief statement agreeing with some aspect of the request—not the basic issue, but some attitude or feeling the reader has expressed. This action paves the way for you to present the reasons why the request cannot be met and then to refuse. You can end on a statement that keeps the door open for future business and keeps the customer's goodwill.

The best plan for a "No" letter is to use the **Stroke-Zing-Stroke** approach. In other words, you sandwich the bad news between good news.

Stroke 1. Begin in a positive way and also restate the original request. (Opening paragraph)

Zing 2. State the reasons for your position; then refuse clearly. (Second—and possibly third—paragraph)

Stroke 3. End with a positive statement. (Final paragraph)

To make this letter effective, you should not begin the opening paragraph or even the second paragraph with a negative statement. It is important to introduce the letter constructively and to present your reasons first so that the reader will remain objective.

In addition to the Stroke-Zing-Stroke plan of action, there are some things to avoid as you write your "No" letter.

1. Do not ever heap blame on the reader.
2. Do not shut the door of communication.
3. Do not forget that you may someday be requesting a favor of the reader.
4. Do not be indefinite; give a clear-cut "No."

Following these guidelines carefully, you should be ready to write a letter that says "No."

ACTIVITY 15-B: Writing a "No" Letter

Using one of the situations in Activity 15-A, write a letter of refusal to a specific request. Remember to restate the request and to use the **Stroke-Zing-Stroke** approach.

SAMPLE "NO" LETTER

The Columbus Villa
605 North Boardwalk
Ocean City, MD 21842

May 15, 2007

Mr. James L. Pike, President
Pike's Art Supplies
501 Main Street
Tamarac, NJ 20092

Dear Mr. Pike:

Preparations for the Mid-Atlantic Craft Fair are well under way! How very thoughtful of you to remember us and to consider our lodging facilities for your company's representatives attending the fair.

Normally, we would have no trouble accommodating your party of 20 people. However, because of expansion of the show, we are almost completely booked for the week in June that you have requested. We regret that we are unable to offer you the accommodations that you require.

If we can be of further service for future shows at Convention Hall, please do not hesitate to contact us. Again, we certainly appreciate your continued patronage.

Sincerely yours,

Fred Baker, Manager

PART VI: RESUMÉ AND LETTER OF APPLICATION

Resumé

A resumé (sometimes called a personal data sheet) and a letter of application work as a pair to help you get a job. To capitalize on this teamwork, use each for its specific purpose: (1) the resumé to show what you have accomplished and (2) the letter of application to show what you can do for the employer.

You should construct your resumé first so that the letter of application can highlight certain items on the resumé. Your first step is to take a personal inventory. What do you have to offer? Your education, internships, and training are important, of course. So is any work experience, whether full time or part time. Even if the experience is not directly related to the job you are seeking, these jobs indicate that you are willing to work. Also evaluate your personality; demonstrate your reliability, resourcefulness, energy, and inventiveness.

The second step in job seeking is to find out which firms have openings for applicants with your qualifications. Among the people who study the needs of companies and could help you are your instructors and department chairpersons. Your college placement service may give you advice and lend you catalogs and other literature. Other productive sources include the college library, which houses the *Occupation Outlook Handbook,* plus newspaper want ads, the local chamber of commerce, and company employees. Get the names of the personnel directors of companies in which you are interested by telephoning the receptionists at their offices. If the plants or offices are within driving distance, take a look at them from the outside. Some may surprise you. Seeing the place to which you will address your letter sometimes helps you get the firm in focus and makes the writing a little easier. If you are answering a classified advertisement of a firm some distance away, check your sources for information, especially your college library or a website.

Once you have decided which companies you would like to work for, match your assets against the requirements of those companies. Determine what you have that the company needs.

Now you are ready to write the resumé. The resumé is a summary of your objectives, education, work experience, and accomplishments—all in one easily digested page. Because employers will use the resumé for quick reference, provide all information in the form of tabulated lists and clearly marked headings, not sentences and paragraphs. Study the following guidelines carefully.

GUIDELINES FOR A RESUMÉ

Essential items:

name, address, phone number (*in prominent place*)
job objective
work experience (*reverse chronological order, including job titles*)

professional memberships or licenses
educational background (*including all degrees and dates received*)
achievements (*honors, publications, awards*)
military service

Optional items:
description of jobs held
readiness to move to another area
computer skills
skill areas
foreign languages
class standing (*if in top 25th percentile*)
summer jobs (*if recent graduate or previous relevant jobs*)
personal qualities, such as dependability, initiative, etc.
special courses or major (*if lacking in work experience*)
community activities

Unnecessary items:
causes for terminating previous employment
salary information
photograph
names of family members
references
high school information (*except honors*)
personal data
hobbies and interests

Appearance:
neatness
balance of white space—good margins
good-quality 8½" × 11" paper (tinted, if desired)
special effects (*selective use of caps, underlining, bold print, tabulation, italicizing, bullets*)
letter-quality printing
double-spacing between headings
dates in prominent locations

Other tips:
Use reverse chronological order for education and work experience.
Use active verbs, such as **audited, assisted, demonstrated, developed, facilitated, maintained, performed, reorganized, scheduled, supervised,** etc.
Use phrases rather than sentences.
Take care not to lie or be too modest.
Proofread carefully for spelling and mechanics.
Place most impressive, either experience or education, at top.
Use parallel wording for entries (*verb phrases, noun phrases,* etc.) and in format (*indentations, use of periods, highlighting, underlining,* etc.).

SAMPLE RESUMÉ

Nancy C. Hopkins
207 West Pine Street
Georgetown, DE 19947
(302) 856-2791

OBJECTIVE	Seeking position requiring office systems skills and knowledge	
EDUCATION	Delaware Technical & Community College, Owens Campus, Georgetown, DE 19947 A.A.S. Degree in Office Administration Technology, May 2007	
COMPUTER SOFTWARE	Microsoft Office: Word, Access, PowerPoint, Excel, Publisher Outlook	
MAJOR COURSES	Keyboarding Accounting Referencing and Transcription Office Systems and Procedures Desktop Publishing Integrated Business Applications	
EXPERIENCE 9/98 to present	Delmarva Cable Company, 110 South Water Street, Georgetown, DE 19947	
	Position:	Office Assistant
	Duties:	Filing, answering telephones, photocopying documents, handling customer requests.
1/00 to 4/02	Delaware Technical & Community College, Owens Campus	
	Position:	Peer Tutor
	Duties:	Tutor fellow students in Keyboarding, Basic Reading, Microsoft Word, and Excel.
6/94 to 8/98	Seaford School District Office, 187 High Street, Seaford, DE 19973	
	Position:	Office Assistant, Business Office (part-time summer job)
	Duties:	Filing, answering telephones, photocopying documents, mailing letters, preparing inventory, assembling employee handbooks
PERSONAL ATTRIBUTES	Organizational abilities Resourceful Self-motivated Adaptable	

ACTIVITY 15-C: Writing a Resumé

Construct the professional resumé which will accompany your letter of application when you begin your job search. The resumé should be printed on $8^1/_2$"× 11" bond stationery.

Letter of Application

As you begin your job search, your letter of application may be your first contact with the prospective company. For this reason, it is one of the most important pieces of correspondence you will write. Its purpose is to introduce yourself to the employer, to mention the position you are interested in, and to state your qualifications for the position. It should underscore your strong points and convince the employer that he or she will profit by granting you an interview.

The letter of application is designed to be accompanied by the resumé, which details your education and work experience. The letter complements the resumé in highlighting aspects of your background that would make the company want to hire you rather than someone else. You should NEVER send a resumé without a letter of application.

As in a standard business letter, the letter of application should maintain the "*you* approach" by letting the employer know how he or she can benefit by hiring you. Keep in mind that neatness and grammatical correctness are of prime consideration.

A well-organized letter of application contains three sections. The introduction should indicate the position you are applying for, if practical. You might also mention where you heard of the opening and arouse the reader's interest in you by mentioning some special qualification you have for the job.

The next section, the body, should emphasize the items on your resumé that you especially want to be noticed. Stress the strongest points of your education, your experience, and your abilities as each relates to the particular job you are seeking. Refer the reader to specific points on your resumé. Save any discussion of salary for the interview.

The main purpose of the conclusion is to secure the job interview. Before requesting a meeting, first summarize your qualifications for the job and comment on what you can do for the company. Then suggest setting up the interview. It is appropriate to give an idea of the times you are available, but be sure to be tactful and not demanding.

GUIDELINES FOR A LETTER OF APPLICATION

Do not use **I** as the first word in the letter.
Use name and title of company representative (*can be obtained by phoning receptionist*).
Mention specific job you are seeking.
Refer to special abilities or achievements.
Mention name of person who told you about job opening.
Include attention-getting statement in opening paragraph.
Place strongest points first, either education or experience.
Indicate your date of availability.
Match your training to employer's needs.
Refer to personal qualities, such as dependability, inventiveness, interest in working with people, etc.
Note outstanding academic record.
Refer to particular items on resumé.
Summarize qualifications for job.
Suggest direct action to secure interview.

Notice how these principles are applied in the following letter of application.

SAMPLE LETTER OF APPLICATION

May 5, 2008

Mr. George V. Ballantyne, Personnel Manager
114 Mellegood Street
Atlanta, GA 30342

Dear Mr. Ballantyne:

The position of draftsman-detailer in your industrial construction section is of interest to me. Word about the opening came through Mr. Harold MacKenzie, our college placement officer at Delaware Technical & Community College, Owens Campus. Mr. MacKenzie thinks that my qualifications might be of special interest to you. On May 10, I will receive my Associate of Applied Science Degree in Architectural Design at Delaware Tech and will be available for employment. Throughout training, my interests have been directed toward industrial design, not only because I prefer it, but also because I was fortunate enough to gain some practical experience assisting designers of poultry construction during the last two summers and on weekends. (See attached resumé.)

This winter at B.A. Brewer, Inc., I worked independently at night and on weekends making detailed shop and field drawings for welded and mechanically assembled steel structures and shop drawings from engineering sketches of grain elevators, screw conveyors, and storage silos.

One of my original designs for improving brooder construction was adopted and made standard equipment by Brewer. The design and model of a solar-heated brooder, which I developed as my Capstone project at college, is now on display at the Chamber of Commerce.

Could I have an interview with you? I am seeking a position outside the poultry industry because I would like to enter a broader field of design where I could gain wider knowledge and find more opportunities to apply my ideas. During the day my phone number is (302) 730-6434.

Your consideration of my application would be greatly appreciated.

Sincerely,

Chris Freeman

Chris Freeman
2371 Newlin Avenue
Milltown, DE 19944

Enclosure

ACTIVITY 15-D: Writing a Letter of Application

Write a letter of application for a specific position. Print the letter on $8^1/_2$" × 11" bond stationery.

PART VII: THE MEMO

Historically, the memorandum (memo) has been a form of communication used to relay information within a company. With electronic mail (email), however, the memo is now used to send messages beyond company walls.

By nature, the memo is usually concerned with one topic, and it should be kept as short as possible. It communicates a message best when it is concise and direct. The memo is usually conversational in tone and free of business jargon, clichés, and slang.

There are three main kinds of memos. The informative memo is the most common type, and it is used to relay announcements and to verify data. A second type, the persuasive memo, tries to persuade the reader to adopt a point of view through the use of logical argument and example. The third kind of memo, used to seek information, consists of specific questions to answer or checklists to mark, or it may simply ask for general comments.

The memo follows the same basic guidelines for all good business writing. It should be organized and have a beginning, a middle, and an end. It should be proper in tone and correct in form, and its message should be clear and concise. Email should not be considered informal and should follow the rules of spelling and good writing practices.

Form

The unique characteristic of the memo is its use of the heading, which consists of four parts. Usually a company will have the four basic parts of the heading preprinted. The format varies with the company, but the following is common practice:

DATE: Various forms
FROM: Name, Title
TO: Name, Title
SUBJECT: Treat Like a Title (capitalize all words of more than four letters)

Sometimes the order of the heading will be different and placement on the page may vary, but all four sections should be present. Memos are usually typed and, unlike the business letter, are not signed. Instead, the sender usually initials the FROM line in ink to authorize distribution of the completed memo after checking it for accuracy. With email, names of senders are automatic, and the time is included with the date.

FROM: Mary Jarvis *MJ*

Memos use traditional paragraph format, which may or may not be indented; most are not. There is no salutation or closing as in the business letter. The memo is single-spaced with double spacing between paragraphs and three spaces between the heading and the first paragraph.

Content

The memo has three basic parts: introduction, body, and conclusion. A properly planned memo communicates the message clearly and eliminates wordiness and repetition.

The introduction of the memo should state the purpose and summarize the most important point. In other words, memos begin with the main message; there is no working up to the major point. To be effective, the memo should deal with one issue at a time. Once the purpose of the memo is established, the succeeding paragraphs can fill in necessary details.

The body of the memo supplies those facts or details the reader needs to make a decision, to understand the purpose of the memo, or to form an opinion. Included are facts, arguments, questions to be answered, historical background, charts, enumerated items, or other relevant material. The content depends on the purpose of the memo. Details should be presented logically and, therefore, need to be stated only once. If the body is extremely long or complicated, headings will help to section the information.

The conclusion is a very important part of the memo that is frequently overlooked. It should leave the reader with some idea of a follow-up. It may give the reader something to think about or do; it may ask for a response by a given date; it may ask the reader to present ideas in writing or to get in touch with the sender of the memo. In a longer memo, it may be a summary of the main points. Frequently, the conclusion consists of an **IF** statement that will give the recipient some idea of the next step in the process.

If you cannot attend the meeting, please send a substitute.
If you have any questions, please contact me.

Sample Memo

This sample is an illustration of how a memo should look in form and how the content can be expressed.

SAMPLE MEMO

TO: All Personnel
FROM: Jason Parker, Chief Security Officer *JP*
SUBJECT: Parking Permits
DATE: September 19, 2007

Due to the increase of illegally parked cars in the parking lots, new parking stickers have been issued and will be distributed to all personnel. As of October 1, any car parked in a lot without a proper sticker will be towed at the owner's expense.

Stickers are available at the Security Office and will be issued during working hours. Each department will be given release time before the end of the month so that all personnel can get needed stickers. To speed up the process, please bring the following information with you:

1. Car registration
2. Company identification card

You will need a separate sticker for each car you possess. You should place the new sticker on the back right bumper for easy verification in the lots.

If you have any questions, please contact me at Extension 32.

Before writing your memo assignment, study the charts comparing the business letter and the memo.

ACTIVITY 15-E: Writing a Memo

Choose one of the following situations and compose a memo using the correct format and tone. Be sure your memo has a purpose section, a body with well-organized details, and a follow-up. The assignments listed below give only sketchy details. Supply all the specific information, such as names, dates, times, places, etc., necessary to make your memo complete and accurate.

COMPARISON OF BUSINESS LETTER AND MEMO FORMATS

Business Letter	*Memo*
___ (heading lines), ___ (inside address), ___: (salutation), body paragraphs, ___, (closing), ___ (signature)	TO: ___ FROM: ___ SUBJECT: ___ DATE: ___

1. You are the in-company Blue Cross-Blue Shield representative. Write a memo to all company personnel to explain that everyone will be required to have a medical checkup every two years. The checkups will be paid for by the company. Announce a meeting (give specifics) at which a Blue Cross-Blue Shield spokesperson will explain the new requirement for physicals.
2. You are the in-company United Fund representative. Announce a meeting for all personnel to discuss the possibility of automatically deducting contributions from employees' paychecks.
3. You are a part-time college student. Write a memo to your supervisor asking for a one-year leave of absence so that you can complete your associate degree.
4. You are in charge of company parking. Schedule a meeting to discuss the parking problems in the company lot and to arrive at a solution to improve the situation.

COMPARISON OF BUSINESS LETTER AND MEMO

	BUSINESS LETTER	ELECTRONIC OR PAPER MEMO
Audience	person outside company	person inside company
Format	heading or letterhead, date, inside address, salutation, body, closing, signature, always has full signature	to, from, subject and date lines; body; initials or signature beside FROM line
	modified block style uses indented paragraphs, block style uses no indented paragraphs 8½" × 11" stationery	usually electronic or may use 8½" × 11" stationery or half sheet if message is short
Tone	positive, conversational, "you" flavor, focus on reader—very few **I**'s and **we**'s	positive, direct, not personal, concentrates on message, not person
Organization of body		
Introduction	cordial greeting and brief statement of purpose	first paragraph direct statement of purpose
Body	background and details of message	background and details of message (often in numbered list)
Conclusion	cordial leave-taking	request for action or follow-up

PART VIII: TRANSMITTAL LETTER AND TRANSMITTAL MEMO

Often in business, a report is written and must be sent to the proper people for review. It is important to have a transmittal (or cover) letter or memo to accompany the report.

The transmittal letter is used if the material is being sent outside the company. Because it is going to another establishment, it is in the form of a business letter and is typed on the firm's letterhead. The transmittal memo, using the standard memorandum form, is used if the material is being circulated within the company.

Because the primary purpose of the transmittal letter or memo is to identify an enclosed report, the correspondence should be relatively short. It should include the title of the report, the name of the person who requested it, and a one- or two-sentence description of the contents. The writer can also acknowledge the help that particular persons gave in compiling the report. Two samples follow.

After reviewing the guidelines for the transmittal letter and memo, proceed to Activity 15-F.

SAMPLE TRANSMITTAL LETTER

Medical Research, Inc.
Suite 541
1012 Arch Avenue
St. Louis, MO 63155

September 27, 2007

Mr. A. B. Jenkins
National Employment Agency, Inc.
4940 Bayview Drive
Chicago, IL 60600

Dear Mr. Jenkins:

We have completed the report, "Projection of Medical Laboratory Technicians' Employment 2008 to 2010," as requested by Mr. Hamilton Rose on May 17.

The survey was conducted among 1,409 recipients at 251 institutions, including public and private hospitals and commercial labs in 41 states. Variation in projected demand is broken down by geographic region.

Our interviewers are grateful for the assistance provided by Mrs. J. B. Brandor of the Health Department and Mr. James R. Glanding of the New York Laboratory Association.

Your comments will be welcome.

Sincerely yours,

Walter Lanahan

Walter Lanahan
Director, Operations Division

WL/pm

Enclosure

pc: Mr. Harold Morakian

SAMPLE TRANSMITTAL MEMO

TO: John Harr, National Director
FROM: Walter Lanahan, Operations Division *WL*
SUBJECT: Employment of Medical Laboratory Technicians
DATE: September 27, 2007

We have completed the report, "Projection of Medical Laboratory Technicians' Employment 2009 to 2010," as requested by Faye O'Hara on May 17.

The survey was conducted among 1,409 recipients at 251 institutions, including public and private hospitals and commercial labs in 41 states. Variation in projected demand is broken down by geographic region.

Our interviewers are grateful for the assistance provided by Mrs. J. B. Brandor of the Health Department and Mr. James R. Glanding of the New York Laboratory Association.

Your comments will be welcome.

ACTIVITY 15-F: Writing a Transmittal Letter or Memo

Using the following details, write appropriate transmittal correspondence. Choose the transmittal letter format if the material goes outside the company or the transmittal memo format if the material is circulated within the company.

1. The report being sent is entitled "Analysis of Maintenance Costs of Cooperative Farm Machinery in Iowa." This material is being sent by Jordan Davies, chief analyst of the John Brix Implement Corporation, 118 Marriott Way, Des Moines, IA 50300, to the attention of Mr. Gentry Yves, AgriBusiness Development Center, 496 Eden Avenue, Boston, MA 02165. The report was requested by Ms. Gale Roper.
2. The report is also being sent to Jordan Davies' supervisor, Calvin Jarvis, president of the John Brix Implement Corporation.

STATE ABBREVIATIONS

State	Abbreviation	State	Abbreviation
Alabama	AL	Montana	MT
Alaska	AK	Nebraska	NE
Arizona	AZ	Nevada	NV
Arkansas	AR	New Hampshire	NH
California	CA	New Jersey	NJ
Colorado	CO	New Mexico	NM
Connecticut	CT	New York	NY
Delaware	DE	North Carolina	NC
District of Columbia	DC	North Dakota	ND
Florida	FL	Ohio	OH
Georgia	GA	Oklahoma	OK
Hawaii	HI	Oregon	OR
Idaho	ID	Pennsylvania	PA
Illinois	IL	Rhode Island	RI
Indiana	IN	South Carolina	SC
Iowa	IA	South Dakota	SD
Kansas	KS	Tennessee	TN
Kentucky	KY	Texas	TX
Louisiana	LA	Utah	UT
Maine	ME	Vermont	VT
Maryland	MD	Virginia	VA
Massachusetts	MA	Washington	WA
Michigan	MI	West Virginia	WV
Minnesota	MN	Wisconsin	WI
Mississippi	MS	Wyoming	WY
Missouri	MO		

Glossary

Action verb (*See also* verb) An action verb shows physical or mental engagement. The action can be done.

Examples: He *typed* the letter. (physical action)
I *thought* about the experiment. (mental action)

Active voice A verb in the active voice shows the subject of the sentence performing or doing the action of the verb.

Examples: *Mr. Jones spoke* to the new employees.

Address (*See also* noun of address *and* comma) When an address appears in a sentence, place a comma after the name, after the street, after the city, and after the zip code. If no zip code is used, place a comma after the state. There is no comma between the state and the zip code.

Examples: Deliver the package to Dr. Marvin Bronson, 112 Oak Lane, Panhandle, Texas 76691, before 5 P.M.

Adjective An adjective describes or modifies a noun or pronoun. It answers the questions: what kind? which one? how many? how much? The articles *a*, *an*, and *the* are classified as adjectives.

Examples: He dictated *a long* letter. (what kind)
That syringe is sterilized. (which one)
The department needed *five* typewriters. (how many)
We ate *enough* lunch. (how much)

Adverb An adverb modifies or describes a verb, an adjective, or another adverb. It answers the questions how, where, when, or how often. Adverbs frequently end in *-ly*.

Examples: She dresses *smartly*. (how)
I put the memo *there*. (where)

He will call the boss *soon*. (when)
The doctor makes rounds *frequently*. (how often)

Agreement (*See* subject–verb agreement or pronoun–antecedent agreement)

Antecedent An antecedent is the word a pronoun stands for.

Example: The *nurse* filled *her* syringe.

Apostrophe The apostrophe (') is a mark of punctuation used to show possession or a contraction.

Examples: architect's drawing (possession)
can't (contraction)

Appositive An appositive is a word or phrase that renames a noun or pronoun immediately preceding it. It is set off by commas.

Example: Mr. Green, *the electrician in charge*, supervised the wiring job.

Body The body is that part of a paragraph or report that develops or supports the topic sentence.

Case of pronouns (*See* pronoun case)

Clause (*See also* dependent clause *or* independent clause) A clause is a group of words containing a subject and verb.

Clause signal A clause signal is a word that introduces a dependent clause. It is sometimes referred to as a subordinate conjunction.

Example: if, when, although, etc.

Cliché A cliché is an expression overused to the point that it loses its effectiveness.

Examples: six of one, half-a-dozen of another
pretty as a picture, sly as a fox

Collective noun A collective noun refers to a group but is singular when the group is thought of as a unit.

Examples: family, team, committee, group, etc.

Comma (*See also* address, appositive, coordinate adjectives, date, independent clause, interrupter, introductory clause, introductory phrase, misreading, negative expression, noun of address, series, transitional expression) A comma (,) is a mark of punctuation used to indicate an address, an appositive, coordinate adjectives, a date, an interrupter, an introductory clause or phrase, a noun of address, or a series. A comma is also used to prevent misreading, to follow a transitional expression, and to separate two independent clauses with a conjunction.

Comparative degree (*See* degree of comparison)

Comparison of adjectives and adverbs (*See* degree of comparison, verb)

Complete verb (*See also* helping verb *and* main verb) The complete verb consists of the main verb and all of its helpers.

Example: The disk *has been sitting* in that spot for years.

Compound subject (*See also* subject) A compound subject consists of two or more subjects linked by a conjunction.

Example: *Typing* and *shorthand* are essential skills for the secretary.

Compound verb (*See also* verb) A compound verb consists of two or more verbs linked by a conjunction.

Examples: A good secretary *types* rapidly and *transcribes* accurately.

Concluding sentence A concluding sentence comes at the end of a paragraph or report and restates the topic sentence in different words.

Conclusion A conclusion is the final paragraph in a report. It sums up the main ideas presented and restates the introduction in different words.

Conjunction (*See also* coordinate conjunction *or* subordinate conjunction) A conjunction is used to join words or groups of words.

Consonant The consonants are those letters of the alphabet that are not vowels. The vowels are *a*, *e*, *i*, *o*, and *u* (and sometimes *y*).

Controlling idea A controlling idea is a word or phrase located in a topic sentence. It narrows the subject or tells the reader what will be said about the subject.

Example: Sponsoring a family of "boat people" can be *a rewarding experience*.

Coordinate adjectives Coordinate adjectives are two or more adjectives that modify the same noun. They are separated by a comma.

Example: The treaty ended a *long, bitter* struggle.

Coordinate conjunction A coordinate conjunction is a word used to join together two words, two phrases, or two clauses.

Examples: and, but, or, nor, for, so, yet
He saw the file, *but* he did not touch it.

Coordination (*See also* coordinate conjunction, independent clause, subordination) Coordination, in sentence structure, refers to connections of two independent clauses with a coordinate conjunction.

Example: The surveyors set up the transit, and they surveyed the property lines.

Correlatives (*See also* parallel structure) Correlatives are pairs of conjunctions that are used together. They require parallel construction.

Examples: not only . . . but also
either . . . or
neither . . . nor
both . . . and

Date In a date, the month and day are treated as a unit, and the year is treated as a unit. In the context of a sentence, follow the day and the year with commas.

Example: He applied for the job on August 12, 2007, after hearing of the opening.

Degree of comparison When using an adjective or an adverb to compare items, the degree of comparison depends on whether you are comparing two items (*comparative degree*) or three or more items (*superlative degree*). The word referring to one item is in the positive degree.

POSITIVE	COMPARATIVE	SUPERLATIVE
good	better	best
smart	smarter	smartest
efficient	more efficient	most efficient

Dependent clause A dependent clause is a group of words containing a subject, a verb, and a clause signal. A dependent clause cannot make sense as a sentence when it stands alone; it is a fragment.

Examples: When the mail comes in. . . .
After the storm hits. . . .
While I was typing. . . .

Direct address A noun of direct address is used when you use a person's name or title to speak directly to that person.

Examples: Mr. Basin, here is the memo.
Call for the ambulance, nurse.
You can see, Ms. Smathers, we have complied with your request.

Direct object (*See also* object) A direct object is a word that receives the action of the verb.

Examples: The nurse gave the *shot.*

First person (*See* person)

Fragment A fragment is a part of a sentence, not a whole sentence. It may be a dependent clause, a prepositional phrase, a verbal phrase, a subject, or a verb.

Examples: Because the machine was broken. (dependent clause)
Out of the office and down the hall. (prepositional phrases)
Breaking the test tubes. (verbal phrase)
The executive of the plant. (subject)
Ordered the new safety policy. (verb)

Future tense (*See also* past tense, present tense, *and* tense) A verb in the future tense shows an action or state of being taking place at a later date.

Example: I *will type* the letter tomorrow.

Gerund A gerund is the *-ing* form of the verb used as a noun. It is also called a verbal.

Examples: *Typing* is a necessary skill.
He is best at *calculating* interest.

Helping verb (*See also* verb) A helping verb is used in conjunction with the main verb. It helps the main verb express action or make a statement.

Examples: She *will be* fired tomorrow.
The memo *has been* typed.

"Imglish" An abbreviated series of letters and numbers.

Examples: LTNS—long time no see.
LOL—laugh out loud.

Indefinite pronoun (*See also* pronoun) An indefinite pronoun refers to a general rather than a specific person, place, thing, or idea.

Examples: each, anyone, everyone, all, few, nobody, anybody, etc.

Indefinite reference In an indefinite reference, a pronoun does not have a specific antecedent.

Examples: *It* says in the paper that costs are rising.

Independent clause An independent clause is a group of words with a subject and a verb. It is not introduced by a clause signal; therefore, it makes a complete sentence. An independent clause standing alone is punctuated as a complete sentence. Two independent clauses in the same sentence can be punctuated several ways: with a comma and a conjunction, with a semicolon, or with a semicolon and a transitional expression followed by a comma.

Examples: The *mail arrives* at ten each morning.

Infinitive (*See also* verbal) An infinitive is a verbal that can be identified by *to* plus a verb.

Examples: to draw, to type, to work, to edit.

Interfering words Interfering words are phrases that come between the subject and the verb and often cause problems with subject–verb agreement.

Examples: *Each* (of the secretaries) *types* well.

Interjection An interjection is one of the eight parts of speech. It usually expresses strong emotion and is not grammatically connected to the rest of the sentence.

Examples: Oh! Heavens! Well!

Interrupter An interrupter is a word or phrase that breaks the grammatical flow of a sentence. It is set off by commas.

Examples: Mr. Blandell, *on the other hand,* is an experienced draftsman.

Interview report (*See also* report) An interview report is the written account of a personal interview. It can be written in the regular report format with an Introduction, Body, and Conclusion, or in a question-and-answer format.

Introduction The introduction is that part of a report or paper that indicates the subject and controlling idea. Coming at the beginning, it sets forth the purpose of the piece of writing.

Introductory clause (*See also* comma *and* dependent clause) An introductory clause is a dependent clause that comes at the beginning of a sentence. It should be followed by a comma.

Examples: While I was typing, the power went off.

Introductory phrase (*See also* comma *and* phrase) An introductory phrase comes at the beginning of a sentence. Usually followed by a comma, it may be a prepositional or verbal phrase.

Examples: Typing the memo quickly, she made several errors.

Irregular verb (*See also* verb) An irregular verb is one that does not form its past tense by adding *-d* or *-ed* to the present tense.

Examples:	wear	wore	worn
	eat	ate	eaten

Linking device (*See* transitional expression)

Linking verb (*See also* subject complement, verb) A linking verb joins the subject to a noun or an adjective that follows the verb. It does not show action; it merely shows a state of being. It acts like an equal sign and is followed by a subject complement.

Examples: The nurse *seems* efficient.
The nurse *is* my friend.

Main clause (*See* independent clause)

Main verb In a sentence containing a verb phrase (the verb and its helpers), the main verb is the last word in the verb phrase.

Examples: *He should have been writing* the report.

Major clause (*See* independent clause)

Minor clause (*See* dependent clause)

Misplaced modifier A misplaced modifier can be a word, phrase, or clause that is positioned incorrectly in the sentence so as to cause misunderstanding or confusion.

Examples	MISPLACED:	The draftsman looked for the pencil in his cabinet that was missing.
	CORRECT:	The draftsman looked in his cabinet for the pencil that was missing.

Misreading, prevention of (*See also* comma) Use a comma after a phrase at the beginning of the sentence when it is necessary to prevent misreading.

Examples: By 2009, 25 of these computers will no longer be in use.
After shooting, the policeman put his gun in the holster.

Negative expression (*See also* comma) A negative expression is a phrase coming at the end of a sentence. It either asks a question or shows contrast. It is preceded by a comma.

Examples: Today is bitterly cold, *isn't it?*

Nonrestrictive element A nonrestrictive element is a word, phrase, or clause modifier that is not essential to the clear identification of the word it modifies. It is set off by commas.

Examples	NONRESTRICTIVE:	Mrs. Landers, *who works in Dr. Burroughs' office*, is an excellent secretary.
	RESTRICTIVE:	The lady *who works in Dr. Burroughs' office* is an excellent secretary.

Noun (*See also* collective noun, gerund, noun of address, subject, object) A noun is a word that names a person, place, thing, or idea. It can be used in a sentence as a subject or as an object.

Examples: A *doctor* was summoned. (person)
He came into the patient's *room*. (place)

He was carrying a black *bag*. (thing)
His *desire* was to make the patient well. (idea)

Note: In the above examples, *doctor* and *desire* are used as subjects, and *room* and *bag* are used as objects.

Noun of address A noun of address is used in a sentence to speak directly to a person by using his or her name. It is set off by commas.

Examples: I see, *Mr. Bowen*, that you have drawn the plans.

Number (*See also* shift) There are only two types of number in the use of nouns and pronouns: singular and plural. Singular refers to one; plural refers to two or more.

Examples: She was reading a *book*. (singular)
She read several *books*. (plural)

Object (*See* direct object, object of preposition, *or* object pronouns)

Object of preposition The object of a preposition is the noun or pronoun following the preposition.

Examples: He got a shot in the *arm*.

Object of verb (*See* direct object)

Object pronouns The object pronouns are used as direct objects, objects of prepositions, and objects of verbals.

Examples: me, you, him, her, it, us, them.
Take *it* to the office. (direct object)
Come with *me*. (object of preposition)
Calling *him*, I made the appointment. (object of verbal)

Outline An outline is a bare skeleton or framework of the ideas to be included in a piece of writing longer than a paragraph. Items can be phrases or complete thoughts. Remember that if you have point 1, you must have point 2. If you have example A, you must have an example B.

Examples: I. Introduction
A.
B.

II. Body
 A.
 B.
 1.
 2.
III. Conclusion
 A.
 B.

Paragraph A paragraph is a group of related sentences with a topic sentence and supporting sentences. If it stands alone, it also has a concluding sentence.

Parallel structure Parallel structure occurs when two or more words, phrases, or clauses are joined by a coordinate conjunction. The items linked in this manner must all be parallel in form; that is, they must all be nouns, all prepositional phrases, all clauses, etc.

Examples: *Typing memos*, *alphabetizing mailing lists*, and *transcribing shorthand* were duties of the new receptionist. (parallel phrases)
The copy editor was *fast*, *accurate*, and *creative*. (parallel adjectives)

Parenthetic element (*See* interrupter)

Participle (*See also* present participle, past participle, *and* verbal) A participle is one of the three types of verbals. It is the *-ing* form or past tense form of the verb used as an adjective.

Examples: The *falling* rocks injured many tourists.
The *barking* dogs kept us from sleeping.

Passive voice (*See also* active voice) A verb in the passive voice shows the subject receiving (rather than doing) the action of the verb. The passive voice is signaled by a form of the verb to be as a helper.

Examples: The new employees *were spoken* to by Ms. Jones.

Past participle The past participle is the form of the verb used with the helper *have* or *has* to show action or state of being completed.

Examples: We *have walked* three miles.
He *has gone* to work.

PRESENT	PAST	PAST PARTICIPLE
walk	walked	(have) walked
go	went	(has) gone

Past tense (*See also* future tense, present tense, *and* tense) A verb in the past tense shows an action completed at a former time.

Examples: I *typed* the letter yesterday.

Person Person indicates the division of pronouns into first person, second person, and third person.

Examples	FIRST PERSON:	(person speaking) I (me, my, mine), we (us, our, ours)
	SECOND PERSON:	(person spoken to) you (your, yours)
	THIRD PERSON:	(person spoken about) he (him, his), she (her, hers), it (its), they (them, their, theirs)

Persuasion report A persuasion report is an essay designed to convince readers of a certain point of view and to urge them to take some form of action.

Phrase (*See also* prepositional phrase, verbal phrase) A phrase is a group of words used to convey a single idea. Although it does not contain a subject or a verb, it is a distinct part of a sentence.

Examples: The boss stomped out *of the office*. (prepositional)
Hearing the phone, she jumped up to answer it. (verbal)

Plural (*See also* singular) The plural form of a word indicates more than one. Generally, a noun forms its plural by adding *-s* or *-es* to the singular; a verb forms its plural by dropping the *-s* or *-es* from the singular.

Examples: *Architects are* in great demand.
Teachers often *strike* for higher wages.

Point of view (*See also* person, shift) Point of view refers to the perspective from which a paragraph or a report is written. It may be told through the writer's eyes in the first person (I–we). It may also address the reader in the second person (you). Finally, it may speak about an individual or group in the third person (he/she, they). The important thing to remember about point of view is to be consistent throughout a piece of writing. Do not shift back and forth from first to second or third person. Also, be consistent with singular or plural throughout.

Examples: *I* was granted a loan. (first person singular)
You were granted a loan. (second person)
They were granted a loan. (third person plural)

Positive degree (*See* degree of comparison)

Possession (*See also* apostrophe *and* possessive pronouns) Nouns or pronouns can show possession or ownership. Nouns use an apostrophe or an apostrophe and an *-s* to show possession ('s). If the noun ends in *-s*, add an apostrophe only; if the noun does not end in *-s*, add an apostrophe and an *-s* ('s). Pronouns never use an apostrophe to show possession.

Examples: The *tree's* trunk was rotten.
The *trees'* trunks were rotten.
Its trunk was rotten.
Their trunks were rotten.

Possessive pronouns (*See also* object pronouns, pronoun, subject pronouns) A possessive pronoun is used to show ownership.

Examples: my, mine, your, his, her, hers, its, their, theirs.
Hand in *his* report.
The report is *mine*.
Their desks are neat.

Preposition (*See also* prepositional phrase) A preposition is a word used to show the relationship between one word and another in the sentence.

Examples: with, in, to, of, on, at, from, etc.
The woman *with* the briefcase is my boss (*With* shows the relationship between *woman* and *briefcase*.)

Prepositional phrase (*See also* preposition) A prepositional phrase is a group of words composed of a preposition, its object, and any modifiers of the object.

Examples: He wrote a script *for a children's television show.*

Present participle (*See also* participle, past participle, *and* verbal) A present participle is the *-ing* form of a verb used as an adjective.

Examples: The *fluttering* flags caught my eye.

Present tense (*See also* tense, future tense, *and* past tense) A verb in the present tense shows an action or state of being occurring at that moment, not in the past or future.

Examples: I *am typing* the letter now.
or I *type* the letter now.

Pro and con paragraph A pro and con paragraph develops two opposing controlling ideas. In the concluding sentence of the paragraph, the writer does not take a stand; he or she merely restates both ideas of the issue.

Process paragraph or Report (*See also* paragraph, report) A process paragraph gives the reader a step-by-step procedure of how something is done.

Pronoun (*See also* possessive pronouns, object pronouns, relative pronouns, *and* subject pronoun) A pronoun takes the place of a noun.

Examples: man (*he, him, his*)
woman (*she, her, hers*)
people (*they, them, their, theirs*)
object (*it, its*)
objects (*they, them, their, theirs*)

Pronoun–antecedent agreement A pronoun must agree (be consistent with) its antecedent in number and person.

Examples: The actress checked *her* daily schedule. (third person singular)
I will retype *my* notes. (first person singular)
The students took *their* books home. (third person plural)

Pronoun case (*See also* possessive pronouns, pronoun, object pronouns, *and* subject pronoun) Case indicates the various forms of pronoun usage: subjective case (pronoun used as subject), objective case (pronoun used as object), and possessive case (pronoun used to show possession).

Pronoun reference (*See* point of view)

Punctuation patterns
IC, cc IC
IC; IC
IC; trans, IC
DC, IC
IC DC

Reasons and examples paragraph (*See also* paragraph) A reasons and examples paragraph develops its topic sentence by using supporting reasons and also giving examples for each reason.

Reasons paragraph (*See also* paragraph) A reasons paragraph develops its topic sentence by using supporting reasons.

Recommendation report A recommendation report is the written account of a comparative study resulting in the recommending of one item or thing over another.

Reflexive pronouns (*See also* pronoun) A reflexive pronoun ends in *-self* or *-selves.* It is used to show that someone did something to oneself or to show emphasis.

Examples: He questioned *himself* about his motives.
Melanie *herself* is in charge.

Relative pronoun A relative pronoun introduces a dependent clause or a question.

Examples: who, whom, that, which, whoever, whomever
The accountant *who* got the job was well qualified.
Which typewriter do you want?

Report (*See also* interview, process, persuasion, recommendation, *and* summary reports) A report is an essay or paper composed of several paragraphs developing an idea more extensively than a single paragraph would.

Restrictive element (*See also* nonrestrictive element) A restrictive element is a word, phrase, or clause modifier that is essential to the clear identification of the word it modifies. It is not set off by commas.

Examples	RESTRICTIVE:	The doctor *who treated me* has office hours tomorrow.
	NONRESTRICTIVE:	Dr. Smathers, *who treated me*, has office hours tomorrow.

Run-on sentence A run-on sentence is an incorrectly punctuated sentence containing two independent clauses. To correct a run-on sentence, separate the independent clause with a semicolon or a period or insert a comma with a coordinate conjunction between the two independent clauses.

Examples	RUN-ON:	The new skating rink was completed, students began using it.
	CORRECT:	The new skating rink was completed; students began using it.
	CORRECT:	The new skating rink was completed, and students began using it.

Second person (*See* person)

Semicolon A semicolon (;) is a mark of punctuation used to indicate a division between separate elements in a sentence.

Examples: The clouds were dark and heavy; a storm was brewing in the west. (between two independent clauses)
He had lived in Seattle, Washington; Boise, Idaho; and New Orleans, Louisiana. (between items of series with internal punctuation)

Sentence (*See also* independent clause) A sentence is a group of words having a subject and a verb and making a complete thought.

Sentence combining To vary sentence structure and to avoid short, choppy sentences, you can employ the techniques of sentence combining, which include use of dependent clauses, prepositional phrases, verbal phrases, and adjectives or nouns to condense ideas.

Examples CHOPPY: Joe was in college.
He studied architectural engineering.
His professor was highly qualified.
He enjoyed the course.
BETTER: While Joe was in college, he studied architectural engineering, which he enjoyed with a highly qualified professor.

Series (*See also* comma) A series is a list of three or more items in sequence in a sentence. Use a comma to separate words, phrases, and clauses in a series.

Examples: We ordered roast beef, baked potatoes, and broccoli for dinner.

Shift (*See also* point of view) A shift is an unnecessary change within a sentence or paragraph or report. Be careful to avoid shifts in number, person, point of view, tense, and voice.

Singular (*See also* plural) The singular form of a word indicates one. Generally, a singular noun does not end in *-s* or *-es*, whereas a singular verb does end in *-s* or *-es*.

Slang Slang is language that is highly informal or unconventional. It is not acceptable in formal or traditional writing or speaking.

Examples: high five (slapping of hands)
fink (undesirable person)

Subject (*See also* noun, pronoun) The subject of a sentence is what the sentence is talking about. It is usually a noun or pronoun.

Examples: *Coffee* increases nervousness.
He is my supervisor.

Subject complement (*See also* linking verb) A subject complement is the noun, pronoun, or adjective that follows a linking verb and renames or describes the subject.

Examples: Mr. Borden is our new *guide*. (noun)
The job applicant is *she*. (pronoun)
The new secretary seems *competent*. (adj)

Subject pronouns (*See also* pronoun, subject) The subject pronouns are *I, you, he, she, it, we, they.* These pronouns are used as subjects.

Examples: *I* would like to speak to the group.
They are coming to work today.

Subject–verb agreement (*See also* plural, singular) A subject must agree with its verb in number. That is, a singular subject uses a singular verb; a plural subject uses a plural verb.

Examples: The *architect draws* house plans.
Architects draw house plans.

Subordinate clause (*See* dependent clause)

Subordinate conjunction (*See* clause signal)

Subordination (*See also* coordination, dependent clause) Subordination, in sentence structure, refers to the use of dependent clauses to make an idea less important to the thought in the independent clause. It is a useful method of varying sentence structure.

Examples: After the surveyors set up the transit, they surveyed the property lines.

Summary report A summary report is a condensation of a larger piece of writing such as a magazine article. It attempts to capture the essence of the article in as brief a form as possible.

Superlative degree (*See* degree of comparison)

Supporting sentence (*See also* topic sentence, concluding sentence, controlling idea) A supporting sentence is one that gives factual detail to aid in proving a topic sentence for a paragraph or longer paper.

Synonym A word that has the same meaning as another word.

Tense (*See also* shift) Tense refers to time expressed by the verb—present, past, or future.

Examples: I *am typing* the lab report. (present tense)
I *typed* the lab report. (past tense)
I *will type* the lab report. (future tense)

Third person (*See* person)

Topic sentence (concluding sentence, controlling idea, supporting sentence) A topic sentence of a paragraph reveals both the subject (what the paragraph is talking about) and the controlling idea (what is being said about the subject).

Examples: Large *computers* are *costly* to produce.

Transitional expression (*See also* semicolon) A transitional expression is a device used to link one idea to another.

Examples: (Therefore, on the other hand, consequently, for example, etc.)
There are many arguments for changing to the metric system;
however, there are a number of opposing ideas as well.

Unclear reference (*See* indefinite reference)

Verb (*See also* linking verb, helping verb, main verb) The verb is the part of the sentence that shows the action or state of being of the subjects.

Examples: My boss *walks* five miles a day. (action)
My boss *is* considerate. (state of being)

Verbal (*See also* gerund, infinitive, participle) A verbal is a word made from a verb but used in another way. The three types of verbals are gerunds, infinitives, and participles.

Verbal phrase (*See also* verbal) A verbal phrase includes the verbal and its object and/or modifiers.

Examples: *Walking rapidly into the room*, he commanded attention.
To be a state police officer is his goal.

Voice (*See* active voice, passive voice, shift)

Vowel The vowels are *a, e, i, o, u,* and sometimes *y*.

Index

A

A, an, 24–25
Abbreviations
  in business letters, 321
  of states of US, 340
About, around, 231
Accelerating techniques
  avoiding clichés and slang, 252–255
  combining like subjects and verbs, 255–256
  eliminating unnecessary words, 249–252
  reducing dependent clauses, 261–266
  subordinating ideas, 257–261
Accept, except, 231
Action verbs, 2–7, 92
Active voice, 200–204
Addresses, 140
Adjective(s)
  adverbs modifying, 27
  comparative, 33–34
  coordinate, 25, 140–141
  defined, 4
  distinguished from adverbs, 30
  ending in *–y*, 29
  good, well, 31–33, 231
  parallel, 236
  possessive form of noun used as, 99
  reducing clauses to, 262
  rules for, 24–28
  use with linking verbs, 26–27
Adjective clauses. *See* Essential clauses; Nonessential clauses
  concerns with, 146–149
Adverb(s)
  comparative, 34–35
  defined, 26
  distinguished from adjectives, 30
  modified by adverb, 29
  reducing clauses to, 262
  rules for, 28–30
  well, 31–33, 231
Adverb clause, 257–259
Advice, advise, 233
Affect, effect, 232
After, 119, 120
Agreement
  indefinite pronouns as subjects, 79–80
  in number, 25, 74, 79
  problems in, 84–86
  pronoun–antecedent. *See* Pronoun–antecedent agreement
  subject–verb. *See* Subject–verb agreement
All, 80
Although, 119, 120
Altogether, all together, 231
Among, between, 232
Amount, number, 231
And
  as clause connector, 123
  as coordinate conjunction, 123
  in parallel constructions, 235
  in pronoun–antecedent agreement, 105
  in subject–verb agreement, 82
  subordinating ideas and, 259
Antecedent(s)
  clarity of reference, 225
  defined, 104
  pronoun agreement, 104–108

Any, none, 80
Anybody, everyone, many, 79
Apostrophe(s)
defined, 57
and possessive nouns, 65
rules for, 57–65
Application letters, 329–332
Appositives, 144
Around, about, 231
Articles, 24–25
As, 102

B

Because, 120, 126, 127
Between, among, 232
Block style letter, 316–317
Both, 80
Business letters. *See* Letters, business
Business writing
format, 316–322
planning, 315–316
psychology of, 313–315
See also Letters, business; Memorandum (Memo)
But, yet, 123

C

Capitalization, in business letters, 321–322
Clarity, need for
misplaced and unclear modifiers, 228–230
parallel construction, 235–242
pronoun reference, 224–228
word usage, 230–235
Clause signal words, 119–120
Clause(s)
defined, 115
essential and nonessential adjectives, 145–146
parallelism by, 236
with pronoun subject, 79–82
in a series, 139
types. *See* Dependent clauses; Independent clauses
Clause connectors, 122
coordinate conjunctions, 123
dependent clause signals, 126–129
transitional expressions, 123–126
Clichés, 252–253
Closing, in business letters, 320
Collective nouns, 54, 76, 210–211
Comma splice, 160
Commas
basic sentence patterns, 135
coordinate adjectives, 25, 140
in dates and addresses, 140
essential and nonessential adjective clauses, 145
in introductory words and phrases, 142
to separate coordinate adjectives, 140–141
in series, 139
to set off interrupters, 143, 180
Company names (possessive form), 64
Complement, compliment, 232
Compound subjects
and verbs, 82–84
defined, 82
Compound verbs, 82
Concluding sentence, 178–179
Conjunction(s), 116
and pronouns, 101–103
Coordinate adjectives, 25
Coordinate conjunctions, 116
Correlatives, 239

D

Dates, 140
Dependent clauses, 118–122
to adjectives, 262
to adverbs, 262
basic sentence punctuation pattern, 134–138
defined, 118
four-step reduction technique, 263–267
to infinitive phrases, 261
to nouns, 262
to participles or participial phrases, 261–262
to prepositional phrases, 261
with pronouns as subjects, 93–94
with pronouns as subject complements, 94–96
signal words, 121–123
Direct address, 143
Direct object, 12–13
Disinterested, uninterested, 232

E

Effect, affect, 232
Either . . . or, 82, 105
Email, 254, 332, 333
Essential clauses, 145, 146
Everybody, 79
Except, accept, 231

F

Farther, further, 233
Fewer, less, 233
First person, 207
For, 123
Fragment(s)
  defined, 156
  types, 157–158
Funnel introduction. *See* Inverted pyramid introduction
Further, Farther, 233
Future perfect progressive tense, 18
Future perfect tense, 17
Future progressive tense, 18
Future tense, 17

G

Gerunds, 45, 47, 73, 100, 235
Good, well, 31–33, 231
Got, have, 233

H

Have, got, 233
Helping verbs, 7–9
Here, there, 84

I

Illegible, ineligible, 232
IMglish, 252, 254–255
Imperative sentences, 143
Imply, infer, 232
Indefinite pronoun subjects, 79–82
Indefinite pronoun(s)
  agreement with verb, 80
  with apostrophe, 57–59
  avoiding shifts in number, 210
  used as adjective, 25
Indefinite references, (*it, they*), 227
Independent clauses, 115–118
  basic punctuation pattern, 134–139
  defined, 115
  run-ons, 159–163
Ineligible, Illegible, 232
Infer, imply, 232
Infinitive phrase, 261
Infinitive, as verbal, 45
Information-seeking memo, 332
Informative memo, 332
Interfering words, 77–79
Interrupters
  additional detail, 144
  defined, 143
  emphasis, 143
Interview reports
  conducting the interview, 293–295
  interveiwee selection, 292
  preparation for interview, 292–293
  report writing, 295–296
  sample, 296–298
Inverted pyramid introduction, 280
Irregular verbs, 9
  confusing, 12–16
  principal parts, 9–12
Its, it's, 233

L

Less, Fewer, 233
Letter address, 319
Letterhead, 319
Letters, business
  appearance, 322
  emphasis, 316
  format, 316–318
  length, 322
  mechanics, 320–322
  outline, 315–316
  parts, 315
  refusal, 324–325
  request, 323–324
  resumé and application, 326–332

Letters, business (*continued*)
sections of, 319–320
summary, 322
transmittal, 336–339
versus memo, 336
Linking verbs, 4–7

M

Main/Major clause. *See* Independent clauses
Memorandum (Memo)
business letter versus, 336
content, 333
form, 332–333
sample, 334–336
transmittal, 336–339
Modified block style letter, 318
Modifier(s)
defined, 228
misplaced and unclear, 228–230
See also Adjective(s); Adverb(s)

N

Negative expression, 143
Neither . . . nor, 82, 105
None, any, 80
Nonessential clauses, 145–146
Nor, or, 123
Noun(s)
adjective with, 24–28
with apostrophe, 57–66
collective, 54, 76, 211
defined, 2, 54
functions of, 55–57
after linking verbs, 4
parallelism by, 236
possessive nouns, 57–66
types of, 54
Number, 74
avoiding shifts in, 210–216
pronoun–antecedent agreement, 104
subject–verb agreement, 74
Number, amount, 231
Numbers, in business letters, 321

O

Object pronouns, 92
Or, nor, 123
Outlining, 276–280

P

Paragraph(s)
coherence development, 181–183
concluding sentence, 178–179
controlling idea selection, 174–178
defined, 171
introduction, 170
organization and writing, 183–184
pro and con, 188–191
process, 191–194
reasons and examples, 186–188
reasons, 184–186
subject selection, 172–174
topic sentence construction, 172
unity development, 180–181
Parallel construction
in correlatives, 239–242
in lists, 235
in outlines, 238–239
in a series, 236–238
with *and,* 235
Parenthetic elements, 143
Participles, as verbals, 45
Passive voice, 200–204
Past participle, 9
Past perfect progressive tense, 18
Past perfect tense, 17
Past progressive tense, 18
Past tense, 17
Persecute, prosecute, 231–232
Personal pronouns. *See* Object pronouns; Possessive pronouns; Subject pronouns
Persuasive report
comparison of introductions, 284–286
outline, 283–284
Phrases
defined, 42
infinitive, 261
kinds of, 42
parallelism by, 236
participial, 261

prepositional. *See* Prepositional phrases
redundant, 250
verbal. *See* Verbal phrases
Plural nouns, 57
Plural. *See* Number
Possession. *See* Apostrophe(s)
Possessive nouns, 57–67
Possessive pronouns
as adjectives modifying gerunds, 100
as adjectives modifying nouns, 99
defined, 92
as subjects, objects, and complements, 100–101
Precede, proceed, 231
Prepositional phrases
defined, 42
as interrupting words, 77
reducing dependent clauses to, 261–262
Prepositions
common, 43
pronouns as objects of, 97–98
Present participle, 9
Present perfect progressive tense, 18
Present perfect tense, 17
Present progressive tense, 18
Present tense, 16
Pro and con paragraphs, 188–191
Proceed, precede, 231
Process paragraphs, 191–194
Pronoun references, 224–227
Pronoun–antecedent agreement, 104–108
Pronouns
antecedent agreement, 104–108
defined, 2, 92
as direct objects, 96–97
as objects of prepositions, 97–99
pronoun–antecedent agreement, 104–108
rules, 101–104
as subject complements, 94–96
as subjects, 93–94
See also Possessive pronouns
Prosecute, Persecute, 231–232
Punctuation
apostrophe. *See* Apostrophe(s)
appositives, 144
basic sentence patterns for, 134–138
commas. *See* Commas
run-ons and, 159–161
in dependent clauses, 119–120
in independent clauses, 116–118
semicolon, 117–118, 123, 136, 160–161
series items, 139

R

Reasons and examples paragraph, 186–188
Reasons paragraph, 184–186
Recommendation report
memorandum format, 298–299
sample, 299–303
Redundant expressions, 250
References, indefinite. *See* Indefinite references, (*it, they*)
Reflexive pronouns, 103
Refusal letters, 324–325
Regular verbs, 9
Report introductions, 280
inverted pyramid introduction, 280
report plan, 280–281
visual representation, 281–282
Report writing
format tips, 282–283
interview report, 292–298
outlining, 276–280
persuasive report, 283–287
recommendation report, 298–303
report introductions, 280–282
review of paragraph writing, 274–276
summary report, 303–310
technical procedure report, 287–291
Request letters, 323–324
Respectively, respectfully, 231
Resumé, 326–329
Return address. *See* Letterhead
Run-ons
defined, 156
types of punctuation errors in, 159–164

S

Salutation, in business letters, 319–320
Scratch outline, 276–277
Second person, 207

Semicolon, 117–118, 123, 136, 160–161
Sentence(s)
  choppy, 257
  clauses. *See* Clause(s)
  concluding, 178–179
  defined, 156
  fragments, 157–159
  parallelism by, 236
  punctuation patterns, 134–139
  run-ons, 159–164
  supporting, 274
  topic. *See* Topic sentence
Series
  parallelism by, 236
  punctuation for items in, 139
Sexist language, 106
Shifts
  defined, 199
  in number, 210–216
  in person/point of view, 207–210
  in tense, 204–207
  in voice, 200–204
Signal words, 119–123
Single-word appositive, 144
Singular. *See* Number
Skeleton outline, 277
Slang, 252, 253
So, 123
Subject complements
  personal pronouns as, 94–96
  possessive pronouns as, 100
Subject–verb agreement, 74–77
  compound subjects, 82–84
  interfering words, 77–79
  problems, 84–86
  recognizing subjects and verbs, 72–74
Subject pronouns, 92
Subject(s)
  combining verbs and, 255–256
  compound, 82
  defined, 2, 73
  indefinite pronouns, 79–82
  possessive pronouns as, 100
  pronouns, 93–94
  recognizing, 72–74
  as sentence fragments, 158
Subordinate clause. *See* Dependent clauses
Subordinating ideas, 257–261
Summary reports, 303–310
Supporting paragraphs, 274
Supporting sentences, 274

T

Technical procedure report
  format, 289
  listing technique, 289
  parts of, 289
  sample, 289–291
  sample procedure, 288
Tense of verb. *See* Verb tense
Than, 102
That, as clause signal, 121
Theirs, there's, 65
Then, 118, 124
There, here, 84
They, indefinite use of, 92
Third person, 207
This, that, these, those, 25
To, too, 233
Topic sentence, 172
Transitional expressions, 117–118
Transmittal letters and memos, 336–339

U

Unclear modifiers, 228–230
Uninterested, disinterested, 232
US states, abbreviations of, 340

V

Verb tense
  future perfect progressive tense, 18
  future perfect tense, 17
  future progressive tense, 18
  future tense, 17
  past perfect progressive tense, 18
  past perfect tense, 17
  past progressive tense, 18
  past tense, 17
  present perfect progressive tense, 18
  present perfect tense, 17

present progressive tense, 18
present tense, 16
Verbal phrases, 45–49
Verbals
defined, 45
types of, 45
Verbs
combining subject and, 255–256
compound subjects and, 82–84
defined, 2
recognizing, 72–74
types, 2
See also Subject–verb agreement
Voice
defined, 200
shifts in, 200–204
See also Active voice; Passive voice

W

Well, good, 31–33, 231
Whose, who's, 65
Words
elimination of unnecessary, 249–252
interrupting, 77
Writing. *See* Accelerating techniques; Letters, business; Memorandum (Memo); Report writing

Y

Yet, but, 123
You, understood, 156